# Killer Poker by the Numbers

# KILLER POKER BY THE NUMBERS

## The Mathematical Edge for Winning Play

**Tony Guerrera**

LYLE STUART
Kensington Publishing Corp.
www.kensingtonbooks.com

LYLE STUART BOOKS are published by

Kensington Publishing Corp.
850 Third Avenue
New York, NY 10022



All Kensington titles, imprints, and distributed lines are available at special quantity discounts for bulk purchases for sales promotions, premiums, fund-raising, educational, or institutional use. Special book excerpts or customized printings can also be created to fit specific needs. For details, write or phone the office of the Kensington special sales manager: Kensington Publishing Corp., 850 Third Avenue, New York, NY 10022. attn: Special Sales Department; phone: 1-800-221-2647.



First printing: January 2007

10 9 8 7 6 5 4 3 2

Printed in the United States of America

ISBN 0-8184-0714-X

*To those who, regardless of the outcome, leave the field of competition confident in these three things:*

1. *They gave it their best effort.*
2. *They learned from the experience.*
3. *They will prepare diligently for the next battle.*

# Contents

# Foreword: Folk Math

## *by John Vorhaus*

When I was coming up in poker, there was such a thing as folk math, a vague understanding of how the numbers of the game matched up to our expectations of outcomes. The classic example of this was the old man's advice to "never draw to an inside straight," the assumption being that hitting your straight was so unlikely as to be unprofitable.

Outside straights we didn't mind drawing to. Those you had twice as many chances to hit, and twice as many was twice as good. Good times!

The first cardroom poker game I played was small stakes, no ante seven-card stud. Low card started the action with a forced bet, and my understanding of poker math was then sufficiently sophisticated so that I knew I'd only have to put money in the pot involuntarily once out of every eight hands on average. I was excited by this, for I got it that I could gamble for next to nothing. Having wasted abundant summer wages at the craps and blackjack tables, I found this a welcome revelation. More good times!

As my poker learning curve slowly steepened, I acquired a dim understanding of *pot odds* and a hazy notion of their relation to my chances of hitting a hand. Aided again by folk math, I learned anecdotally to chase my draws if the pot was big and to pass if the pot was small. I also learned about these marvelous things called *outs*, the cards I needed to complete my hand. I learned that if I multiplied my number of outs times the number of cards to come times 2 percent, I could get a rough approximation of my real chances. Armed with this crucially useful piece of folk math, I could now start to make more informed guesses as to whether the pot was laying me the right price for my call. I could genuinely begin to get my money in with the best of it. Triple good times!

But times change and poker has changed. Driven by the twin engines of TV poker and internet poker, a flood of young—and terribly intelligent—new players have entered the game. Having come of age in the computer age, they bring with them an innate level of math awareness that gives them a huge edge over us old fogies who cling to such hoary shibboleths as "bad cards bad, good cards good." In the face of this new class of competition, the message to practitioners of folk math is both dire and clear: get with the math of poker or get blown to smithereens.

This is not welcome news to me, folks. My eyes glaze over at the mere mention of words like *permutation, combination,* or *interval notation*. In fact, math has always made my mind go walkabout. Way back in school, when they used to ask me how long it would take a train traveling ninety miles an hour to get from Philadelphia to Cincinnati, I couldn't help wondering who all the passengers on that train were and why they were in such a hurry to get to Cincinnati in the first place.

But now, thankfully, here comes Tony Guerrera's literate and lucid *Killer Poker by the Numbers,* and what this book accomplishes is no mean feat: It makes poker math manageable, even to a math weenie like me. Using clear examples, a measured approach, and a straightforward (yet strangely elegant) writing style, Tony has peeled back the layers of poker play and exposed the ticking clockwork underneath. With every page I read, I found my confidence growing—confidence not only in my ability to master the math of poker but in the comforting fact that there's such a strong underlying logic to it all. I suppose I knew this all along on the level of folk math (don't draw to inside straights), but thanks to Tony, the picture is now just vividly clear in my mind.

And guess what? There's a lot of terrific nonmath value in this book as well: simple, plain-spoken truths of poker (e.g., "being good at reading players means not allowing your emotions to influence you") that can help anybody's game. So if you're browsing this book in a bookstore and wondering whether it's worth putting down your shekels for or investing your mental energy in, let me just say this: don't let the math of the matter daunt you. You'll get plenty of good "food value" out of this book, on the math and the nonmath level alike.

In fairness (and as Tony warns), what you'll get out of *Killer Poker by the Numbers* will be a function of what you put in. I suspect that some will choose to "harvest" the book, ignoring the higher math and deeper logic, but absorbing its important conclusions and integrating them into their poker play. Others will embrace the math in all its textured glory and use the book the way Tony intends: to devise tools of their own with which they can dominate and crush their foes. Both approaches work. You'll find the one that works for you.

I'm reminded of a late-night bull session in a college dorm many long years ago, when some smartass upperclassmen declaimed that the beauty of the New Testament was how it worked on two levels. There were simple parables for simple minds but much deeper meaning and esoteric wisdom for those with the intellectual tools to dig them out. That, claimed the upperclassmen, was the key to the book's enduring popularity: It offered something for everyone. (I have since heard a contrary theory, that the New Testament is enduringly popular because it's the derived word of God, but that's a discussion for another time and place and dorm room.) Listen, I'm not comparing *Killer Poker by the Numbers* to the New Testament—though it may very well become the Bible of Poker Math—but I do stand in frank awe of how it works on those two levels, with simple math for simple minds and a much deeper, and much more rewarding, math path for those who care to walk it.

So if the prospect of heavy math scares you, take heart. It scared the bejeezus out of me until I actually sat down and spent some quality time with this book. Then I found out what you'll find out: that with every page you'll be thinking more deeply and diligently and precisely about your poker. And if you're diligent enough to be able to absorb, if you will, the math of math, you're about to lock onto an astounding analytical apparatus that will take your game to the next level. No, not the next level—to unimaginable heights. Armed with Tony's tools is to be armed to the teeth.

And that's good times. Very good times indeed.

# Introduction

Hi, my name is Tony Guerrera, and I'd like to welcome you back to Killer Poker. Over the past few years, John Vorhaus (JV) and I have battled each other in many home games, and on occasion, we have taken road trips to some of the nearby cardrooms in Los Angeles. Our common love of poker has led to countless discussions about theory and strategy. These discussions, combined with my winning record of play, have afforded me this wonderful opportunity to contribute to JV's Killer Poker series. You may simply be an avid fan of the World Poker Tour on The Travel Channel and play weekly $10 tournaments with your friends, or you may be a battle-hardened veteran who, on a nightly basis, confidently buys in for $100,000+ in The Bellagio's high-limit room in Las Vegas. Regardless of where you are in the spectrum of poker players, I am sure that there will be something in this book for you.

The strength of Killer Poker, to date, is its philosophy of fearlessness tempered with honesty and discipline. The lessons contained in the first four Killer Poker titles are well worth the price of admission. Through his books, magazine articles, and association with Ultimate Bet, JV has established himself as a premier poker theorist. However, this reputation isn't what impresses me about JV. Rather, JV impresses me with the down-to-earth mentality he maintains despite the accolades he's received. Instead of walking in a mist of grandeur and placing himself on a magical pedestal, he's the first to acknowledge his weaknesses and mistakes. The success he enjoys by adhering to his philosophy of honest self-introspection exemplifies the power of Killer Poker.

A few months ago, I watched JV play a $2–$5 blind no-limit (NL) game ($300–$500 buy-in) at the Bicycle Casino via a time-delayed webcast. The announcers heavily criticized him for a bad laydown he made, going so far as to say that the poker authors playing at The Bike need to back their words up with solid play. JV could have hidden from his mistake, trying to cloak it with a veil of well-crafted excuses. Instead, he not only admitted his mistake, but he actually put it back into the public's eye by writing an article about the hand. He turned a negative situation into an opportunity to evaluate and discuss his own play. In that hand, JV lost money by folding when he should have called, but he made that money back—and then some—with his article and the subsequent adjustments he made to his game. In a game filled with inflated egos, it's refreshing to see someone with JV's approach. Even though we've seen a fair share of egomaniacs win money in big televised tournaments, the players with JV's Killer Poker approach have the greatest chance of success in poker—and in the greater game known as life.

JV's Killer Poker books have mainly covered managing your psychological state and getting a line on your opponents' play. They offer a different look at the game than what is seen in most books, and that's their strength. With all their great insights, the Killer Poker books do lack something—rigorous mathematical analysis of the game. To change that, JV suggested that I write this book. I've performed countless calculations in my effort to stay on top of the hold'em games I play online and in the casinos. Hell, I sit at home and do calculations on all the crazy games we play in our monthly dealer's choice game (the types of games JV covers in *Poker Night* [St. Martins, 2004]). For this reason, JV thought I would be the perfect candidate to fill the mathematical void, and I am confident that this addition to the Killer Poker books will not disappoint. After all, JV would never allow me to publish a Killer Poker title—putting his own reputation on the line—unless he genuinely thought I had something insightful to offer.

When I submitted the proposal for this book to Kensington, there was one section in which I compared my book to other poker titles on the market and talked about what unique offerings my title would have. I found myself making comparisons to great books from powerhouse names. Such books included Brunson's *Supersystem* (Cardoza Publishing, 2002), Harrington's *Harrington on Hold'em* (Two Plus Two, 2004 and 2005), and Sklansky and Malmuth's *Hold'em for Advanced Players* (Two Plus Two, 1999). As of this writing (January–March 2006), I haven't competed in any World Poker Tour or World Series of Poker events, and none of you know me by name. A handful of you may know me from the name I made for myself at the $500NL cash games on the Party Poker Million IV Cruise. A few others may know me from my days as a regular in the middle-limit cash games at the Commerce Casino, and the Bicycle Club. Most of you out there who know me, though, probably know me by my online poker handles, and, well, I'm not going to reveal them here.

Over the past year, I've spent most of my poker-playing time online where I play up to ten tables concurrently, mostly cash games and single-table tournaments. Unfortunately, online cash games and single-table tournaments have no trophies or scantily clad women bringing out chests of $100 bills. The only glory comes in the form of bank wires from my online poker accounts to my bank accounts. However, that's fine with me—after all, isn't money the means by which we keep score in poker?

My approach to poker is something that hasn't really been seen before. Some concepts have been touched upon, but not to the depth or from the viewpoint presented here. You will learn to analyze poker by using mathematics to process information gained from psychological cues and betting patterns at the table. My approach and the way I present it are slightly unconventional for a poker book. Lou Krieger, in his foreword to *Killer Poker: Strategy and Tactics for Winning Poker Play* (Lyle Stuart, 2002), writes, "Ass backwards! That's right. John Vorhaus wrote a book about poker and he's gotten it ass backwards. But that's a good thing." While my approach isn't necessarily "ass backwards," it might be considered "ass sideways" or "ass perpendicular." From an early age, I've viewed problems from a different perspective. Doing so led me to Caltech, and in my post-Caltech days, it has proven immensely helpful in my rapid evolution from a novice poker player to one who can beat up to ten online games at once.

In the following pages, I dissect many possible lines of play. Most of the time, I carefully guide you through as precise an analytic treatment as possible. *This* is the type of analysis that you should do in front of your computer or on a Denny's restaurant napkin during a 4:00 A.M. meal with your poker buddies following a trip to the casino. Applying the pure theoretical analysis is too cumbersome to carry out at the poker table, so after presenting detailed results, I deconstruct some calculations, showing where appropriate approximations and shortcuts can be made, and I make sure that the major results of my calculations are summarized immediately following them.

We live in a black-box society. What I mean by this is that we do not know how many things work; we simply know how to use them. TVs, computers, cars, cell phones, and microwaves are just a few of the myriad black-boxes that we take for granted. Those accustomed to the black box mentality may wonder why I don't take the space I use for theory and make this book consist entirely of simple approximations that you can memorize and take with you to battle. I don't take that approach because poker is a very situational game. If I only gave you mathematical tables, you would finish reading this book with very little understanding of the underlying framework of the game.

If you find yourself in a situation that is even slightly different from what I present here, you would not know how to handle it. My goal in this book isn't to produce robots; my goal is to produce flexible problem solvers who can think their way through any unique situation in which they may find themselves. Good poker players are adaptive, and the only way to be adaptive is to understand the underlying theory. Consequently, this book will not have magical answers to generalized questions such as "should I play KQs *under the gun* in an eight-handed game?"

When I started writing this book, I envisioned a no-limit hold'em bible that would discuss the underlying theory and contain an unrivaled encyclopedia of playing situations. However, it quickly became clear that the book was trying to accomplish too much. The most important lesson I want to emphasize in this book is the theoretical framework through which poker problems should be viewed, and that lesson was being hidden in the encyclopedic approach. Therefore, I tossed the encyclopedic approach aside in favor of making *Killer Poker by the Numbers,* a book that focuses mostly on the theory unifying all situations. With the theory in hand, you can personally analyze the specific circumstances that you find yourself in. Having said that, I am confident that you will be satisfied with the sampling of situations that I do discuss; they are drawn from my wide range of experiences in casinos and online. I encourage those of you seeking more situational analysis to visit my website at www.killerpokerbythenumbers.com.

Many people aren't good at math, and even those proficient at it don't necessarily enjoy it. People eschew math for widely varying reasons. However, the bottom line is that this book is driven by math. As a result, some of you may be unsure if this book will be right for you or even comprehensible. For those having such thoughts, it's vital that you be willing to step out of your personal comfort zones. There will be concepts that you have never seen before, but my straightforward approach to powerful mathematical ideas will put readers from all educational backgrounds on equal footing. My beloved mother, who neither plays poker nor knows a lot of math, understood this book; you will also understand it.

The Killer Poker books have always encouraged their readers to be active participants. JV has asked you to write lists and recall past experiences so that you dig deep into your minds. *Killer Poker by the Numbers* is no exception. Poker is an exercise in problem solving, and the only way to become good at problem solving is to "practice, practice, practice."

I hope that you find me to be a well-informed, enthusiastic, and empathetic guide. You should find that I'm not your stereotypical mathematical player who lacks an understanding of the psychology of the game. The mathematical analysis I use is simply a way of processing all the information I obtain from my opponents. The information gathering happens first, and the math only happens once it's my turn to act and I've weighed all available information. This mentality is reinforced through the example hands found throughout the text. In short, we're about to embark on a marvelous journey into the nitty-gritty of NL hold'em theory (and poker theory in general). Let's all pause for a moment, take a relaxing breath, close our eyes, and imagine the dwindling stacks of our competition. It's once again time for some Killer Poker. As always, it's for blood, but this time, it's also by the numbers.*

* Poker is a gender-neutral game, but to avoid awkward constructions such as "he or she," I use male singular pronouns throughout.

# Acknowledgments

My family, my friends, and I coexist with a mutual awareness of our appreciation for each other and all that we do to help each other out. Despite that, there are times to give thanks and to outwardly show our appreciation, and this is one of them. I am indebted to so many people that I not only worry about the order of acknowledgment but also the possibility of leaving people out. It's currently 5:00 A.M. PST in Pasadena, California, March 16, 2006, the extended due date of my manuscript, and I still don't know quite what to say. I guess the thoughts that matter most in times like these are sometimes the thoughts that stream from spontaneity.

With that in mind, I first have to give thanks to my parents who've supported me all along. Without your support and the great education that you provided me with, I wouldn't be living the life that I lead (of course, most people wouldn't be envious of the sleep deprivation and energy drink consumption I've succumbed to in the past month or so, but I certainly can't complain). My mother also deserves thanks for taking the time to read a good chunk of my manuscript. She doesn't know a lot of math, and she's never played a hand of poker in her life (other than the penny games of 5-card draw we used to play with my grandfather when I was young). As a result, her understanding of my words gave me much confidence going into the second half of my book.

I also have to thank all my teachers from kindergarten all the way up through my education at Caltech. A special thanks goes to everyone at The Taft School in Watertown, Connecticut. I hope that being mentioned in a poker book doesn't ruin its reputation because the four years I spent at Taft were some of the most enjoyable, influential, and motivational years of my life. If it wasn't for Taft, I wouldn't have had the opportunity to attend Caltech, and without Caltech, I probably wouldn't be sitting here writing this book. It's not the Nobel Prize–winning paper people expected from me (that's in a few years), but it does have a lot of good game theory in it, and game theory applies to many decisions outside the realm of poker!

The next shout-out goes to JV. I first met JV at Caltech while we were playing ultimate frisbee back in 1998 or 1999, before the first *Killer Poker* title was even published and before I had begun playing poker. Somehow, around the summer of 2003, I participated in a home game with him, and since then, he's been great to discuss theory with. I thank JV for all the good times and for the willingness to present my work to his agent and to Kensington. Oh, I also have to thank him for including my work in his *Killer Poker Online 2* (Lyle Stuart, 2006). Without his backing, I'd never have this opportunity. I'm sure that the work I've produced won't let him down. JV, whenever you need a calculation for a magazine article, just let me know!

Having thanked JV, I'd also like to thank all the people in the literary world who JV hooked me up with. Greg Dinkin and Frank Scatoni at Venture Literary, you guys have been awesome, and I look forward to a successful, ongoing relationship in the years to come. Richard Ember at Kensington also deserves many thanks for dealing with my frantic emails over the past month. Writing this first book hasn't always been the smooth process that I envisioned, and Richard's patience has been much appreciated.

This book wouldn't be as good as it is without the direct help from a few people who went beyond the call of duty. First, Marcie Braden was an awesome editor! She helped out a ton with everything from the intro through most of Chapter 4. I'm still amazed at all the effort she put into this project. In addition to being an awesome editor, Marcie also designed all the figures in the book. She did a much better job than I could have ever done. For everything she's done, I owe her at least one more multi-table victory on Party Poker. Marcie, just call me the next time your internet goes down, and we'll get another first place! Dan McArdle was also helpful in the editing process. He checked all my work on the problems in the first few chapters. He also deserves thanks for being the questioning soul that he is. Oh, wait, Dan and I don't believe in souls. The final person who contributed directly to this manuscript was Ryan Patterson. Without him, there's no way I would have been able to do the simulations I use in the tournament chapter (chapter 7). Thanks to Ryan, his access to insane amounts of computing power, and his ability to code Monte Carlo simulations so quickly!

Marcie, Dan, and Ryan also deserve thanks for all the great poker theorizing over the past few years. With respect to great poker conversation, there are a few more people to thank. Craig Vieregg is an endless source of interesting situations and viewpoints, and talking to him always expands my thoughts on the game. I shouldn't thank Ben Brantley because he took all his money and moved to Colorado, but in all seriousness, Ben deserves a big thanks for all the tricky decisions he's put me to in the home games we used to play! Britt Boras deserves thanks for the days of playing heads-up limit hold'em when we were on Caltech's tennis team. Other players from the Caltech home-game scene have also provided me with great practice and poker debate: Tony "Chicago Stud" Nannini, Tom Vanderslice, and Jon Bird. Finally, a mad shout-out goes to everyone who's part of what I refer to as "The Caltech Poker Posse." As I write, these guys are probably winning grandusands upon grandusands on Party Poker and the Party Poker Million V (PPMV) Cruise (grandusands is our term for the amount of money we win). Scott Jordan, Eugene Yanayt, Dan "Young Tiger" Yi, and Akshay Singal—keep doing what you're doing and remember that Knish always has a few more tricks up his sleeves!

All the people just mentioned, besides being poker buddies, have been great friends, and I thank them all for that. In addition, I thank all my other good friends who didn't get specifically named in a shout-out here. My other friends who weren't specifically mentioned here don't play poker, and I sincerely appreciate them for the times that they drag me away from my computer or from the cardrooms. I can be single-mindedly driven at times (perhaps all the time), and I sincerely thank you guys for showing me life outside of the hustle and grind.

My final thanks go to you, the reader. Without books and people looking to expand their minds, the world would be a crazier place than it already is. I hope that what you read helps you at the poker tables and beyond!

# 1

♣♠♦♥

# ANALYTIC TOOLS

## A Motivational Example

How many times have you raised with AK only to miss the flop completely? Suppose you have just raised with A♣K♠, got one caller, and the flop is 9♠4♥2♦. A standard play in this situation is to make a *continuation bet*. A continuation bet is a bet made on the flop by the last preflop raiser when he misses the flop and no one else has bet. How profitable is a continuation bet? Let's perform simple analysis to answer this question.

Our cursory analysis of this situation will assume that your opponent calls your raise with any two cards. We will also assume that he only calls your bet if the board cards match at least one card in his hand. There are 47 unknown cards in the deck, and of those, 9 match the rank of one of the board cards. Therefore, the probability that your opponent doesn't hold a card matching the rank of a board card is given by $\left(\frac{38}{47}\right)\left(\frac{37}{46}\right) \approx .65$.* Our initial approximation is that

* For those not familiar with the symbol $\approx$, it means "approximately equal to." I use this symbol wherever I round off an answer. For presen-

your opponent misses the flop 65% of the time, meaning that if you bet here, your opponent will fold 65% of the time. Now, instead of one opponent, suppose you have two such opponents. The probability that neither has a card matching the rank of a board card is $\left(\frac{38}{47}\right)\left(\frac{37}{46}\right)\left(\frac{36}{45}\right)\left(\frac{35}{44}\right) \approx .41$. Thus, both opponents will fold to a bet on the flop 41% of the time. Table 1.1 summarizes the results of this calculation when the number of opponents ranges from 1 to 9:

**TABLE 1.1: Probability That None of Your Opponents Have a Hole Card Matching a Board Card on an Unpaired Flop If They Have Random Hands**

| NUMBER OF OPPONENTS | P (NONE MATCH A BOARD CARD) |
|---|---|
| 1 | 0.65 |
| 2 | 0.41 |
| 3 | 0.26 |
| 4 | 0.16 |
| 5 | 0.09 |
| 6 | 0.05 |
| 7 | 0.03 |
| 8 | 0.01 |
| 9 | 0.01 |

Given these *probabilities*, and assuming that your opponents call only when they match a board card, let's calculate the profitability of a $\frac{2}{3}$pot continuation bet. Let the pot size equal *P*. When you have one opponent, you will win an amount of money equal to *P* with a frequency of .65 (the

tation purposes, I round off displayed answers to two decimal places; however, if I use an answer from one calculation in another calculation, I always use exact expressions to avoid errors that result from rounding.

continuation bet is successful when your opponent misses the flop). You will lose an amount of money equal to $\frac{2}{3}P$ with a frequency of .35 (your continuation bet fails when your opponent hits the flop). Equation 1.1 gives your expected profit against one opponent:

$$(.65)(+P) + (.35)(-\tfrac{2}{3}P) = +\tfrac{5}{12}P \tag{1.1}$$

Given opponents who act as described, you expect to win an amount of money equal to $\frac{5}{12}$ pot every time you fire this continuation bet. If the pot is \$120, and you make an \$80 continuation bet into one opponent, your expected profit is $(\frac{5}{12})(\$120) = \$50$. When you have 2 opponents, equation 1.2 gives your expected profit.

$$(.41)(+P) + (.59)(-\tfrac{2}{3}P) = +\tfrac{1}{60}P \tag{1.2}$$

Thus, with two opponents, the same \$80 bet into a \$120 pot yields a profit of \$2. Equation 1.3 shows that you expect to lose money by continuation betting into 3 opponents.

$$(.26)(+P) + (.74)(-\tfrac{2}{3}P) = -\tfrac{7}{30}P \tag{1.3}$$

By using mathematical analysis, we see that a $\frac{2}{3}$ pot continuation bet is profitable against one or two opponents. When you have three or more opponents, continuation betting is a losing play. The analysis needs some improvement, but this is a good initial look at the problem.

Now, you could generalize this result and make a rule to never continuation bet into more than two opponents, and I'll be honest in telling you that's not a bad route to go. However, the preceding analysis only scratches the surface. To determine the profitability of a continuation bet for a specific instance, we need to consider a number of variables. First, I assumed your opponents called your raise with any two hole cards. Honestly, I've been in some juicy games where this actually isn't a bad assumption, but in all likelihood, even your *loosest* opponents will have *some* starting requirements. Second, I assumed your opponents needed a board card to match the rank of a hole card to call your continuation bet on the flop. If your opponents hold an overpair, for example, my assumptions dictate that they actually fold. Our opponents may also have draws that they will call with. In addition, some sophisticated opponents may actually call you with nothing, intending to bluff on a later round. Third, postflop play hasn't been considered—perhaps you hit the turn or river and win the hand. There is virtually an endless list of such critiques—can you think of any other problems with the assumptions I used?

Poker calculations are only as good as the assumptions that go into them. For our first calculation, I chose assumptions that led to a straightforward computation. What we really want to do, though, is to take assumptions mimicking the conditions of play that we actually encounter. Accounting for these assumptions can lead to some tricky lines of thought and some seemingly intimidating calculations, so before we can move on, I must show you some tools that I'll be using. The rest of this chapter introduces you to these tools and also exposes you to the persistent, probing mindset needed to dissect no limit (NL) Texas hold'em.*

* Note that even though the numbers and situations won't be the same, the general procedures I use in this book can be applied to any variant of poker—everything from razz to seven-card stud hi/lo with a chip declare. In fact, some material can also be used to step through nonpoker situations. For example, should you buy the extended warranty for your new DVD player? The people trying to rob you aren't just your opponents at the poker table!

## The Analytic Mentality: "Be Prepared"

I was never a Boy Scout, but success in my life has usually been the result of subconsciously adhering to the Scouts' aphorism, "Be Prepared." Since I've met some unsavory characters in casinos, I guess I should also draw inspiration from society's darker element or, at least, Hollywood's depiction of society's darker element. In my favorite movie, *The Godfather*, an arrangement is made for a gun to be planted in the restroom of a restaurant where the protagonist, Michael Corleone, is to kill two enemies of the Corleone family. Before Michael carries out these murders, his oldest brother, Sonny, says the following infamous words: "Hey, listen, I want somebody good, and I mean very good, to plant that gun. I don't want my brother coming out of that toilet with just his dick in his hands, alright?" Whether it's the Boy Scouts or *The Godfather* that inspires you, the point is that you need the right tools for the right job, and you need adequate preparation to do things correctly. In the words of JV, "Go big, or go home!"

In the introduction, I encouraged you to be an active reader. You might be able to absorb everything if you are reading this book in bed, half asleep after downing some NyQuil, but somehow, I highly doubt it. You will be a much more efficient learner if you are sitting ready with paper on the side and a pencil in your hand. "Be prepared" to read actively. With paper and pencil ready, you will more easily follow the work that I do. In addition, you are much more likely to do the problems at the end of each chapter carefully instead of simply half-heartedly thinking of answers and then filling in the gaps by reading the answers I provide. In short, by reading actively, you will no longer just scan over words with your eyes. Instead, the words will permeate into your deepest thoughts where they can do the most damage to your foes at the poker table.

If you are sitting in your favorite recliner and the nearest pencil is in another room, you will probably say, "I'll get a pencil later," but most likely, you will never get one. You will have important thoughts and questions only to forget them later and lament that you didn't take thirty seconds to fully prepare yourself. Laziness is a barrier that separates many people from their potential—don't let it be yours.

In addition to paper and a pencil, it would also be helpful to have a calculator. I have a TI-83, a graphing calculator with a big, multiline display and all sorts of crazy functionality, including a handy library of functions commonly used in statistics and probability.* For readers unfamiliar with this item, all I can say is that I love this calculator more than I love my ex-girlfriends, but its $100ish price tag, its many buttons, and its huge instruction manual might not appeal to you. If the $100 means nothing to you, don't let the buttons or the manual stop you. The calculator is simpler to use than a PDA, and you only need the manual as a reference—to find what you're looking to do in the index. For those who either don't want to drop a Benjamin on a calculator or don't want to deal with it, the good news is that you don't *need* anything that fancy. Theoretically, a simple four-function calculator is enough for everything, but I'd recommend having at least a scientific calculator—the added functionality expedites some calculations.

While on the topic of computations, you should have some type of *hand simulator* on your computer. A hand simulator is a program that takes a situation and evaluates the probability that each hand will win or tie. For example, if I have A♣K♦ and I am all-in preflop against an opponent

* I am not receiving any compensation for this or any other references to products in this book. Such information is provided solely to benefit you, the reader.

holding 9♥9♠, a hand simulator will find the outcome for each of the 1,712,304 possible boards and spit out the chance that each hand wins or ties. You could do this calculation by hand, but I doubt it would be a constructive use of your time; the sheer number of possible boards in Texas hold'em makes a hand simulator necessary for most hand analysis. I use one all the time, and so should you—it will be an invaluable asset when you go off and solve your own poker problems. My hand simulator of choice is Poker Stove, and it is available at www.pokerstove.com.

In terms of active reading and away-from-the-table hand analysis, all you really need are a pencil, some paper, a calculator, and a hand simulator. To become a real tiger at the tables, there are some additional items to consider. If you play online, there is no excuse for not having *hand-tracking* software. Hand-tracking software, referred to in *Killer Poker Online 2* as *sniffers*, keeps track of every hand you and your opponents play and calculates various statistics. Such statistics include percentage of flops seen and the relative frequency of bets to checks on the flop. Sniffers also let you sort through hands intelligently, looking for specific situations that you might want to analyze. Perhaps you want to look at all the hands where you played AJ *under the gun*. Eventually, you will want to perform the analysis that I do in this book on your own play, and if you are an online player, the bottom line is that the best way to have past hands available is to record them with a sniffer. Sniffers are also a great way to keep tabs on your foes—you can use them to replay hands against commonly faced opponents. From experience, finding good hand-tracking software for free is tricky. However, a few good programs are available that aren't too expensive. You can easily lose $25 to $50 in a session, so you might as well take that money and use it to purchase something that will immediately influence your game for the better. My favorite sniffer is Poker Tracker; it provides many useful statistics, and its instant replay feature is unrivaled. Poker Tracker is available at www.pokertracker.com.*

If you are like me, you also play in casinos. Obviously, you can't have software recording every hand you play in a casino, even though I guess you could try wearing a hidden camera. My piece of advice concerning live play is to keep scrap paper and a pen in your pocket, or a notebook in your car, so that immediately after your sessions, you can record the most noteworthy hands while they are still fresh in your head.

If you are an online player, you must have one final tool. No online player should be without software that works with sniffers to overlay opponents' statistics in real time while you play online. A piece of software that does this is called a *heads-up display (HUD)*.† The information provided by HUDs will not let you discern every nuance of your opponents' betting patterns. In other words, to play optimally, you still have to pay very close attention. However, a HUD gives you a tremendous edge in that it picks up information that you may have missed. Did you notice that the person who went all-in over the top of your QQ has only played 1 out of 100 hands? If not, you might mistakenly get entangled in a very expensive pot against his AA or KK. With the knowledge from your HUD, however, you can confidently fold. Finding the maniacs at an online table is easy, but keeping track of *tight* players online is sometimes difficult—good luck knowing that your online opponent has only played 1 out of 100 hands!

A HUD also gives instant feedback regarding your observations. For example, you are the *button*, and you have a

* For a more in-depth look at sniffers, check out the appendix I wrote for *Killer Poker Online 2* (Appendix B: Information Overlord).

† The creator of PokerAce HUD pronounces the acronym HUD as a word that rhymes with "thud," so I'm going with that convention as well.

hunch that the *big blind* does not defend the *blinds* often. Your HUD tells you that he has folded to 15 out of 16 blind steal attempts. You were fairly confident in stealing before, but now you can steal pretty much regardless of what two cards you hold, provided that the *small blind* isn't loose. My ability to multitask and my ability to interpret the information from a HUD let me profitably play up to ten tables at the same time. My HUD of choice is PokerAce HUD. PokerAce HUD interacts with the Poker Tracker database and has an easily customizable display. PokerAce HUD is available at www.pokeracesoftware.com.

Now that you are ready to be an active reader and have opened yourself to the analytic mindset, the next issue is making sure we are speaking the same language. A fair amount of jargon exists in the poker world, and a lot of this jargon makes poker easier to talk about. In my interest to make this book accessible to all readers, I was tempted to have a section in this chapter that defined commonly used terms, abbreviations, and acronyms. However, as I started to write it, I realized that such a section would end up being a boring list of words, and isn't that what a glossary is? My glossary is very comprehensive, so if you encounter any unknown words or abbreviations, I am quite confident that you'll find them there.

The only issue I'd like to talk about regarding jargon has to do with position. Refer to figure 1.1 (p. 10) throughout this discussion. In a hand of hold'em, there is always a button (B) and a big blind (BB). Most of the time, there is also a small blind (SB). The person to the left of the BB, who acts first preflop, is referred to as under the gun (UTG). The person immediately to his left is referred to as UTG+1, the person two to his left is referred to as UTG+2, and so on. The person to the right of the button, who therefore acts immediately before the button, is referred to as the *cutoff (CO).*

**Figure 1.1: Table Position Diagrams**

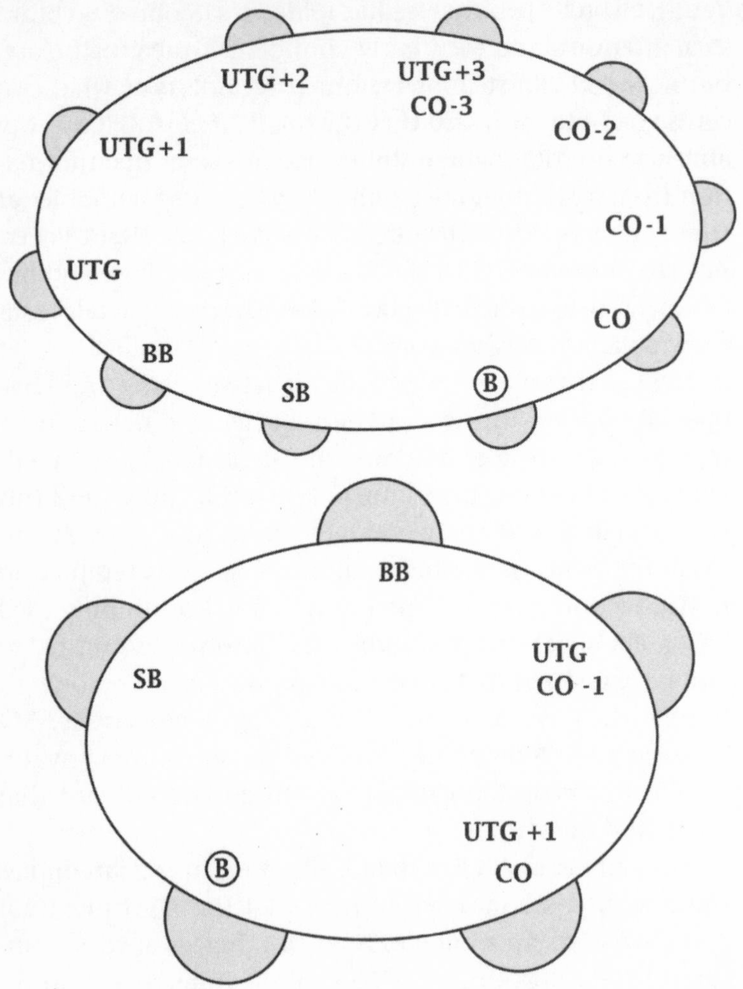


The reason this person is called the cutoff is that, often, when action is folded to the CO, he will raise preflop, thereby "cutting off" the button from entering the pot. The person immediately to the CO's right is referred to as CO −1, the person two to his right is referred to as CO –2, and so on. In other words, the convention is that you add as you go later in position and you subtract as you go earlier in position. At shorthanded tables, it is possible to occupy more than one commonly referred to role. For example, if you are UTG at a four-handed table where the SB and BB have been posted normally, you also happen to be the CO. Most people would refer to this person as being UTG; the UTG label seems to be stronger than the CO label. What if you are at a ten-handed table and are 5 to the left of the BB? In that case, you can be referred to as either UTG+4 or CO –2. Since 2 is smaller than 4, you would probably be referred to as CO –2; however, UTG+4 is still acceptable, and depending on the point of view from which you are talking, it may actually be preferred. It doesn't really matter, though, as long as you are comfortable with how the nomenclature works. Just note that if you are the SB, BB, or B, you won't be referred to with respect to UTG or CO designations.

Having addressed positional semantics, let's now look at how I present the play of hands.

## Modified MCU Poker Charts

A big difference between weak players and expert players is the way in which they talk about hands that they played. A poker story from a weak player often sounds something like this:

> Man, this was such a bad beat. I got pocket aces and raised. The flop was jack high. I bet and was called. The turn was the ace of hearts. I bet and was check-raised. I went all-in and was immediately called. He had a flush with K♥Q♥. . . . I can't believe he sucked out on my rockets.

Now, let's put an experienced, winning player in the same situation. Here's how he would tell the story:

> I was in a $500NL game with $3–$5 blinds. The table was eight handed, and I was under the gun. I was dealt pocket aces and raised to $20. Two players in late position called me as well as the big blind. I didn't knew much about the late position players, but I knew that the big blind was relatively conservative, even though I had seen him make some moves at a few pots when he smelled weakness. The flop was J-6-2 with two hearts. The big blind checked to me and I bet $60. One of the late position players called, as did the big blind. The turn was the ace of hearts. The small blind checked to me. At this point, I was worried about one of my opponents having completed a flush draw. However, with my set, I could not let a free fourth heart fall. And even if one of my opponents did complete a flush, I still had 10 *outs* to complete either a full house or quads. The pot at this point was about $260, so I fired $150. The late position player folded, but the big blind *check-raised* to $300. At this point, I had $250 left in front of me. If I just called, I would have called the rest of my chips on the river anyway in the instance that the big blind was pulling a move on me; thus, I *pushed* all-in. My opponent called, and the river was no help to me. The check-raise on the turn was fairly compelling evidence that my opponent had the flush. If I had just called on the turn, could I really have laid down top set on the river against the big blind given the 8:1 or 9:1 *pot odds?**

* Whether our "experienced, winning" player played this hand optimally is up for debate, but we will be doing more than our fair share of hand analysis later. For now, just take the story to be an example of how you should think about your poker.

The difference between these two stories, of course, is the detail with which the stories are told. This difference in detail illustrates the difference in how the two players think. The weak player focuses on two things: what he had and what his opponent had. Ultimately, he is only concerned about having lost. He recalls some betting action information, but not nearly enough to reconstruct the hand. He doesn't tell us the number of callers there were, the values of the bets and raises, or any information about how the players in the hand played. In contrast, the experienced, winning player gives lots of detail. While it is not possible to convey every nuance about each player, he provides information about his general state of knowledge of his opponents. He also does an excellent job of recapping the betting action. If we are going to do any work with analyzing hands that we've played, we have to remember hands and talk about them like our experienced, winning player does.

To conduct solid hand analysis, we must have a precisely defined situation. Talking about the action in a hand can be done in paragraph form, but a graphical presentation is more convenient, compact, and understandable. My inspiration comes from Mike Caro; in *Caro's Book of Poker Tells* (Cardoza Publishing, 2003), he presents *MCU Poker Charts* (MCU stands for "Mike Caro University"). He discourages modifications so that the poker world can have a universal way of presenting hands, but I thought a few minor changes were in order. If you go to *Caro's Book of Poker Tells*, you'll see that I haven't changed much. I opt for a textual representation of cards instead of a graphical presentation to save space, and I eliminate symbols indicating raises and calls, since the wager amounts themselves are enough to convey that information. I also add some abbreviations to account for actions like betting *in the dark*. This is pretty much the extent of my changes, though. Table 1.2 (pp. 14–15) is an example chart for a NL hold'em hand.

**Table 1.2: Sample Modified MCU Poker Chart**

**Game:** $200NL Hold'em
**Structure:** Small Blind: $2 Big Blind: $5
**Comments:** P6 is an extremely tight player who has been in very few pots.

| | **1(SB)** | **2(BB)** | **3** | **4** | **5** |
|---|---|---|---|---|---|
| | **XX** | **XX** | **XX** | **XX** | **XX** |
| **STACKS** | $240 | $140 | $500 | $367 | $300 |
| **PREFLOP** | b$2 | b$5 | >- | - | - |
| | $20 | -< | | | |
| **STACKS** | $220 | | | | |
| **FLOP** | >$0 | | | | |
| **J♠9♥5♣** | - | | | | |
| **STACKS** | | | | | |
| **TURN** | | | | | |
| **3♦** | | | | | |
| **E:(8♥)** | | | | | |
| **STACKS** | | | | | |
| **RIVER** | | | | | |
| **4♦** | | | | | |
| **HOLE** | | | | | |

**Comments:** P10's call of P6's preflop raise is questionable given the tight image of P6, and as we see, his preflop call got him in a lot of trouble.

**Legend:** SB = Small Blind; BB = Big Blind; B = Button; X = Unknown Hole Card; b = Blind or Straddle; > = Beginning of Betting Round Action; < = End of Betting Round Action; - = Fold; d = Action in the Dark; c = Call; r = Raise; E = Exposed Card; M = Main Pot; S = Side Pot; AI = All-In; R = Rake

| 6 | 7 | 8 | 9 | *10(B)* | POT |
|---|---|---|---|---|---|
| XX | XX | XX | XX | A♠J♥ | |
| $725 | $225 | $300 | $400 | $300 | |
| $20 | - | - | - | $20 | M = $61<br>R = $4 |
| $705 | | | | $280 | |
| $40<br>$120< | | | | $120 | M = $301<br>E:(9♠) |
| $585 | | | | $160 | |
| >d$300 | | | | $160< | M = $621<br>S1 = $140<br>S1(P6) |
| $285 | | | | $0 | |
| AI | | | | AI | M = $621<br>S1 = $140<br>S1(P6) |
| K♠K♣<br>Win S1<br>Win M | | | | A♠J♥<br>Mucked | |

The first row of this chart informs us of the game and the blind structure. It also has room for comments that give background information such as knowledge about players. The next row identifies each player by number and indicates the SB, the BB, and the B. If the hand is presented from the point of view of a specific player, then asterisks enclose that player's designation. This row also tells us what players are holding. An X is used to represent unknown cards. If we know one hole card, but not both (perhaps there's a slightly careless player to our right who exposes a hole card when he looks at his hand), then we can represent the situation with something like A♦X. The next row, labeled Stacks, tells us how much money each player has before the hand is dealt. The other Stacks rows tell us how much money each player has at specific points in the hand. For example, the Stacks row between the Preflop and Flop rows tells us how much money players left in the hand have when the flop hits. The preflop row outlines the action that occurs preflop. A "b" prefaces blinds and *straddles*. When someone calls without looking at his cards, the prefix "cd," for "calls in the dark," is used. In the event that someone raises without looking at his cards, the prefix rb, for "raises blind," is used. The beginning of voluntary action in a betting round is denoted by a "greater than" symbol (>) since it looks like an arrowhead pointing to the right. Folds are indicated by dashes (-), and numbers indicate the total amount to which the player has completed betting. The end of betting action is denoted by a "less than" symbol (<). The > and < act as parentheses containing all the action occurring within a round of betting.

The Flop, Turn, and River rows follow the same format, and the cards that hit on each round are displayed appropriately. Note that $0, a "bet" of zero, is used to designate a check. If any additional cards are exposed during the hand, they are displayed in the location designating when exactly they were exposed, and they are followed by E:(), with the *exposed cards* appearing in the parentheses. For example, if the nine of clubs is exposed, E:(9♣) denotes this. The letter "d" prefaces actions in the dark. AI indicates that a player is all-in. The row entitled Hole shows what hands are shown down. In the event that someone folds and shows his hand, the word "Shown" will appear below it. In the event that the hand is mucked without showing, the word "Mucked" appears in the "Hole" row. The row labeled Comments allows room for analysis of the hand. I do so much analysis in the main text that I usually forego using the Comments row, but it's nice to have just in case I need it. The final row is a legend concisely displaying all the information covered in this paragraph.

Having explained the poker chart, let's walk our way through this hand in paragraph form, just to make sure that you understand the play. The first row tells us that this hand is taken from a $200NL game with $2–$5 blinds. To begin, all hands are unknown except for P10's, and the asterisks around 10(B) indicate that you are effectively P10 in that you are dealing with his information set.* P1 posts the small blind, P2 posts the big blind, and P10 is the button. The preflop betting action starts with P3. P3–P5 fold, P6 raises to $20, and P7–P9 fold. P10 calls, as does P1. P2 folds, and preflop betting action concludes with the total amount in the pot being $61 after the casino takes a $4 *rake*.

The flop is J♠9♥5♣. Three players are left in the hand (P1, P6, and P10), and their respective stack sizes are $220, $705, and $280. P1 begins betting action on the flop by checking. P6 bets $40, P10 raises to $120, P1 folds, and P6 calls. $301 is

* Instead of typing things like "player 10," I will use the letter "P" followed by the identifying number of the player. So, "player 10" becomes "P10."

now in the pot. After the flop, the 9♠ is exposed. On the turn, P6 has $585, and P10 has $160. P6 bets $300 in the dark. The turn card is a 3♦, and in addition, the 8♥ is exposed. P10 calls his remaining $160. The main pot (M) is $621, and since P6 has P10 covered, he is eligible for side pot 1 (S1), which contains $140. There is only one player here, so you usually will not see a side pot in a real-life cardroom. The notation designating the players eligible for each side pot is what is important here. The river card is a 4♦, and P6 wins the main pot, M ($621), and side pot 1, S1 ($140), with his pocket kings. P10 mucks his hand without showing.

It took a lengthy, at times confusing, paragraph to describe all the information contained in the chart. MCU charts don't use a large number of obscure abbreviations and symbols, and since there's a legend with every chart, I hope that you find them helpful to you in your reading.

## Interval Notation

Another convenient tool used throughout this text is *interval notation*, a shorthand method for describing *hand distributions*. A hand distribution is the set of all possible holdings a player may have. For example, we will later examine distributions your opponents push all-in with late in a single-table tournament (STT). Suppose that your opponent is pushing all-in with any ace, any king, any pocket pair, QJ, QT, or JT. While that sentence isn't nearly as cumbersome as a paragraph outlining the play of a hand, we can convey this hand distribution in a more compact way with interval notation.

In mathematics, interval notation is often used to represent a set of numbers. For example, if I want to represent the set of all the numbers from 1 to 8, with 1 and 8 included, I can simply write [1,8]. A Texas hold'em hand contains two hole cards; however, the notation is still applicable. Instead of intervals such as [1,8], we have intervals such as [AK,A9]. The way this notation works is that we count from the first card in the first hand to the first card in the second hand while, simultaneously, counting from the second card in the first hand to the second card in the second hand. If the cards are suited, an "s" follows, and if they are unsuited, an "o" follows. If the cards are either suited or unsuited, then no letter is used. Cards of a specific suit are identified with a ♣, ♦, ♥, or ♠. Now, let's look at a few examples:

[AK,A9] = AK, AQ, AJ, AT, and A9

[KQs,JTs] = KQ (suited), QJ (suited), and JT (suited)

[JJ,77] = JJ, TT, 99, 88, and 77

Each interval represents a set of hands. Now, what happens if we want to talk about a hand distribution like "all aces and any pocket pair?" In that case, we need two separate intervals. To do this, I borrow a symbol from computer programming. "||" is the logical OR operator in the C programming language, and I use it with interval notation to take the union of two or more sets. [AK,A2]||[AA,22] represents the hand distribution of all aces and pocket pairs. The way it's read is that the player has either an unpaired ace *or* a pocket pair. A few more examples are below:

[AK,AT]||[KQ,KJ]||[AA,TT] = AK, AQ, AJ, AT, KQ, KJ, AA, KK, QQ, JJ, and TT

[AKs,A2s]||[JT,54] = AKs, AQs, AJs, ATs, A9s, A8s, A7s, A6s, A5s, A4s, A3s, A2s, JT, T9, 98, 87, 76, 65 and 54

Why should we be so concerned about hand distributions in the first place? Well, when we *put a player on a hand,* what we should really do is put him on a range of hands. Sometimes, it's possible to have a read so good that the distribution contains only one hand, but most of the time, it's ridiculous to say something like, "I put you on AK with that preflop raise since you wouldn't have raised to four big blinds with AA."

## Probability, Permutations, and Combinations

With notational business taken care of, it's now time to discuss the type of math I'll be using. Much of my analysis consists of probability calculations that take into account knowledge of opponents' hand distributions. Probability, after all, is the mathematics of *random events*. The probability of an event, simply defined, is the number of outcomes for the event divided by the total number of possible outcomes. As an equation, this idea is expressed in equation 1.4, with P(event) meaning "the probability of an event."

$$P(event) = \frac{Outcomes\_for\_Event}{Total\_Number\_of\_Possible\_Outcomes} \qquad (1.4)$$

Using this definition, the probability of drawing an ace out of a deck of 52 cards is:

$$P(Ace) = \tfrac{4}{52} \qquad (1.5)$$

This is because there are 4 aces in the deck out of 52 total cards in the deck. Finding probabilities is, therefore, really just a problem in counting, and if all the counting we were going to do was as simple as counting the number of aces in a deck, I wouldn't have to say anything else. Unfortunately, most of the counting needed to analyze Texas hold'em is more complicated than this. *Fortunately*, it's not complicated to the point of being really difficult. To assist in our counting efforts, we're going to use two related ideas: *permutations* and *combinations*.

A permutation is an ordering of elements in a set. For example, let's take the set {a, b, c}. The permutations of this set are the following: {a, b, c}; {a, c, b}; {b, a, c}; {b, c, a}; {c, a, b}; {c, b, a}. To find the number of permutations of objects in a set, what you do is take the number of ways to choose the first element and multiply that by the number of ways to choose the second element. If there is a third element, you then multiply by the number of ways to choose the third element, and you repeat this process until there are no more elements to choose. Let's follow this procedure for the example above. There are three ways to choose the first element (a, b, or c). Once the first element is chosen, there are only two elements left, and once the second element is chosen, the last one is completely determined since there are only three objects. By doing the multiplication out as described, we get that there are $3 \cdot 2 \cdot 1 = 6$ permutations of the set {a, b, c}.

Now, let's bring this back to hold'em—after all, that's why we're all here. Suppose you are dealt 2 cards from a regular 52-card deck. There are 52 ways to get dealt the first card and 51 remaining ways to get dealt the second card. The total number of ways that two cards can be dealt to you is therefore:

$$52 \cdot 51 = 2{,}652 \tag{1.6}$$

In other words, there are 2,652 permutations. Notice that order matters in this calculation—for example, A♣K♣ and K♣A♣ are different.

From the definition of permutations and the definition of probability in equation 1.4, we see that one way of calculating probabilities is to take the number of permutations of an event and then to divide by the total number of possible permutations—a permutation is considered an outcome. As an example, let's calculate the probability of getting dealt AKs [written as P(AKs)]. First, we must find the number of AKs permutations. There are 4 aces and 4 kings that we can receive for the first card. Given that the first card is an ace or king, there is only one possibility for the second card—the card of the same suit as the first card. Suppose the first card is K♣. The only possible second card that gives us AKs is A♣. The number of AKs permutations is therefore 8•1 = 8. To find P(AKs), we must now divide 8, the number of AKs permutations, by the total number of permutations for two cards. Equation 1.6 tells us that there are 2,652 permutations of 2 cards. Thus, P(AKs) is given by:

$$P(AKs) = \tfrac{8}{2{,}652} = \tfrac{1}{331.5} \approx .00302. \qquad (1.7)$$

Note that probabilities don't have units. Also note that I don't put a leading zero before the decimal point. This is because a probability can never be more than 1. To convert to a percentage, take the probability and multiply by 100. Having brought percentages into the picture, we now have two ways to refer to equation 1.7's result. We can say that the probability of getting dealt AKs is .00302, or we can say that we will be dealt AKs 0.302% of the time.

Now, let's say we want to know how many ways a deck of 52 cards can be ordered—in other words, we want to know the number of permutations that exist for a deck of cards. To figure that out, use the same method as before. We know that there are 52 possibilities for the 1st card, 51 possibilities for the 2nd card, 50 possibilities for the 3rd card, and so on, all the way down to the last card. Thus, we have to multiply 52•51•50•. . . •3•2•1. Writing out products like this can be quite cumbersome, but luckily, there is a notational device to help us out. The product, 52•51•50•. . . •3•2•1, can be represented as 52!. The exclamation point tells us to start with 52 and to keep on multiplying until we get down to 1. This is called a factorial. A few examples follow:

$$6! = 6 \cdot 5 \cdot 4 \cdot 3 \cdot 2 \cdot 1 = 720 \tag{1.8}$$

$$20! = 20 \cdot 19 \cdot 18 \cdot \ldots \cdot 3 \cdot 2 \cdot 1 = 2{,}432{,}902{,}008{,}176{,}640{,}000 \tag{1.9}$$

As we can see, the factorial function grows extremely fast! Imagine that we are at a ten-handed table. That means that 20 cards have been dealt, and in addition, there are 5 more cards for the flop, the turn, and the river. The total number of permutations is 25! = 15,511,210,043,330,985,984,000,000. In general, if you have *n* objects, there are *n*! permutations of those objects. This is why a lot of computer power is needed to do simulations for poker situations at a full table where players have random hands.

Now, let's say that we don't care about card order. In other words, we want to treat A♣K♣ and K♣A♣ as the same outcome. A♣K♣ then becomes a combination as opposed to a permutation—a combination is an unordered sampling of objects. To determine the number of combinations of AKs, we know that there are 4 aces in the deck, and for each ace, there's only 1 king of the same suit. Thus, there are 4 combinations of AKs. Notice how the counting here is different from when we counted permutations of AKs. Since AKs and KAs are now the same, we can simply consider *one* of the orderings.

Another way to find the number of AKs combinations is to start with the fact that there are 8 *permutations* of AKs. To find the number of AKs *combinations*, we need to divide out the permutations leading to doubly counted combinations (e.g., we don't want to double count A♣K♣ and K♣A♣ since they're the same combination). There are two cards, meaning that there are 2! = 2 permutations for each combination. Using the 8 AKs permutations and the fact that there are 2 permutations of 2 objects, we get that there are $\frac{8}{2} = 4$ combinations of AKs, just as we did before.* In general, we can find the number of combinations by taking the total number of permutations and dividing that by the permutations of the number of elements comprising a permutation.

We can use combinations in the same way that we used permutations to find probabilities. To find the probability of getting dealt AKs in the combinations paradigm, we now need to know how many total combinations of hole cards there are. Well, there are 52•51 = 2,652 permutations. Now, all we need to do is divide out the doubly counted combinations. There are 2 cards; therefore, there are 2! permutations for each combination, meaning that the total number of combinations is:

$$\frac{2{,}652}{2} = 1{,}326 \tag{1.10}$$

Because there are 4 AKs combinations, the probability of getting dealt AKs is $\frac{4}{1{,}326} \approx .00302$, the same number we got before for P(AKs). Some counting is more easily done using permutations while other counting is more easily done using combinations, so it is convenient to have a choice of which to use.

Now, what about everyone's favorite hand, AA (if AA is not your favorite hand, then you must not like making money)? There are $\frac{4 \cdot 3}{2} = 6$ combinations of AA (4•3 total permutations and 2! permutations of 2 cards). Thus, P(AA) is $\frac{6}{1{,}326} = \frac{1}{221} \approx .00452$. In other words, you will get dealt AA 1 out of every

* A great way of checking answers is to do problems multiple ways, making sure each yields the same answer.

221 hands. This same process can be used to find the probability of getting dealt any hand in hold'em.

One way of organizing the possible starting hands is to put them into three classes: pocket pairs; unsuited, unpaired cards; and suited, unpaired cards. The probabilities of getting a specific hand from each class are summarized in table 1.3. I did the calculation for getting a specific set of suited, unpaired cards (there's nothing special about AKs as a set of suited, unpaired cards). I also did the calculation for getting dealt a specific pocket pair (the probability of getting AA is going to be the same as getting 22, 77, or any other pocket pair). Therefore, I leave it as an exercise for you to compute the probability of getting a specific set of unsuited, unpaired cards.

**TABLE 1.3: Probability of Being Dealt Certain Starting Hands**

| STARTING HAND | PROBABILITY |
|---|---|
| Specific Pocket Pair (AA, for example) | $\frac{1}{221}$ |
| Specific Unsuited, Unpaired (J9o, for example) | $\frac{1}{110.5}$ |
| Specific Suited, Unpaired (KQs, for example) | $\frac{1}{331.5}$ |

You'll see that I use the combinations approach for most of the probabilities that I calculate (there are a few instances where permutations must be used, though). If you wish, you can always just count permutations instead. In addition, you can multiply the probabilities of independent events—events that don't depend on each other—as I did in the continuation bet example at the beginning of the chapter.

There are different styles for handling probability problems, and in time, you'll find the style that you prefer. If you have valid, logical justifications for everything you do, you should be just fine with the material I've given you.

## Using Complements to Find Probabilities of Certain Events

I have one more trick for finding probabilities that deserves its own section. When I first defined probability, I talked about the probability of events happening. However, we can also discuss the probability of events *not* happening. If we have a particular event in mind, all the outcomes not part of that event, when put together, form the complement. Knowing how to use complements can expedite many probability calculations. To motivate the discussion, let's assume that you have AK. What is the probability that you will flop one or more aces or kings? There are two ways to solve this problem. Method 1 employs what you learned in the previous section (see p. 20) while Method 2 employs a useful trick.

**METHOD 1:** You know 2 cards in the deck, so now we are left with a deck of 50 cards. There are $\frac{50 \cdot 49 \cdot 48}{3!}$ = 19,600 combinations of flops—50•49•48 gives the total number of permutations and 3! = 3•2•1 = 6 is the number of permutations of 3 cards. We now need to count how many of these flops give us one or more aces or kings. The problem breaks into three steps: finding the number of combinations with 1 ace or king, the number of combinations with 2 aces or kings (meaning both are aces, both are kings, or one of each), and the number of combinations with 3 aces or kings (meaning all aces, all kings, or some mixture of aces and kings).

The number of flops containing 1 ace or king is found as follows: We constrain the first card to be an ace or king, meaning that there are 6 combinations for the first card. The second and third cards cannot be an ace or a king, so for the last two cards, we are choosing from 44 cards. There are 44 ways to choose the second card and 43 ways to choose the last card. 44•43 is the number of permutations for the last two cards. To get the number of combinations, we have to divide by 2! since there are 2! = 2 permutations for a group of 2 objects. The number of flops containing 1 ace or king is then $(6)\left(\frac{44 \cdot 43}{2!}\right) = 5{,}676$.

To find the number of flops containing 2 aces or kings, we constrain the first 2 cards to be aces or kings. We are choosing 2 aces or kings from a pool of 6, meaning that the number of combinations of aces and kings is given by $\frac{6 \cdot 5}{2!} =$ 15. For each combination of aces and kings, there are 44 cards left that can be chosen for the last card. Thus, there are 15•44 = 660 flops containing 2 aces or kings.

To find the number of flops containing 3 aces or kings, we choose 3 cards out of the 6 aces and kings available. The number of combinations for choosing 3 objects out of a pool of 6 objects is given by $\frac{6 \cdot 5 \cdot 4}{3!} = 20$. 3! is in the denominator since there are 3! permutations of 3 objects.

To find the probability of flopping at least one ace or king, all we have to do now is add up the number of flops of interest and divide by the total number of possible flops. The probability is therefore:

$$\frac{5{,}676 + 660 + 20}{19{,}600} = \frac{6{,}356}{19{,}600} \approx .32 \qquad (1.11)$$

**METHOD 2:** We know that each *outcome of interest* is associated with one, two, or three of the remaining aces and kings coming out on the flop. Note that the only other possible outcome is flopping no aces or kings. Mathematicians refer to the set of all possible outcomes for a random event as an *outcome space.* The complete outcome space of flops, with respect to aces and kings, is that 0, 1, 2, or 3 show up. These are disjoint outcomes, meaning that they have no overlap and that we can therefore add and subtract their probabilities to answer questions like, "What is the probability that 0 or 3 aces or kings come out on the flop?" In Method 1, we added the probabilities of flopping 1, 2, or 3 aces or kings. Since 0 is the only other possible outcome and since the probabilities of all disjoint events in a completely defined outcome space must add up to 1, it makes sense that we can find the probability of flopping 0 aces or kings and then subtract that number from 1. The outcome, 0 aces or kings, is the complement of the outcome of 1, 2, or 3 aces or kings showing up. More formally, two sets of outcomes are complementary if they are disjoint and their probabilities add up to 1.

With that in mind, let's find the probability of 0 aces or kings showing up on the flop. There are 44 cards in the deck that aren't aces or kings, and we are going to choose three of them. Thus, the number of combinations is $\frac{44 \cdot 43 \cdot 42}{3!} = 13{,}244$. The number of combinations that, therefore, contain at least 1 ace or king is $19{,}600 - 13{,}244 = 6{,}356$, and as in Method 1, we see that the probability of flopping at least 1 ace or king is equal to $\frac{6{,}356}{19{,}600} \approx .32$. By using the idea of complements, we are able to reduce the number of calculations required. So when you find yourself in a similar situation, you should employ them as I did here.

## Chapter Summary and Preview of What's to Come

In this chapter, I put you in the analytic mindset, set up some notational conventions, and gave you a crash course on calculating probabilities. We did a lot of essential foundation building to set us up for what's to come.

In the next chapter, I continue building a foundation as we delve into *expectation value* (EV). EV is a concept applicable to making decisions in many contexts (gambling, insurance, and warranties, just to name a few), and optimizing EV in situations encountered in Texas hold'em will be the focus of the rest of this book. In talking about expectation value, I will also expose you to what I call the "hand distribution model" (HDM) of Texas hold'em. The HDM is the theoretical framework through which I view the game.

## Problems

1. a. Using a hand simulator, find the winning and tying probabilities associated with the preflop matchup of A♣K♦ vs. 9♥9♠.

   b. Using a hand simulator, find the winning and tying probabilities associated with the preflop matchup of AK vs. 99.

   c. Using a hand simulator, find the winning and tying probabilities associated with A♣K♦ vs. 9♥9♠ when the flop is J♦T♠8♣.

2. Congratulations! You are heads-up in a long multi-table tournament. You and your opponent both have 200,000 chips, and the blinds are at a monstrous 20,000–40,000. You post the big blind and are dealt K7s.* Your opponent pushes all-in. Use a hand simula-

* For those not familiar with heads-up play, the button posts the small blind and the other player posts the big blind. The button therefore acts

tor to find your winning and tying percentages if your opponent is pushing all-in with the following distributions (Poker Stove allows me to input a distribution so that I only have to run one calculation—should you choose a different simulator, it should do that too):

a. [AA,22]|||[AK,A2]|||[KQ,K2]|||[QJ,Q8]|||[JT]|||[T9s,65s]

b. [AA,22]|||[AK,A2]|||[KQ,K2]|||[QJ,Q8]

c. [AA,55]|||[AK,A2]|||[KQ,K8]|||[QJ,QT]

3. Show that the probability of getting dealt a specific unsuited, unpaired starting hand in hold'em matches the result in table 1.3 ($\frac{1}{110.5}$).

4. a. If you hold two hearts, what is the probability that you will flop either a flush or 4 to a flush?

   b. If you hold two hearts and are able to see the flop, the turn, and the river, what is the probability that you will get a flush?

5. If you hold a pocket pair, what is the probability that you will flop a set or better, excluding full houses where the flop contains three of a kind?

6. You have AK. What is the probability that you will flop at least 1 ace or king given that an ace was exposed preflop?

---

first preflop and acts last all other betting rounds. It is supposed to work like this in cash games and tournaments, but at the time of writing, there is at least one online poker site that screws this up in cash games.

## Answers to Problems

1a. Using Poker Stove, I find that P(win) for A♣K♦ is .4416 and P(tie) for A♣K♦ is .0032 when against 9♥9♠.

1b. Using Poker Stove, I find that P(win) for AK is .4520 and P(tie) for AK is .0040 when against 99.

*Explanation:* Contrasting this result to the answer to 1a, we see that the particular suits involved in a preflop matchup like this make a slight difference in the results. However, unless your opponent exposes his cards, you won't know what particular suits you are up against, so simulations like those done for 1b are more along the lines of what you'll be using in your analysis.

1c. When the flop is J♦T♠8♣, Poker Stove shows that P(win) for A♣K♦is .3717 and P(tie) for A♣K♦ is .0080 when against 9♥9♠.

2a. Against [AA,22]|||[AK,A2]|||[KQ,K2]|||[QJ,Q8]|||[JT]|||[T9s, 65s], Poker Stove shows that your K7s will win .4195 times and tie .0682 times.

2b. Against [AA,22]|||[AK,A2]|||[KQ,K2]|||[QJ,Q8], Poker Stove shows that your K7s will win .4072 times and tie .0726 times.

2c. Against [AA,55]|||[AK,A2]|||[KQ,K8]|||[QJ,QT], Poker Stove shows that your K7s will win .3746 times and tie .0258 times.

3. The probability is $\frac{1}{110.5} \approx .009$, matching the result in table 1.3.

   *Explanation:* Consider a specific unsuited, unpaired hand like J9o. If you choose the jack first, there are 4 ways to choose the jack. If you then choose a 9, there are only 3 nines left since one of the nines is the same suit as the jack. Therefore, there are $4 \cdot 3 = 12$ combinations of J9o. There is nothing special about J9o—this analysis works out the same whether you are looking at AKo or 72o. Thus, for any specific unpaired, unsuited hand, there are 12 combinations. From equation 1.10, there are $\frac{52 \cdot 51}{2!} = 1{,}326$ combinations of hole cards. Thus, the probability of getting dealt a specific unsuited, unpaired hand is $\frac{12}{1{,}326} = \frac{1}{110.5} \approx .009$, which matches the result in table 1.3.

4a. The probability is about .12.

   *Explanation:* You hold 2 hearts, meaning that there are 11 hearts left in the deck. There are 4 outcomes in the flop outcome space with respect to hearts: {0 hearts, 1 heart, 2 hearts, 3 hearts}. If you flop a flush or 4 to a flush, what you are looking for is the probability of seeing either 2 hearts or 3 hearts on the flop. To find this probability, first compute the number of combinations for each outcome. The number of combinations of flops containing 2 hearts is given by the number of combinations of 2 hearts, $\frac{11 \cdot 10}{2!} = 55$, times the number of nonhearts for the last card, 39. The number of combinations of flops that give you a flush draw is therefore $55 \cdot 39 = 2{,}145$. The number of combinations of flops containing 3 hearts is given by $\frac{11 \cdot 10 \cdot 9}{3!} = 165$. Therefore, the total number of combinations giving you either a flush or 4 to a flush is 2,145 + 165 = 2,310.

You now need to know how many total combinations of flops there are. You are given that you hold two hearts. You don't know what cards they are specifically; however, the rank of the cards isn't used at all in this calculation. Thus, you must treat the deck as a deck of 50 cards. Recall from the reading that the number of combinations for the flop, when you know two cards, is given by $\frac{50\cdot49\cdot48}{3!} = 19{,}600$. The probability of flopping a flush or a flush draw is therefore $\frac{2{,}310}{19{,}600} \approx .12$.

4b. The probability is about .064.

*Explanation:* Again, you hold 2 hearts, meaning that there are 11 hearts left in the deck. The only things different about this problem are that you are now only considering the outcomes where you make a flush (after all, you don't care if you have a four flush on the river) and that you are getting 5 cards instead of just 3. The outcome space with respect to the number of hearts that show up on the board is {0,1,2,3,4,5}. You get a flush if there are 3, 4, or 5 hearts on the board. Granted, if you don't hold the highest or possibly second highest heart in your hand, a board with 4 or 5 hearts isn't exactly what you want. However, we'll be calculating each outcome separately, so we'll be able to see the effect of each on the total.

The number of combinations of boards with 3 hearts is given by $\left(\frac{11\cdot10\cdot9}{3!}\right)\left(\frac{39\cdot38}{2!}\right) = 122{,}265$. The first part of this product, $\left(\frac{11\cdot10\cdot9}{3!}\right)$, represents the number of ways to choose 3 hearts from a pool of 11 hearts.

The second part of this product, $\left(\frac{39\cdot38}{2!}\right)$, represents the number of ways to choose two nonhearts from the remaining pool of 39 nonhearts. Similarly, the number of combinations of boards with 4 hearts is $\left(\frac{11\cdot10\cdot9\cdot8}{4!}\right)(39) = 12{,}870$, and the number of combinations of boards with 5 hearts is $\left(\frac{11\cdot10\cdot9\cdot8\cdot7}{5!}\right) = 462$. The total number of combinations of 5-card boards is $\frac{50\cdot49\cdot48\cdot47\cdot46}{5!} = 2{,}118{,}760$. Therefore, the probability of getting a flush is $\frac{122{,}265+12{,}870+462}{2{,}118{,}760} = \frac{135{,}597}{2{,}118{,}760} \approx .064$.

We've answered the question, but let's delve a bit deeper. The probability of getting a flush with 3 hearts on the board is $\frac{122{,}265}{2{,}118{,}760} \approx .058$. The probability of getting a flush with 4 or 5 hearts on the board is $\frac{12{,}870+462}{2{,}118{,}760} \approx .006$. From these probabilities, we see that the instances that you get a flush with 4 or 5 hearts on the board are outweighed by the times you get a flush with 3 hearts on the board. In fact, out of the times you get a flush, the probability that you have a flush with 3 hearts on the board is $\frac{122{,}265}{122{,}265+12{,}870+462} \approx .90$.

5. The probability is about .12.

*Explanation:* Let's say you hold 55. This question is really asking, what is the probability that you will flop one or two 5's. {0,1,2} is the outcome space with respect to the number of flopped 5's. The quickest way to solve this problem is, therefore, to find out how many flops have no 5, and then to subtract that number from the total number of flops. In other words, find the complement of what you are interested in so that you can ultimately get the answer you're actually looking for. The number of flops not containing a 5 is $\left(\frac{48\cdot47\cdot46}{3!}\right) = 17{,}296$. There are $\frac{50\cdot49\cdot48}{3!} = 19{,}600$ total flops since you know two cards. (I continue to show this calculation for pedagogical purposes, but if you've committed it to memory and understand how to derive it, then you don't have to do the same work repeatedly.) There are 19,600 total flops and 17,296 flops not containing a 5; thus, the number of flops containing at least one 5 is 19,600 – 17,296 = 2,304. The probability of flopping at least one 5 is therefore $\frac{2{,}304}{19{,}600} \approx .12$.

6. The probability is about .28.

*Explanation:* This problem is very similar to the example problem in this chapter. In the chapter, we had a pool of 6 aces or kings to draw from (see p. 26). Now, the pool of aces or kings only contains 5 cards. Also, you know your hole cards and the exposed ace, so at this point the deck has 49 cards instead of the 50 cards that we have been using in most of the flop examples. Complements are the best way to solve this problem. Thus, the first order of business is finding the probability that there are no aces or kings on the flop. There are $\frac{44 \cdot 43 \cdot 42}{3!}$ = 13,244 flops containing neither an ace nor a king, and there are $\frac{49 \cdot 48 \cdot 47}{3!}$ = 18,424 possible flops in total. In all, there are 18,424 – 13,244 = 5,180 flops containing at least 1 ace or king. The probability of flopping an ace or a king if you hold AK and an ace is exposed is therefore $\frac{5{,}180}{18{,}424} \approx .28$. This result shows that if one of your unpaired cards is dead, your probability of flopping at least one of your remaining 5 outs decreases from .32 to .28.

# 2

# EXPECTATION VALUE AND ODDS

♧♤◇♡

## Expectation Value Part 1: Complete Information

When we play poker, our goal is to optimize our profit. For a specific hand, the nature of poker is that we don't know what the actual outcome is going to be. Despite that, if we know the probabilities of winning, P(win), tying, P(tie); and losing, P(lose), we can come up with the average gain or loss for a decision. This average gain or loss for a decision is called expectation value (EV). Understanding EV and knowing how to calculate it are essential to poker success.

EV refers to the amount of money that you expect to win or lose *in the long run* per wager on a random event. Recalling from the motivational problem in chapter 1, your expected profit from making a $\frac{2}{3}$ pot continuation bet into one opponent in that situation is $(.65)(P) - (.35)(\frac{2}{3}P) = +\frac{5}{12}P$. For a numerical example, if the pot is \$120 and you make an \$80 continuation bet into one opponent, you expect a profit of $(\frac{5}{12})(\$120) = \$50$. Notice how I used the words "expect" and "expected." The reason is that because, in the long term, this is how much money that we predict you'll make per continuation bet. In the short term, though, you won't necessarily make $50 per continuation bet (after all, we don't always get what we expect in life). In fact, if we consider just the first continuation bet you ever make, you either gain $120 or lose $80—it's *impossible* to make $50. It's only after averaging your results over many continuation bets that your average profit per bet would be close to $50. Of course, it doesn't *have* to be close to $50; an improbable string of events, like your opponent folding 300 out of 300 times, can occur.* The idea, though, is that if you made an infinite number of continuation bets, the average would be $50.

Now that we understand what EV is, it would be nice to be able to calculate it. Calculating EV for a random event requires three pieces of information. First, we must be able to enumerate all possible outcomes of the random event—recall from the last chapter that this set of all possible outcomes is called an outcome space. Second, we must know the probability of each event in the outcome space. Finally, we must know the payout for each event in the outcome space—in other words, the monetary loss or gain for each outcome.

Once you have these three pieces of knowledge, EV is found by multiplying each payout by its probability of happening and adding everything together. Let's run through a sample calculation based on the situation in table 2.1 (pp. 38–39).

* Don't confuse improbable with impossible. The probability that your opponent folds 300 consecutive times is given by $(.65)^{300} \approx 7.48 \cdot 10^{-57}$. That's 748 with 56 zeroes in front of it! This incredibly small probability indicates that you probably won't see a string of 300 consecutive folds in your lifetime (unless you are immortal); however, this is *not* the same as it being impossible.

## Table 2.1: Sample Situation of an EV Calculation with Complete Information

**Game:** $200NL Hold'em
**Structure:** Small Blind: $2 Big Blind: $5
**Comments:** Home game with no rake. Action only recorded until P5's bet on the turn. When P5 bets the turn, he exposes his hole cards before you (P4) act, thinking that you had folded. Given P5's hole cards, what's your EV for the $150 call?

| | 1(SB) | 2(BB) | 3 | *4* | 5(B) |
|---|---|---|---|---|---|
| | XX | XX | XX | A♣T♣ | XX |
| **STACKS** | $250 | $150 | $425 | $270 | $290 |
| **PREFLOP** | b$2 | b$5 | >$5 | $5 | $20 |
| | - | - | - | $20< | |
| **STACKS** | | | | $250 | $270 |
| **FLOP** | | | | >$40 | $100 |
| **Q♣J♣2♥** | | | | $100< | |
| **STACKS** | | | | $150 | $170 |
| **TURN** | | | | >$0 | $170 |
| **4♠** | | | | | E(Q♠Q♦) |
| **STACKS** | | | | | |
| **RIVER** | | | | | |
| **HOLE** | | | | | |

**Comments:** See text for analysis.

**Legend:** SB = Small Blind; BB = Big Blind; B = Button; X = Unknown Hole Card; b = Blind or Straddle; > = Beginning of Betting Round Action; < = End of Betting Round Action; - = Fold; d = Action in the Dark; c = Call; r = Raise; E = Exposed Card; M = Main Pot; S = Side Pot; AI = All-In; R = Rake

| POT |
| --- |
| |
| M = $52 |
| |
| M = $252 |
| |
| |
| |

Because P5 wasn't paying full attention, we have full knowledge of his hole cards. You, in contrast to P5, are on top of things—you didn't immediately fold when you saw the set of queens. If you are fortunate enough to get information about one or both of your opponents' hole cards, take a breath and take the opportunity to think.* Most of the time, you have *incomplete information* at the poker table, so take advantage of any break that you get.

So, let's take advantage of the break given by P5 by figuring out the precise EV of calling your remaining $150 on the turn. If you call, the outcome space is {win, tie, lose}. With a properly defined outcome space, we can now calculate the probability of each outcome. There is one card to come, and we know that 9 clubs in the deck give you a flush. However, 2 of these give P5 a full house (2♣ and 4♣), leaving only 7 flush outs. In addition, there are 3 uncounted kings that give you a straight—K♣ was already counted as a flush out.† In all, there are 10 cards in the deck that will win the hand for you. You know 8 cards in the deck—your hole cards (2 cards), P5's

* In fact, you should always take a breath and pause to think before you make any decisions at the poker table. Because I profitably play many tables at once against extremely weak opponents online, I am susceptible to what I refer to as *autopilot* poker, where my decisions are made instantaneously without any deep thought. Other people may go on autopilot for other reasons: watching the basketball game on the big screen, eating dinner, or checking out the cute cocktail waitress, just to name a few. Regardless of the cause, if you let yourself go on autopilot, I guarantee that you will hurt your results. So, let's make a pact, shall we? We will always think about our decisions before committing to them—no autopilot at the poker table!

† When we learned to count as youngsters, all we were taught was "1,2,3..." This type of basic counting is something we can all do. Avoiding double counting, as we had to do here, is the next step in learning how to count. It sounds a bit funny, but a lot of probability really is just about learning ways to count objects that are tricky to count because of double-counting possibilities or large quantities. Avoiding

hole cards (2 cards), the flop (3 cards), and the turn (1 card). This leaves $52 - 8 = 44$ cards in the deck.*

Since 10 cards in the deck win the hand for you and the deck has 44 cards, the probability that you will win is $\frac{10}{44}$. No cards result in a tie, making the probability of a tie $\frac{0}{44}$, and 34 cards in the deck result in a loss, making the probability of a loss $\frac{34}{44}$. Note that a great sanity check for your assigned probabilities is to make sure that they all add up to 1, and sure enough, $\frac{10}{44} + \frac{0}{44} + \frac{34}{44} + \frac{44}{44} = 1$. A big part of solid analysis is checking your work for errors along the way. It's also nice to have multiple ways of doing a problem; by making sure that all methods lead to consistent results, you can have more confidence in your results.

We have defined the outcome space, {win, tie, lose}, and calculated the probability of each outcome, $\{\frac{10}{44}, \frac{0}{44}, \frac{34}{44}\}$. The only task remaining is to assign a payout to each outcome. P5 bet \$170 on the turn; however, you only have \$150 remaining, meaning that the decision is whether to call \$150. The pot is \$252 + \$150 = \$402. Therefore, if you call and lose,

---

double counting is tough to teach; I think I've done my job by making you aware of it. Counting large quantities is mostly done using permutations and combinations, as seen at the end of chapter 1.

* Some players playing in live games with burn cards believe that there are only 42 cards left in the deck because of the burn cards. For those who believe this, I'm going to settle an issue of semantics. Even though Texas hold'em is played with one deck, there are really two decks to talk about: the physical deck that the dealer holds and the theoretical deck. It's true that the physical deck has 42 cards—if you could take the deck out of the dealer's hands and count the remaining cards, you would count 42 cards (if you don't have 42 cards, you better switch casinos). However, probability calculations are done based on our knowledge, so even though there are only 42 cards in the physical deck, we have no knowledge of what the burn cards are. Thus, the river card is equally likely to be any one of the remaining 44 cards in the theoretical deck, and therefore, the theoretical deck is what must be used in probability calculations.

you lose \$150, but if you call and win, you profit \$402. The EV for your call is therefore the following sum:

$$(P(win)(+\$402) + (P(lose)(-\$150) = \left(\tfrac{10}{44}\right)(+\$402) + \left(\tfrac{34}{44}\right)(-\$150) \approx -\$24.55 \quad (2.1)$$

On average, making this call results in a loss of about \$24.55. Obviously, you will either win \$402 or lose \$150 on this hand if you call. However, if you were to make this exact call 100 times, we expect that you would lose about \$24.55 per call, meaning that your total loss over 100 hands is expected to be \$2,455 (ouch!). Does this mean that you would actually lose \$2,455 if you made this call 100 times? No. The nature of random events is that there is *variance* associated with them. All we can say is that if you make this call, then the *expectation* is that you will lose \$24.55 per call on average. Recall our definition of EV as the amount of money that you would expect to win or lose per wager *in the long run*. Whenever we make decisions about random events, the idea is to make decisions that yield the highest possible profit in the long run. So, for those gamblers out there who might pay \$150 to catch that club, your understanding of EV should now tell you how foolish that call is in the long run. Vice versa, for the timid and meek, if I gave a situation where the \$150 call was very slightly +EV, let's say +\$0.01, you should, in general, have no qualms about calling since you are expecting a long term profit—if the variance of the call scares you, you are playing for too much money to begin with.* By thinking about EV, you are thinking about the

* One situation where I personally avoid a very slightly + EV call like this is when I'm in a restricted buy-in game, I have multiple buy-ins in front of me, and losing the amount of money for the call will bring my stack below that of a weak player that I'm looking to bust. As an example of this, let's say I'm in a \$100 buy-in game with \$300 in front of me, and

long term, and this is why the focus of Killer Poker has always been about the process and not the immediate outcomes.

## Expectation Value Part 2: Incomplete Information and the Hand Distribution Model (HDM)*

In the hand we just looked at, we were fortunate enough to know exactly what your opponent held. We all know how rarely that happens, though: we usually do not know the precise hand held by an opponent. Therefore, we must learn how to make the optimal decision based on incomplete information.

Again, consider the hand from the previous section, but this time, P5 is paying more attention and does not show his hand. The hand is outlined in table 2.2 (pp. 44–45).

---

there's a weak player with $300 in front of him. Why would I put myself in a situation where I have a $\frac{2}{3}$ chance of having only $150 in front of me, putting me out of contention for getting an easy $300 later on in the session?

* Hand Distribution Model (HDM) bears some similarities to material that has already been published. In particular, some may note similarities between HDM and Dan Harrington's Structured Hand Analysis (SHAL), which appears in *Harrington on Hold'em Volume 2* (Two Plus Two, 2005). While Dan Harrington's SHAL is applied to tournament preflop all-in situations, it can really be applied to any poker situation. HDM, therefore, may be considered by some to be an extension of SHAL as presented by Harrington, and as a result, I should acknowledge SHAL and Harrington's great book.

## Table 2.2: Sample Situation for an EV Calculation with Incomplete Information

**Game:** $200NL Hold'em
**Structure:** Small Blind: $2 Big Blind: $5
**Comments:** Home game with no rake. Action only recorded until P5's bet on the turn. What's your EV for the $150 call (you are P4)?

| | 1(SB) | 2(BB) | 3 | *4* | 5(B) |
|---|---|---|---|---|---|
| | XX | XX | XX | A♣T♣ | XX |
| **STACKS** | $250 | $150 | $425 | $270 | $290 |
| **PREFLOP** | b$2 | b$5 | >$5 | $5 | $20 |
| | - | - | - | $20< | |
| **STACKS** | | | | $250 | $270 |
| **FLOP** | | | | >$40 | $100 |
| **Q♣J♣2♥** | | | | $100< | |
| **STACKS** | | | | $150 | $170 |
| **TURN** | | | | >$0 | $170 |
| **4♠** | | | | | |
| **STACKS** | | | | | |
| **RIVER** | | | | | |
| **HOLE** | | | | | |

**Comments:** See text for analysis.

**Legend:** SB = Small Blind; BB = Big Blind; B = Button; X = Unknown Hole Card; b = Blind or Straddle; > = Beginning of Betting Round Action; < = End of Betting Round Action; - = Fold; d = Action in the Dark; c = Call; r = Raise; E = Exposed Card; M = Main Pot; S = Side Pot; AI = All-In; R = Rake

| POT |
| --- |
| |
| M = $52 |
| |
| M = $252 |
| |
| |
| |

You are faced with the same $150 call on the turn for a $402 pot, but this time, you don't know what P5 has. Our task as Killer Poker players is now to put P5 on a range of hands. Before making any decision during a poker game, it's imperative that you deduce what your opponents' possible holdings are and how they will react to your actions. Their reactions will be based on their cards and their perceptions of your play. The only way to have all this information is to pay attention constantly when you're at the table. If you are playing online, definitely take advantage of the sniffers I mentioned in chapter 1.

From your observations of P5, his raise preflop indicates that he most likely has a hand in the following distribution: [AA,88]|||[AK,AT]|||[KQ,KJ]|||[QJ]. I use "most likely" because no distribution that you ever assign to an opponent will be exact. A big part of understanding this process is being comfortable with the uncertainty involved. The only times you can possibly be certain about a read are when your opponents exhibit obvious physical tells, such as uncontrollable shaking indicating that they have the stone cold *nuts*, or when they bet in an extremely predictable fashion given their prior betting patterns.* In general, as the hand progresses, you will add and subtract hands from your opponents' distributions to have the most accurate pictures of them possible.

With your *overcard*, nut flush draw, and *gutshot straight draw,* you decide to bet into your opponent on the flop, and

* Even uncontrollable shaking is unreliable sometimes, especially when playing extremely old players or jittery players who haven't had their coffee. Unfortunately, these players always exhibit the uncontrollable hand tremor that's traditionally assigned to players who are excited about their monstrous hands. The best tell ever that I've witnessed was in a home game I played. A player looked at her hole cards and muttered "king-jack" under her breath without realizing it!

your opponent raises you. After raising preflop, he makes a lot of continuation bets when checked to on the flop; however, he usually folds when bet into. The times he has raised when bet into on the flop are situations where he has *semi-bluffed* big draws or when he has had at least top pair with a pretty good kicker.

Knowing these things about your opponent, let's think of the possible draws that he could have. You have A♣T♣, meaning that your opponent can't have the nut flush draw (you have it)—don't neglect the information from your hole cards when deducing your opponents' possible hole cards. He can't have an *outside straight draw* with a draw to a king-high flush since he would need K♣T♣ for that, and you hold the T♣. Some players would semi-bluff here with K♣T♦, K♣T♥, or K♣T♥, given that they have an outside straight draw with the king of clubs. In fact, some would semi-bluff here with any KT; however, from your observations of P5, you don't believe that he has KT. The only drawing hand you could be up against here is, therefore, K♣9♣, but given P5's preflop raise and his prior behavior, you can't put him on it. Note that if K♣T♣ were possible, I would consider adding it to our P5's distribution at this point. Even though it wasn't in the initial preflop raising distribution, it's close enough where putting it in now could be justified. K9s seems a little low relative to the preflop raising distribution, though.

We have deduced that given our present state of information about P5's game, there is no drawing hand that we can put him on. Does this mean that you would bet your mother's life on the fact that P5 does not have a draw on the flop? Of course not, unless you harbor some deep resentment toward your mother, but such feelings are your business and possibly your therapist's. The point is that to do any analysis, you need to have some courage in your convictions. If your convictions end up being wrong, figure out how to improve the accuracy of future convictions.

Now, we must go through all the possible made hands that P5 may hold. From our observations, we assume that he has at least top pair with a good kicker. The original preflop raising distribution was [AA,88]|||[AK,AT]|||[KQ,KJ]|||[QJ]. Out of these, the hole cards that give P5 top pair or better are [AA,JJ]|||[AQ,KQ]|||[QJ]. Even though QT wasn't in the original preflop raising distribution, we might be inclined to include it here. There's a fine line between being confident with your reads and adapting them to information gained as the hand develops.* In this situation, I'm going to hypothesize that you've seen your opponent limp with QT before, and you've never seen him raise with it. This doesn't mean that your opponent will never raise with QT, but it's a reasonable assumption. The other hand not in the original preflop raising distribution that has you beaten at this point is 22. It seems very unlikely that P5 raised preflop with 22 since it is so far from his preflop raising distribution, so we can discount the possibility that P5 has a set of 2s. We have therefore narrowed P5's distribution to [AA,JJ]|||[AQ,KQ]|||[QJ].

The next step is figuring out P(win), P(tie), and P(lose) against each of P5's possible holdings. As I cover commonly encountered situations later in the book, you'll learn approximations that you can use at the table, but whenever I

* There are two errors made by players when they put their opponents on hands. First, they avoid putting opponents on hands because they've prematurely fallen in love with their premium hole cards (e.g., they have AA and do not flinch when the board is J-J-T, or they play their KK fearlessly against 4 opponents when an ace flops). Second, players unreasonably put their opponents on hands that beat them because they're playing scared. Being good at reading players means not allowing your emotions to influence you. Let your observations and information guide you—nothing else. Assign your distributions first, and only after having done so, then figure out how your hand compares.

am away from the table, I do exact calculations on situations like these. Doing the exact calculations helps me commit the numbers to memory and learn new ones, and most likely, doing the exact calculations will benefit you as well. The bulleted list below gives P(win), P(tie), and P(lose) against each of P5's possible holdings:

- AA: You need to complete the flush (9 outs) or the straight (3 more outs since K♣ was included with the flush outs) to win. We know the 4 board cards, our 2 hole cards, and our opponent's 2 hole cards (either A♦A♥, A♦A♠, or A♥A♠), leaving 44 cards in the deck.* $P(win) = \frac{12}{44}$; $P(tie) = \frac{0}{44}$; $P(lose) = \frac{32}{44}$.
- KK: There are six combinations of cards that he can have (K♣K♦, K♣K♥, K♣K♠, K♦K♥, K♦K♠, and K♥K♠). Besides getting a straight or a flush, you can also hit an ace to win the hand. If your opponent holds the K♣, then you have 8 flush outs, 2 straight outs, and 3 ace outs: $P(win) = \frac{13}{44}$, $P(tie) = \frac{0}{44}$, and $P(lose) = \frac{31}{44}$. If your opponent does not have the K♣, then you have 9 flush outs, 1 straight out (we counted the K♣ as a flush out, and your opponent holds 2 kings, meaning that only 1 king remains), and 3 ace outs: $P(win) = \frac{13}{44}$, $P(tie) = \frac{0}{44}$, and $P(lose) = \frac{31}{44}$.
- QQ: There are 3 combinations (Q♦Q♥, Q♦Q♠, and Q♥Q♠). Against each, you have 7 flush outs (4♣ and 2♣ do not count since they make a full house for your op-

* All the combinations of AA are equivalent since you have the same number of outs against each, but each combination of AA is only 2 cards. That's why we gain 2 hole cards of information as opposed to 6 or some other number. This line of reasoning indicates that the mere process of putting an opponent on a hand reduces the number of cards in the deck by 2.

ponent) and 3 straight outs: $P(win) = \frac{10}{44}$; $P(tie) = \frac{0}{44}$; $P(lose) = \frac{34}{44}$.

- JJ: Same as QQ; just substitute J for Q in the combinations: $P(win) = \frac{10}{44}$; $P(tie) = \frac{0}{44}$; $P(lose) = \frac{34}{44}$.

- AQ: There are 3 aces left and 3 queens left, meaning that there are 3•3=9 combinations. Against each, you have 9 flush outs and 3 straight outs: $P(win) = \frac{12}{44}$; $P(tie) = \frac{0}{44}$; $P(lose) = \frac{32}{44}$.

- KQ: There are 4 kings left and 3 queens left, meaning that there are 4•3=12 combinations. If P5 has the K♣, you have 8 flush outs, 3 straight outs, and 3 ace outs: $P(win) = \frac{14}{44}$; $P(tie) = \frac{0}{44}$; $P(lose) = \frac{30}{44}$. If P5 does not hold the K♣, then you have 9 flush outs, 2 straight outs, and 3 ace outs, so again: $P(win) = \frac{14}{44}$; $P(tie) = \frac{0}{44}$; $P(lose) = \frac{30}{44}$.

- QJ: There are 3 queens left and 3 jacks left meaning that there are 9 combinations. Against each, you have 9 flush outs and 3 straight outs:$P(win) = \frac{12}{44}$; $P(tie) = \frac{0}{44}$; $P(lose) = \frac{32}{44}$.

Table 2.3 summarizes these results.

With the information in table 2.3, we can now do the EV calculation. Recall that winning the pot has a payout of +\$402 and that losing the pot has a payout of –\$150. In total, there are 18 terms to add together (9 winning terms and 9 losing terms). Eighteen terms are a lot; to reduce the number of terms by half, I use a little trick. I'm going to consider your EV when your \$150 call is in the pot. Putting the \$150 call in the pot, the payouts are now +\$552 for a win and \$0 for a loss. The payouts have changed, but the situation is the same. By making the payout for a loss \$0, all the terms involving losing situations go away since any number multi-

**TABLE 2.3: Number of Combinations for Each of P5's Possible Holdings and the Corresponding Values of P(Win) and P(Tie)**

| HAND | COMBINATIONS | P(WIN) | P(TIE) |
|---|---|---|---|
| AA | 3 | $\frac{12}{44}$ | $\frac{0}{44}$ |
| KK (with ♣) | 3 | $\frac{13}{44}$ | $\frac{0}{44}$ |
| KK (no ♣) | 3 | $\frac{13}{44}$ | $\frac{0}{44}$ |
| QQ | 3 | $\frac{10}{44}$ | $\frac{0}{44}$ |
| JJ | 3 | $\frac{10}{44}$ | $\frac{0}{44}$ |
| AQ | 9 | $\frac{12}{44}$ | $\frac{0}{44}$ |
| KQ (with K♣) | 3 | $\frac{14}{44}$ | $\frac{0}{44}$ |
| KQ (no K♣) | 9 | $\frac{14}{44}$ | $\frac{0}{44}$ |
| QJ | 9 | $\frac{12}{44}$ | $\frac{0}{44}$ |

plied by 0 is equal to 0. Thus, assuming that your $150 call is in the pot, your EV is the following:

$$\underbrace{\left(\tfrac{3}{45}\right)\left(\tfrac{12}{44}\right)(\$552)}_{\text{AA}}+\underbrace{\left(\tfrac{3}{45}\right)\left(\tfrac{13}{44}\right)(\$552)}_{\text{KK(with K♣)}}+\underbrace{\left(\tfrac{3}{45}\right)\left(\tfrac{13}{44}\right)(\$552)}_{\text{KK(no K♣)}}+\underbrace{\left(\tfrac{3}{45}\right)\left(\tfrac{10}{44}\right)(\$552)}_{\text{QQ}}+\underbrace{\left(\tfrac{3}{45}\right)\left(\tfrac{10}{44}\right)(\$552)}_{\text{JJ}}+$$

$$\underbrace{\left(\tfrac{9}{45}\right)\left(\tfrac{12}{44}\right)(\$552)}_{\text{AQ}}+\underbrace{\left(\tfrac{3}{45}\right)\left(\tfrac{14}{44}\right)(\$552)}_{\text{KQ(with K♣)}}+\underbrace{\left(\tfrac{9}{45}\right)\left(\tfrac{14}{44}\right)(\$552)}_{\text{KQ(no K♣)}}+\underbrace{\left(\tfrac{9}{45}\right)\left(\tfrac{12}{44}\right)(\$552)}_{\text{QJ}}\approx \$155.56 \quad (2.2)$$

Each term contains three numbers being multiplied by each other. The first two numbers when multiplied together give the probability of each event. For example, in the AA term, the probability that you win against AA is:*

* The " " in the expression is read as "given that" Thus, the probability that you win against AA is the probability that you are up against

$$[P(\text{vs. AA})][P(\text{win}|\text{vs. AA})] = \left(\tfrac{3}{45}\right)\left(\tfrac{12}{44}\right) \quad (2.3)$$

We see then that I originally figured out the number of combinations for each of P5's possible holdings to get the probabilities of being against each one. Some people mistakenly say that since 9 hand categories exist, the chance of being up against each is $\frac{1}{9}$. Those who say that forget there are a total number of hand combinations that they are up against, and the true probability of being up against a specific hand is therefore the number of combinations available for the specific hand divided by the total number of combinations. Thinking about it qualitatively, there are more AQ combinations possible than QQ combinations in this example, so it couldn't possibly be right to weigh them equally.

Going back to the result of equation 2.2, given P5 has the defined set of hands, you'll get $155.56 on average after investing $150. In other words, your expected profit from this call is $5.56. With your current, incomplete knowledge, the call is +$5.56, where before it was –$24.55. Notice how changes in information can significantly affect the outcomes of these calculations. Because changes in information change the results of these calculations, and we can never be precisely sure of our information, these calculations are part of an imprecise science. Despite that, this process is at the heart of playing poker. Once you know how to perform these calculations, poker becomes an art of deducing what your opponents hold, because then you take these hand distributions and crank them through this process. The more you pay attention and the more skilled you are, the more accurate your assigned distributions be-

---

AA times the probability that you win, given that you are up against AA. Formally, this concept is known as *conditional probability*.

come, and this is why it's so important to pay attention and to get data about all your opponents.

Are you going to do this type of calculation on the fly when you are playing? Probably not. However, it is important to understand the theory behind it. This calculation is at the heart of all poker playing, yet it is understood by only a small fraction of *winning* players, never mind the poker-playing population as a whole. Understanding HDM will put you well ahead of the curve. Combined with the ability to read your opponents as narrowly and accurately as possible, HDM will make you an optimal decision-making machine.* When I conduct my analysis away from the table, I often do exact calculations like those just mentioned assisted by computer software (spreadsheets and Poker Stove). By doing enough of these calculations, I have been able to come up with results that apply to situations that I commonly find myself in. Chapters 3 and beyond cover some commonly encountered situations using a combination of HDM analysis and simplifying approximations in cases where the full HDM analysis becomes overly cumbersome.

## Tree Diagrams

The reason that HDM analysis becomes cumbersome is that there are situations for which many possibilities exist. This usually happens because of the *conditional probabilities* involved. In solving the example hand from the last section, I

* The reason I say "narrowly and accurately" is that there are some very loose opponents for which the best hand distribution to assign is, in fact, the random distribution of all remaining cards in the deck. By assigning a narrower distribution against such an opponent, you'd actually be making a mistake.

used a bulleted list to pedagogically step through each of the nine possibilities for P5's hole cards. For situations with more possibilities, a bulleted list can get pretty long. To help with more complicated situations, I sometimes use a graphical tool known as a *tree diagram.*

In a tree diagram, each different outcome is represented as a branch, and the probabilities of each outcome are listed on the branches. The branches can split into subbranches, and the subbranches can continue to split into more subbranches. To trace through a set of outcomes, you simply trace through the branches. The probability of a set of outcomes is found by multiplying the probabilities of each branch along the path representing the set of outcomes of interest. Then, if you know the payout associated with the path, you can easily find its EV. With that overall picture in mind, see figure 2.1, a tree diagram of the same situation that I did the bulleted list for in the last section (since tree diagrams are awkward when all possibilities are not included, I did this tree diagram under the paradigm where winning is +$402 and losing is –$150):

We see that the sum of the EVs at the end of each line of branches matches the result from the previous section. If you're a visually oriented person, then you'll probably prefer tree diagrams to using tables or other such methods for sorting through these problems. If you start using tree diagrams, realize that you don't have to use the exact format that I use here or provide the amount of detail that I provide (unless, of course, you are putting your tree diagrams in a book). Just with everything else I present, the key is taking what I'm giving you and making it work for you. So long as you aren't violating any fundamental theories or concepts, there's no problem. As you may have gathered, one drawback to tree diagrams is that more complicated situations end up having more branches, meaning that there's a limit to the complex-

## Figure 2.1: Tree Diagram for the Situation Described in Table 2.2

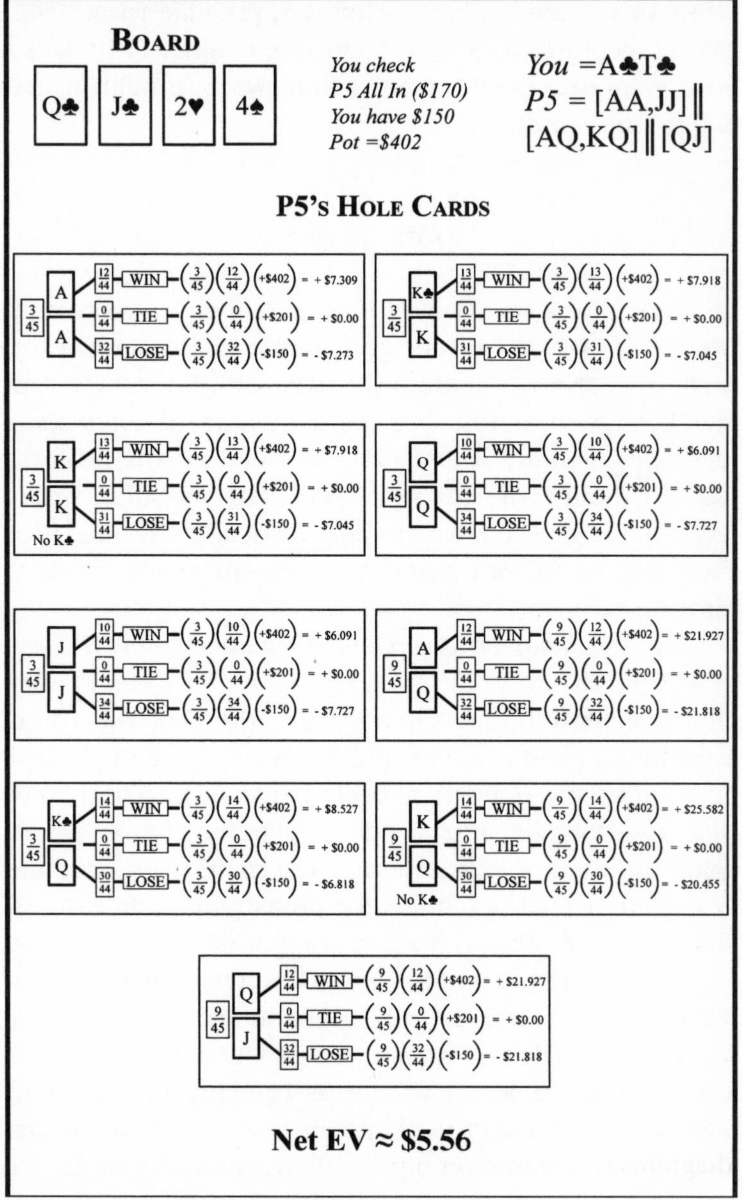

ity of the situations that can be solved in an acceptable time frame using tree diagrams. However, just like with HDM, simply becoming acquainted with tree diagrams will have a positive impact on the mental framework through which you see the game.

## Pot Odds

EV calculations are essential for evaluating play away from the table, and part of our goal is to educate ourselves to perform analysis away from the table whose results we can take back with us to battle. Even though there are some regularly encountered situations in hold'em, the reality is that the number of situations in hold'em is practically endless. Thus, we need a way to do EV calculations quickly at the table, so we can perform intelligent analysis during play.

Since EV calculations can be quite cumbersome, the way to do this is to shift our thinking from probabilities to *odds*. Odds are really nothing more than a different way of expressing probabilities. Probabilities refer to the number of outcomes of interest with respect to the total number of possible outcomes. In contrast, odds refer to the number of outcomes of interest with respect to the number of outcomes not of interest. For example, the probability of drawing an ace from a full deck is $\frac{4}{52} = \frac{1}{13}$ (1 ace out of 13 total draws). Expressed in terms of odds, we say the odds in favor of drawing an ace are 1:12 (said 1 to 12). There are 13 total draws, one of them being an ace. Therefore, $13 - 1 = 12$ outcomes are not aces, making the odds 1:12. Notice that when talking about odds, a colon is usually used instead of a fraction bar. We can also talk about the odds against drawing an ace, which are 12:1, the reciprocal of the odds in favor of drawing an ace.

When evaluating decisions in poker, you are usually considering the odds *against*.

With this understanding of odds, calculating EV becomes much easier. For example, let's play a game. I give you $10 every time you draw an ace, and you give me $1 every time you draw a card other than an ace. On average, if we were to play thirteen times, you would have to pay me $1 twelve times, and I would have to pay you $10 one time. In other words, you would pay me $12:$10, meaning that I make $2 per 13 draws. You didn't think I would take the negative end of a proposition bet, did you?

To settle an issue of semantics quickly, I refer to $10:$1 as the *payout odds*. The payout odds tell you the amount of money you stand to win given the amount of money you wager. Meanwhile, the odds pertaining to the random event itself (12:1 in this case) are called the *event odds*.

The important question, of course, is when does this game become fair? Well, the game becomes fair when the payout odds match the event odds. In other words, I'd have to pay you $12:$1 to make the game fair, and if I paid you more than $12:$1, you'd be profiting. The key concept is that you come out ahead if the payout odds are larger than the odds against the event you're wagering on.

Let's say you are playing on a popular online site that offers a side bet paying 7:1 on a bet that the flop will contain 3 red cards. Is this a profitable bet to make? You are forced to make this bet before you are dealt cards, so the deck contains 52 cards. Thus, there are $\frac{52 \cdot 51 \cdot 50}{3 \cdot 2 \cdot 1} = 22{,}100$ possible flops.* Out

* Notice how our state of knowledge makes subtle, but important, changes in probability calculations. In chapter 1, when we considered flops when we held AK, we only had 19,600 possible flops to deal with, but when we don't know any cards, the number of possible flops becomes 22,100.

of those 22,100 flops, there are $\frac{26 \cdot 25 \cdot 24}{3 \cdot 2 \cdot 1}$ = 2,600 that contain three red cards. The odds against you flopping 3 red cards are $\frac{\text{Not All Red}}{\text{All Red}} = \frac{22100 - 2600}{2{,}600}$ = 7.5:1. Thus, for every $7 you make from the site, you are giving back $7.50. You are losing $.50 for every $8.50 wagered (the odds in this case are considered in cycles of 8.5 trials since 1 + 7.5 = 8.5), meaning that in the long run, you are losing about $.06 per dollar wagered on this proposition. A Killer Poker player would never waste money on a –EV proposition, so do not burn your bankroll just to "test your luck."*

Now that we understand odds, let's apply them to the play of a poker hand. It's the turn, and you have to hit a flush draw to win. Your opponent bets $100 into a pot of $300. Do you have odds to call here? To figure this out, we need to know the odds against hitting your flush with one card to come. There are 4 cards on the board, and 2 cards in your hand, meaning that you know 6 cards in the deck: 52 – 6 = 46 cards left in the deck. Out of those 46 cards, 9 complete your flush. Therefore, the odds against your completing your flush are (46 – 9):9 = 37:9, or a little worse than 4:1 (about 4.11:1). Meanwhile, the pot has $300 + $100 = $400, and you have to call $100, meaning that the pot odds are 4:1. Since the odds against your hitting your flush are worse than 4:1, analysis of the strict pot odds dictates that you should fold. To break even, you need an approximately $411 return for every $100 you invest. If you call, you lose about $\frac{\$11}{5.11} \approx \$2.15$ per call because you put up this imaginary $11 over the span of 5.11 hands. The 5.11 comes from the fact that our approximate

* At live poker tables, meanwhile, there are opportunities to find suckers who will take the negative end of a proposition bet. In fact, some players willingly take the EV end of a bet just to show that they have so much money that they don't care about losing a few hundred dollars (nothing like a big ego to cloud your judgment). If you have a bet that you know the odds for, take the +EV end of the bet and reel your fish in!

odds against hitting the flush are 4.11:1, meaning that there are 4.11 + 1 = 5.11 total trials to consider.*

We see that by shifting our thinking from probabilities to odds, EV calculations become simpler. By now, you should have a solid understanding of EV and how you can use pot odds to determine your EV at the table. We are almost finished with this important chapter, but there is one more point to consider. Up to now, our decisions concerning EV have all been in situations where there will be no future betting action. Usually, though, we must also consider future betting rounds.

## Implied Odds and Reverse Implied Odds

We now need to account for action in future betting rounds. In some hold'em situations, you will find yourself –EV with respect to the pot odds when you are actually in a +EV situation. The reason for this is that you can account for money that will enter the pot in future betting rounds when you make your hand. Consider the flush drawing example from the previous section. Hypothesize that when you make your flush, your opponent will call a $150 bet on the river. This means that you now profit $400 + $150 = $550 when you win the hand. Your payout odds have changed from $400:$100 to $550:$100, turning the $100 call on the turn

* Observant readers who may have done the EV calculation on their own may have noticed that the actual expected loss per call is about $2.17. We can get this precise result from the odds as follows: The odds against hitting the flush are 37:9. Thus, in 46 trials, the payout odds are 37($100):9($400) = $3,700:$3,600. Over the span of 46 hands, you lose $100 if you make this call, and $100/46 ≈ $2.17 per hand. This shows that when you use rounded results, you are going to introduce some errors in your calculations unless you carry one or two additional decimal places throughout your work.

into a +EV play (recall you only need $411:$100). The extra $150:$100 you are getting from play on the river are referred to as your *implied odds.* We see from this example that implied odds must also be taken into consideration when evaluating EV.

A huge word of caution here: many poker players have some gamble in them, and people who want to gamble love to use inflated implied odds estimates to justify bad plays. Don't be one of those people! As an example, many people *open* in late position by limping in with small pocket pairs. Assuming that the small blind completes, the big blind checks, and this hand has no rake, they're getting 2:1 on their money. Meanwhile, the only time these players proceed past the flop is pretty much when they flop a set or better. Using the results from chapter 1, problem 5, the odds against this happening are 7.5:1. To be +EV, they need to get 5.5 more big blinds in the pot against two opponents who haven't shown much interest preflop. The likelihood of this happening isn't great, so the lesson to be learned is that unless you have lines of effective postflop play that occur when you don't hit a set or better, limping with your pocket pair is a horrible play here.

Suppose that you do manage to get 5.5 more big blinds in the pot when you hit the flop. Will you win every time you do so? The answer to this question is, "Hell no." In fact, many times you get action are when you hit a set against an opponent who is drawing to either a flush or a straight. If your opponent hits, you have redraws to a full house or quads, but the point is that you need to expect more than 5.5 big blinds to go in the pot to account for the times that you hit the flop but still end up losing. The amount of money that you expect to lose in future betting rounds when you hit your hand is referred to as your *reverse implied odds.* A complete analysis of EV, therefore, takes into account pot odds, implied odds, and reverse implied odds.

## Chapter Summary and Preview of What's to Come

In this chapter, we talked about expectation value (EV), how to calculate it precisely in poker situations using HDM, and how to use odds to help with approximations. Now that you've made it through this material, you have the tools to do away-from-the-table analysis of Texas hold'em cash game situations. You also have some tools to help with approximations when you're at the table. The remainder of this book will give specific applications of EV calculations involving HDM. The importance of HDM can't be stressed enough. Most players make decisions by arbitrarily putting an opponent on a specific hand, but the reality of poker is that you can very rarely do so. People are slowly becoming aware of how individual hands match up, and it's important to have that basic knowledge in order to do what we ultimately wish to do. However, there isn't much knowledge of how hand *distributions* match up. If you can master this concept of hand distribution matchups, you'll be well ahead of your competition.

Having said that, I must add that exact HDM analysis without the aid of a high-powered network of computers to run simulations can only be done in an acceptable time frame if the number of opponents you face is small. Thus, in addition to precise HDM analysis, I will also be placing increased emphasis on approximations and assumptions that make these calculations easier. I will also be highlighting many results that are easily taken to the table. Just keep in mind that in an ideal world, the proper way to solve any poker problem is through exact HDM analysis.

The next chapter explores how play evolves from unpaired flops and paired flops. We examine what types of hands you need to compete in multiway pots and what boards present potentially lucrative bluffing opportunities. Before moving on to that stuff, here are some problems to make sure that you understand the theory that I've put forth for the decision-making process in NL Texas hold'em.

## Problems

1. You are P10 in the hand given in table 2.4.

### Table 2.4: Hand for Problem 1

**Game:** $50NL Hold'em
**Structure:** Small Blind: $.25 Big Blind: $.50
**Comments:** Online game with a negligible rake that will not be considered. You are P10 in a situation where you are reraised all-in, and there is a fair amount of dead money in the pot. The action is recorded until it is your turn to respond to the all-in.

| | 1(SB) | 2(BB) | 3 | 4 | 5 |
|---|---|---|---|---|---|
| | XX | XX | XX | XX | XX |
| **STACKS** | $82.50 | $43 | $55 | $35 | $27.50 |
| **PREFLOP** | b$.25 | b$.50 | >$.50 | $2.50 | $2.50 |
| | - | - | - | $35 | - |
| **STACKS** | | | | | |
| **FLOP** | | | | | |
| **STACKS** | | | | | |
| **TURN** | | | | | |
| **STACKS** | | | | | |
| **RIVER** | | | | | |
| **HOLE** | | | | | |

**Comments:** None.

**Legend:** SB = Small Blind; BB = Big Blind; B = Button; X = Unknown Hole Card; b = Blind or Straddle; > = Beginning of Betting Round Action; < = End of Betting Round Action; - = Fold; d = Action in the Dark; c = Call; r = Raise; E = Exposed Card; M = Main Pot; S = Side Pot; AI = All-In; R = Rake

You are faced with a $15 call into a $68.75 pot. Figure out whether you should call or fold given the following hand distributions for P4:

a. [AA,KK]

b. [AA]

c. [AA,QQ]

| 6 | 7 | 8 | 9 | *10(B)* | POT |
|---|---|---|---|---|---|
| XX | XX | XX | XX | Q♥Q♠ | |
| $85 | $73.25 | $40 | $63 | $70 | |
| $2.50 | $2.50 | $2.50 | $2.50 | $20 | M = $68.75 |
| - | - | - | - | | |

2. You are P5 in the hand given in table 2.5.

**Table 2.5: Hand for Problem 2**

**Game:** $1,000NL Hold'em
**Structure:** Small Blind: $5 Big Blind: $10
**Comments:** Casino game with a timed collection. You are P5. You have been in this game for a while, and you know that P2, P4, and P8 are tight, straightforward players. P1 and P3 are loose, aggressive players who can be a tad tricky at times, but for the most part, they overplay their hands. The rest of the players are calling stations who do a lot of calling but rarely bet or raise (yeah, for those of you who have never played in games this big, there are some games out there where people call their chips away just like they do in lower limit games).

| | 1(SB) | 2(BB) | 3 | 4 | *5* |
|---|---|---|---|---|---|
| | XX | XX | XX | XX | 8♥8♣ |
| **STACKS** | $2,500 | $725 | $1,500 | $1,800 | $2,200 |
| **PREFLOP** | b$5<br>$30 | b$10<br>-< | >$30 | $30 | $30 |
| **STACKS** | $2,470 | | $1,470 | $1,770 | $2,170 |
| **FLOP**<br>**T♠8♠4♦** | >$0<br>$400 | | $100<br>$400 | $100<br>- | $100<br>$400< |
| **STACKS** | $2,070 | | $1,070 | | $1,670 |
| **TURN**<br>**J♠** | >$2,070 | | - | | |
| **STACKS** | | | | | |
| **RIVER** | | | | | |
| **HOLE** | | | | | |

**Comments:** None.

**Legend:** SB = Small Blind; BB = Big Blind; B = Button; X = Unknown Hole Card; b = Blind or Straddle; > = Beginning of Betting Round Action; < = End of Betting Round Action; - = Fold; d = Action in the Dark; c = Call; r = Raise; E = Exposed Card; M = Main Pot; S = Side Pot; AI = All-In; R = Rake

| 6 XX | 7 XX | 8(B) XX | POT |
|---|---|---|---|
| $500 | $1,250 | $800 | |
| $30 | $30 | - | M = $190 |
| $470 | $1,220 | | |
| - | - | | M = $1,490 |
| | | | |
| | | | M = $3,560 |
| | | | |
| | | | |

Put P1 on a hand distribution and figure out whether you should call with your set of 8's. Of course, the problem with setting up scenarios in a poker book is that you don't have as much information as you would have at a poker table, but the point of doing this is to get comfortable using HDM.

3. You hold Q♣6♣ and the board is J♣T♦5♣2♠. You are up against one opponent on the turn. He is in *early position,* and he bets $200 into a pot of $250. After his bet, he has $400 left in front of him. You have more than enough in front of you to cover him. You are inclined to think that he has [AA,TT]|||[AJ]. No matter what card falls, let's assume that we know that your opponent will bet his last $400. Can you call the bet on the turn?

**Answers to Problems**

1a. You should call.

*Explanation:* Poker Stove indicates that you win .1803 times, tie .0044 times, and lose .8152 times against the [AA,KK] distribution. If you make the $15 call, the pot will contain $68.75 + $15 = $83.75. Your EV is therefore:

$$(.1803)(\$83.75) + (.0044)\left(\tfrac{\$83.75}{2}\right) + (.8152)(\$0) \approx \$15.28 \qquad (2.4)$$

The call yields an expected profit of $15.28 – $15 = $0.28. Since your net EV is positive, you should call. Notice that by including the amount of the call in the pot, one of the terms in the EV calculation becomes zero. This trick was mentioned in the reading; and it is a good way to simplify these calculations, especially if you are at the table where you have to do them in your head.

1b. You should call.

*Explanation:* Poker Stove indicates that you win .1824 times, tie .0044 times, and lose .8133 times against AA. If you make the \$15 call, the pot will contain \$68.75 + \$15 = \$83.75. Your EV is therefore:

$$(.1824)(\$83.75) + (.0044)\left(\tfrac{\$83.75}{2}\right) + (.8133)(\$0) \approx \$15.46 \qquad (2.5)$$

Calling yields an expected profit of \$15.46 – \$15 = \$0.46. Wow, this is actually a bigger profit than when KK was included in the distribution. Thinking about it, this makes sense, though. If P4 possibly holds KK, less possible straights can be made with QQ. Since your net EV is positive, you should call.

1c. You should call.

*Explanation:* Poker Stove indicates that you win .1681 times, tie .0778 times, and lose .7541 times. Again, if you make the \$15 call, the pot will contain \$83.75. Your EV is therefore:

$$(.1681)(\$83.75) + (.0778)\left(\tfrac{\$83.75}{2}\right) + (.7541)(\$0) \approx \$17.34 \qquad (2.6)$$

Calling yields an expected profit of \$17.34 – \$15 = \$2.34. Your net EV is positive, so you should call.

2. It ultimately depends on what hand distribution you assign to P1. In one case, I get that you should fold; in another case, I get that you should call.

*Explanation:* The first task is to assign a hand distribution to P1. Preflop, he called a raise from the small blind after four other players had called it. The problem states that P1 is loose-aggressive, so, unfortunately, we can't really put much of a read on him that would help narrow his distribution of hands. Some loose-aggressive players call with any two cards here. Others exercise some selection and muck hands such as 72o and K3o. A typical loose-aggressive player is at least calling with any two suited cards and any unsuited *connector*, especially given the multiway action here. In addition, he's staying in with high cards and pocket pairs. There's such a wide range of holdings, that preflop, I'd say that P1's hand distribution is all hands except for hands that he would reraise with [AK]|||[AA,JJ]. There's a chance that he might reraise with [AQ]|||[TT,88], and possibly more, especially given the obvious *squeeze play* possibility and his loose-aggressive nature. I'll be honest in saying that I wouldn't be surprised one way or another. We have to commit to something, though, so I'm assigning a reraising distribution of [AK]|||[AA,JJ]. Remember that we can add and subtract hands later as we get more information.

The action on the flop is quite interesting. P1 checks, and as expected, P3 follows his preflop raise with a bet. Whether or not he has an overpair, hits the flop, or completely misses it, who knows? P4, a tight player, just calls. He may be slow playing a big hand against aggressive opponents, he may have something like AT for top pair, or he may have a flush draw. After P4 calls, you just call. I really hate just calling here, but that's how I set up the hand, so we have to live with it. Now, here is the fun part of the hand—P1 raises, P3 calls, and P4 folds.

What the hell do these guys have? Who knows,

especially since they are both loose-aggressive. However, all but the craziest maniacs have *something* with this kind of betting pattern. There's a decent chance that you are up against a flush draw and a made hand such as an overpair. Suffice to say, you are happy to have middle set at this point. I would reraise to about $1,400 here, forcing these guys to put their money in now, when you know for sure that you are ahead in the hand (unless you are unlucky enough to be up against a set of tens). With the flush draw and straight draw possibilities, there are many tricky turn cards. Despite all the good reasons for raising, you just call.

The turn comes, and it is about the worst possible card, the J♠. P1 overbets the pot by pushing all-in. Given your stack, P1 effectively bets $1,670 into a pot of $1,490. P3 folds, meaning that he wasn't drawing to a flush. P4 folds on the flop, meaning that most likely, he did not have a flush draw. Was it possible that you were up against three made hands on the flop, or did P1 turn a flush? Well, check-raise semi-bluffing a flush draw is not an unheard of play, especially if the player holds an overcard or two. P1 may have had a straight draw and a flush draw with Q♠T♠. It is very feasible that P1 check-raised on the flop with a drawing hand, especially given his aggressive style. He most likely would have just called on the flop with a low flush draw or a straight draw though—in other words, if he had a draw, it was either a high flush draw or a flush/straight draw combo.

Taking this into account, P1's possible flushes are A♠Q♠, A♠9♠, A♠7♠, A♠6♠, A♠5♠, A♠4♠, A♠3♠, A♠2♠,

K♠Q♠, K♠9♠, K♠7♠, K♠6♠, K♠5♠, K♠4♠, K♠3♠, K♠2♠, Q♠9♠, Q♠7♠, Q♠6♠, Q♠5♠, Q♠4♠, Q♠3♠, Q♠2♠, 9♠7♠, 9♠6♠, 9♠5♠, 9♠4♠, 9♠3♠, and 9♠2♠. I acknowledge that with the lower end of an inside straight draw, 7♠6♠ could belong in this distribution as well. It's hard to say, but I made a decision not to include it. In addition to a flush, P1 may have TT or 44 for a set. I'm sticking to the assumption that he would have reraised with JJ, meaning that he does not have it, even though an adjustment may be justified against some players. There is also a chance that he has two pair: JT, T8, T4, or 84. I am assuming that J8 and J4 are not possible since it takes a special type of loose-aggressive player to check raise into three opponents with just middle or bottom pair.

Of course, some may ask why he would overbet the pot on the turn with a made hand or a hand that would only get called by a hand that beats him. That's a good question, and there is some probability that he is on a naked bluff. It would be tough to bluff on the turn after all the interest in the flop, though. Along similar lines, he probably wouldn't make this play with just two pair since, if he is beaten, he will only have 4 outs on the river with which to catch a full house. P1 is therefore making this play with a set (figuring he has 10 outs to a full house or quads if he's beaten) or a flush (figuring that his opponents may read the overbet as a bluff attempt).

Having gone through this thought process, the hand distribution I put P1 on is all the flush drawing hands from the flop discussion, TT, and 44. Table 2.6 summarizes P(Win) and P(Tie) against each class of hands.

Did you assign the same hand distribution to P1?

**TABLE 2.6: Combinations of Each Possible Holding Along with P(Win) and P(Tie)**

| HAND AGAINST | COMBINATIONS | P(WIN) | P(TIE) |
|---|---|---|---|
| Straight Flush (Q♠9♠,9♠7♠) | 2 | $\frac{0}{44}$ | $\frac{0}{44}$ |
| Flush (no 4♠) | 23 | $\frac{10}{44}$ | $\frac{0}{44}$ |
| Flush (with 4♠) | 4 | $\frac{9}{44}$ | $\frac{0}{44}$ |
| TT | 3 | $\frac{1}{44}$ | $\frac{0}{44}$ |
| 44 | 3 | $\frac{43}{44}$ | $\frac{0}{44}$ |

You probably didn't come up with the exact hand distribution I came up with, but that's fine. The point of this problem is to get you thinking about HDM and to get you accurately filling in tables like table 2.6. Coming up with the particular hand distributions to plug into HDM is another topic matter entirely, and it's largely a function of experience and your ability to focus at the table.

Now that we have a hand distribution and the winning and tying probabilities against each hand in it, all that's left is calculating the EV of a call. As noted before, P1 is effectively betting \$1,670 into a pot of \$1,490 since you only have \$1,670 left. Thus, you are faced with a call of \$1,670 into a pot of \$1,670 + \$1,490 = \$3,160 If you call, the pot will be \$1,670 + \$3,160 = \$4,830. Given a call, your EV is:

$$\left(\tfrac{2}{35}\right)\left(\tfrac{0}{44}\right)(\$4830) + \left(\tfrac{23}{35}\right)\left(\tfrac{10}{44}\right)(\$4830) + \left(\tfrac{4}{35}\right)\left(\tfrac{9}{44}\right)(\$4830) + \left(\tfrac{3}{35}\right)\left(\tfrac{1}{44}\right)(\$4830) + \left(\tfrac{3}{35}\right)\left(\tfrac{43}{44}\right)(\$4830) \approx \$1248.27 \qquad (2.7)$$

Your net EV is therefore \$1,248.27 – \$1,670 = –\$421.73 if the hand distribution I assigned is correct. Against this hand distribution, you should fold. Let's now suppose that P1 could've made this move with two pair (holding either JT, T8, T4, or 84). P1's new distribution is in table 2.7.

**TABLE 2.7: P1's New Distribution with Combinations, P(Win) and P(Tie)**

| HAND AGAINST | COMBINATIONS | P(WIN) | P(TIE) |
|---|---|---|---|
| Straight Flush (Q♠9♠,9♠7♠) | 2 | $\frac{0}{44}$ | $\frac{0}{44}$ |
| Flush (no 4♠) | 23 | $\frac{10}{44}$ | $\frac{0}{44}$ |
| Flush (with 4♠) | 4 | $\frac{9}{44}$ | $\frac{0}{44}$ |
| TT | 3 | $\frac{1}{44}$ | $\frac{0}{44}$ |
| 44 | 3 | $\frac{43}{44}$ | $\frac{0}{44}$ |
| JT | 9 | $\frac{40}{44}$ | $\frac{0}{44}$ |
| T8 | 3 | $\frac{42}{44}$ | $\frac{0}{44}$ |
| T4 | 9 | $\frac{42}{44}$ | $\frac{0}{44}$ |
| 84 | 3 | $\frac{44}{44}$ | $\frac{0}{44}$ |

Given a call, your EV is given by equation 2.8.

$$\left(\tfrac{2}{59}\right)\left(\tfrac{0}{44}\right)(\$4830) + \left(\tfrac{23}{59}\right)\left(\tfrac{10}{44}\right)(\$4830) + \left(\tfrac{4}{59}\right)\left(\tfrac{9}{44}\right)(\$4830) + \left(\tfrac{3}{59}\right)\left(\tfrac{1}{44}\right)(\$4830) +$$
$$\left(\tfrac{3}{59}\right)\left(\tfrac{43}{44}\right)(\$4830) + \left(\tfrac{9}{59}\right)\left(\tfrac{40}{44}\right)(\$4830) + \left(\tfrac{3}{59}\right)\left(\tfrac{42}{44}\right)(\$4830) + \left(\tfrac{9}{59}\right)\left(\tfrac{42}{44}\right)(\$4830) +$$
$$\left(\tfrac{3}{59}\right)\left(\tfrac{44}{44}\right)(\$4830) \approx \$2593.61 \qquad (2.8)$$

In this case, your net EV is \$2,593.61 – \$1,670 = +\$923.61, meaning that you should call. The addition of the two pair possibilities makes a formerly –EV call a highly profitable one. This analysis serves as evidence for how important it is to read your opponents accurately. Without accurate reads, all the fancy mathematical analysis in the world isn't going to help you!

Is it possible to lay down a set in the face of heavy betting action on the turn when you are not given proper odds to draw to a full house or quads? This problem should show you that there are times to lay down a set on the flop or the turn. When you aren't given odds to draw and the number of completed draws that your opponent(s) could have made are large, then you may be forced to fold. When you do make this fold, *do not* show your opponents; if they see that you are capable of laying down a set, they are going to play back at you a lot, making your play of top pair, overpairs, and possibly even two pair very tricky, and a bulk of your made hands are going to be top pair, overpairs, or two pair.

3. You should fold.

   *Explanation:* You're faced with the decision to call \$200 into a pot of \$450, knowing that your opponent will be betting \$400 on the end and knowing that you will call when you hit your flush. Thus, when you make a flush and win the hand, you make \$850. When you don't make a flush, you lose \$200. If you make a flush and you're beaten by a full house, you lose \$600. Table 2.8 gives the probability of winning against each hand [P(Win)], the probability of missing your flush [P(Lose and Fold)], and the probability of hitting a flush and losing, meaning that you call on the river with a losing hand [P(Lose and Call)].

**TABLE 2.8: Opponent's Distribution with Combinations, P(Win) and P(Tie)**

| HAND | COMBINATIONS | P (WIN) | P (LOSE AND FOLD) | P (LOSE AND FOLD) |
|---|---|---|---|---|
| AA (no A♣) | 3 | $\frac{9}{44}$ | $\frac{35}{44}$ | $\frac{0}{44}$ |
| A♣A | 3 | $\frac{8}{44}$ | $\frac{36}{44}$ | $\frac{0}{44}$ |
| KK (no K♣) | 3 | $\frac{9}{44}$ | $\frac{35}{44}$ | $\frac{0}{44}$ |
| K♣K | 3 | $\frac{8}{44}$ | $\frac{36}{44}$ | $\frac{0}{44}$ |
| QQ | 3 | $\frac{9}{44}$ | $\frac{35}{44}$ | $\frac{0}{44}$ |
| JJ | 3 | $\frac{7}{44}$ | $\frac{35}{44}$ | $\frac{2}{44}$ |
| TT (no T♣) | 1 | $\frac{7}{44}$ | $\frac{35}{44}$ | $\frac{2}{44}$ |
| T♣T | 2 | $\frac{7}{44}$ | $\frac{36}{44}$ | $\frac{1}{44}$ |
| AJ (no A♣) | 9 | $\frac{9}{44}$ | $\frac{35}{44}$ | $\frac{0}{44}$ |
| A♣J | 3 | $\frac{8}{44}$ | $\frac{36}{44}$ | $\frac{0}{44}$ |

*Total number of combinations = 33*

Your EV is the following, broken up into parts to make the sum look less intimidating:

Contribution from AA

$$\left(\tfrac{3}{33}\right)\left(\tfrac{9}{44}\right)(\$850) + \left(\tfrac{3}{33}\right)\left(\tfrac{35}{44}\right)(-\$200) + \left(\tfrac{3}{33}\right)\left(\tfrac{8}{44}\right)(\$850) + \left(\tfrac{3}{33}\right)\left(\tfrac{36}{44}\right)(-\$200) \approx \$0.52 \qquad (2.9)$$

Contribution from KK

$$\left(\tfrac{3}{33}\right)\left(\tfrac{9}{44}\right)(\$850) + \left(\tfrac{3}{33}\right)\left(\tfrac{35}{44}\right)(-\$200) + \left(\tfrac{3}{33}\right)\left(\tfrac{8}{44}\right)(\$850) + \left(\tfrac{3}{33}\right)\left(\tfrac{36}{44}\right)(-\$200) \approx \$0.52 \qquad (2.10)$$

Contribution from QQ

$$\left(\tfrac{3}{33}\right)\left(\tfrac{9}{44}\right)(\$850) + \left(\tfrac{3}{33}\right)\left(\tfrac{35}{44}\right)(-\$200) \approx \$1.34 \qquad (2.11)$$

Contribution from JJ

$$\left(\tfrac{3}{33}\right)\left(\tfrac{7}{44}\right)(\$850) + \left(\tfrac{3}{33}\right)\left(\tfrac{35}{44}\right)(-\$200) + \left(\tfrac{3}{33}\right)\left(\tfrac{2}{44}\right)(-\$600) \approx -\$4.65 \qquad (2.12)$$

Contribution from TT

$$\left(\tfrac{1}{33}\right)\left(\tfrac{7}{44}\right)(\$850) + \left(\tfrac{1}{33}\right)\left(\tfrac{35}{44}\right)(-\$200) + \left(\tfrac{1}{33}\right)\left(\tfrac{2}{44}\right)(-\$600) + \left(\tfrac{2}{33}\right)\left(\tfrac{7}{44}\right)(\$850) + \left(\tfrac{2}{33}\right)\left(\tfrac{36}{44}\right)(-\$200) + \left(\tfrac{2}{33}\right)\left(\tfrac{1}{44}\right)(-\$600) \approx \$4.10 \qquad (2.13)$$

Contribution from AJ

$$\left(\tfrac{9}{33}\right)\left(\tfrac{9}{44}\right)(\$850) + \left(\tfrac{9}{33}\right)\left(\tfrac{35}{44}\right)(-\$200) + \left(\tfrac{3}{33}\right)\left(\tfrac{8}{44}\right)(\$850) + \left(\tfrac{3}{33}\right)\left(\tfrac{36}{44}\right)(-\$200) \approx \$3.20 \qquad (2.14)$$

Your net EV is found by adding these individual EVs together. The result is that this line of play has a net EV of \$0.52 + \$0.52 + \$1.34 – \$4.65 – \$4.10 + \$3.20 = –\$3.17. Thus, the correct play here is to fold.

Now, some of you out there may be wondering why you simply can't fold when the board pairs to make this line +EV. It's a valid question, and if you've thought of it, then it's good that you're beginning to think about multiple ways to play situations. After all, if you don't think of all the ways to play a situation, how can you decide what the best way is? In the spirit of the rigorous analysis we should always strive for, suppose that the 2♣ falls on the river. In that case, your opponent's distribution is the same one defined in table 2.8. If your opponent has JJ or TT (6 total combinations), you lose, or else (27 total combinations), you win. If you called on the turn, the pot has $650, meaning that including your opponent's $400 bet, you're facing a $400 call into a pot of $1,050. The EV of this call is $\left(\frac{27}{33}\right)(+\$1050) + \left(\frac{6}{33}\right)(-\$400) \approx +\$786.36$. This is pretty high +EV! By calling on the turn, you're therefore locking yourself into calling on the river when you hit your flush, meaning that the line of play suggested in the problem is the line of play you have to take when you call on the turn. Since the overall line of play is –EV, you should simply fold on the turn, as said before.

A common mistake made by many players is the following: They assume that whenever they hit a flush, they win the hand. Since they know their hole cards and the board, the deck has 46 cards left. They have 9 outs; thus, the odds against hitting a flush are 37:9, which is $4.\overline{1}$:1.*

* The bar over the 1 means that the 1's repeat forever. By the way, to figure this number out on the spot when I'm playing, I use the fact that 37/9 is 4 with a remainder of 1. I know that 1/9 is .1; thus, 37.9 is 4.1:1. . . . I simply add .1 to 4.

implied odds, they figure that they are getting \$850:\$200 = 4.25:1 odds, meaning that the call is +EV. They are neglecting to account for the reverse implied odds associated with making their flush and losing.

# 3

# UNPAIRED FLOPS AND PAIRED FLOPS

## Introduction

Congratulations! You've just made it through some very difficult material. HDM can be time consuming at times; however, just understanding the process should make you a more formidable foe at the poker table. Now that you're well versed in the theoretic framework governing NL Texas hold'em, it's now time to examine some common situations. In this chapter, we'll examine the implications of unpaired flops and paired flops relative to your opponents hitting them.

## The Importance of Having Top Pair or Better in Multiway Pots

When you enter a hand, you need to be aware of how postflop play will evolve. In typical ring games with seven to ten players, where three or more players see the flop, you typically win pots with top pair or better. To see why this is true, assume that you have three opponents with random cards.

If you don't have top pair, the probability that your opponents don't either is:

$$\left(\tfrac{44}{47}\right)\left(\tfrac{43}{46}\right)\left(\tfrac{42}{45}\right)\left(\tfrac{41}{44}\right)\left(\tfrac{40}{43}\right)\left(\tfrac{39}{42}\right) \approx .66 \qquad (3.1)$$

The probability that one of your three opponents with random cards has top pair is the complement, .34. Of course, most of your opponents aren't playing random cards. Furthermore, your opponents will sometimes have overpairs and draws—more adventurous opponents will give you resistance with a lot more. To know precisely where you stand in a particular hand, you need to account for everyone's preflop hand distributions and to know how they relate to specific flops. While we can't possibly enumerate this for every set of opponents and flops that you'll encounter, let's come up with some qualitative corrections to equation 3.1 to see which way they shift your opponents' interest in the pot (see table 3.1).

**TABLE 3.1: Shift in Opponents' Interest in a Pot**

| CORRECTION | SHIFT IN OPPONENTS' INTEREST |
|---|---|
| Opponents who voluntarily enter the pot typically do so with high cards | More Likely (Especially when the top card is a face card) |
| Opponents who raise typically do so with high cards or high pocket pairs | More Likely (Given a preflop raise) |
| Opponents with overpairs will stay in | More Likely |
| Opponents with draws will stay in | More Likely |
| Opponents with bottom two pair or sets will stay in | More Likely |

Each correction increases the likelihood of resistance in the form of calls or raises. When you have three opponents, this resistance will often come from someone with a better hand if your hand is not at least top pair. I can't assign numerical weights to the factors in table 3.1 (and others that may exist) without defined hand distributions for your opponents. However, everything discussed so far suggests that we want at least top pair on an unpaired flop when we have three opponents if we want to make our decisions on later rounds straightforward. Since having more opponents increases the likelihood of facing someone interested in the pot, it makes sense that you are playing "hit-to-win" whenever you have three or more opponents postflop. The probabilities of being up against top pair as a function of the number of opponents with random cards are in table 3.2.

**TABLE 3.2: Probability That You Are Up Against Top Pair on an Unpaired Flop Against *N* Opponents with Random Hands**

| NUMBER OF OPPONENTS | P(AT LEAST ONE OPPONENT HAS TOP PAIR) |
|---|---|
| 1 | .12 |
| 2 | .24 |
| 3 | .34 |
| 4 | .44 |
| 5 | .52 |
| 6 | .60 |
| 7 | .66 |
| 8 | .72 |
| 9 | .77 |

## Playability of Paired Boards

Now, what if the board is paired? How much do we need to worry about opponents having trips?

Consider the case when your opponents have random hands. With one opponent, the probability that he doesn't have trips is $\left(\frac{45}{47}\right)\left(\frac{44}{46}\right) \approx .92$, meaning that the probability that he has trips is about .08. If you have two opponents, the probability that they don't have trips is $\left(\frac{45}{47}\right)\left(\frac{44}{46}\right)\left(\frac{43}{45}\right)\left(\frac{42}{44}\right) \approx .84$, meaning that the probability that they do have trips is about .16. The probabilities from these calculations when you have 1–9 opponents with random cards are summarized in table 3.3.

**TABLE 3.3: Probability That You Are Against Trips When the Flop Is Paired and Your Opponents Hold Random Hands**

| NUMBER OF OPPONENTS | P(AGAINST TRIPS) |
|---|---|
| 1 | 0.08 |
| 2 | 0.16 |
| 3 | 0.24 |
| 4 | 0.31 |
| 5 | 0.38 |
| 6 | 0.45 |
| 7 | 0.51 |
| 8 | 0.57 |
| 9 | 0.62 |

Table 3.3 indicates that betting into a *paired board* can be a very powerful bluff against opponents who fold unless they hit the flop hard. It follows that betting into these pots with pocket pairs, especially those higher than the unpaired board card, is also a powerful play. Just realize that when you

get resistance of any kind on a paired board when you hold a pocket pair, the turn and the river are tricky to handle. Does your opponent have trips? Does he have two pair? Is your opponent calling you with ace high? Is he on a draw? It's tough to know where you stand in the hand.

Occasionally, you do know where you stand. Suppose that you raise preflop with JJ and get three callers. The following two flops, though paired, are completely different: AA3 and 553. With your raise and 3 callers, table 3.3 indicates that you are up against trips 24 percent of the time. Table 3.3 was produced assuming that your opponents are holding random hands—your opponents aren't calling your preflop raise with random hands (well, most of them aren't). Most likely, they're on distributions such as [JJ,22]|||[AK,AJ]|||[KQ]. Let's analyze the AA3 flop and the 553 flop assuming that your opponents are on the [JJ,22]|||[AK,AJ]|||[KQ] distribution.

The AA3 flop is a complete disaster. Many opponents will give you resistance with a pocket pair, and when they don't have two pair, they have an ace, or a full house with 33. When you get resistance, either you have your opponent crushed or your opponent has you crushed, but it's tough to know where you stand. If you are against one opponent and he's on [JJ,22]|||[AK,AJ]|||[KQ], table 3.4 gives a summary of his distribution with respect to combinations.

From table 3.4, the probability that you are beaten is $\frac{3+8+8+4}{88} = \frac{23}{88} \approx .26$. The probability that you are beaten when you are up against two or more players on the [JJ,22]|||[AK,AJ]||| [KQ] distribution is more difficult to calculate. This probability is given by the following qualitative expression:

$$P(P1\_ahead)+P(P1\_not\_ahead)P(P2\_ahead)=P(beaten) \quad (3.2)$$

In Equation 3.2, *P*(*P*1_*ahead*) is the probability that P1 is a favorite to win the hand, *P*(*P*1_*not_ahead*) is the probability

**TABLE 3.4: Distribution of 1 Opponent on [JJ,22]||[AK,AJ]||[KQ] with Respect to Combinations Given That You Hold JJ and the Flop Is AA3**

| HAND | COMBINATIONS |
|---|---|
| JJ | 1 |
| TT | 6 |
| 99 | 6 |
| 88 | 6 |
| 77 | 6 |
| 66 | 6 |
| 55 | 6 |
| 44 | 6 |
| 33 | 3 |
| 22 | 6 |
| AK | 8 |
| AQ | 8 |
| AJ | 4 |
| KQ | 16 |

*Total number of combinations = 88*

that P1 is not a favorite to win the hand, *P(P2_ahead)* is the probability that P2 is a favorite to win the hand, and *P(beaten)* is the probability that you are beaten. The first term of this expression is equal to .26—it's simply the same as the calculation for when you have one opponent (it doesn't matter if P2 has you beaten when you know P1 has you beaten). The second term of this expression is the tricky part of this calculation. We know that *P(P1_not_ahead)* = .74, the complement of .26. The problem is that given P1 doesn't have you beaten, *P(P2_ahead)* ≠ .26. If P1 doesn't have you beaten, he has [JJ,44]||[22]||[KQ], altering the number of available combinations for P2's [JJ,22]||[AK,AJ]||[KQ] distribution. The probabilities are not independent, which makes dealing with them a big hassle—what we have to do is assign new distributions to P2, one for each of P1's possible holdings. P1's distribution of holdings, given that he doesn't have you beaten, is given in table 3.5.

**TABLE 3.5: P1's [JJ,44]||[22]||[KQ] Distribution with Respect to Combinations, Given That You Hold JJ and the Flop Is AA3**

| HAND | COMBINATIONS |
|---|---|
| JJ | 1 |
| TT | 6 |
| 99 | 6 |
| 88 | 6 |
| 77 | 6 |
| 66 | 6 |
| 55 | 6 |
| 44 | 6 |
| 22 | 6 |
| KQ | 16 |

*Total number of combinations = 65*

This table is included because we'll need to know the probability of each combination in order to weigh P2's distributions properly. Now, if P1 has JJ, P2's adjusted distribution is given by Table 3.6 (opposite).

The probability that P2 has you beaten, given P1 has JJ, is $\frac{3+8+8}{83} = \frac{19}{83} \approx .23$. From table 3.5, we know that P2 will have this distribution $\frac{1}{65}$ times. P2's hand distribution when P1 holds TT is in table 3.7 (see p. 86).

The chance that P2 has you beaten is now $\frac{3+8+8+4}{83} = \frac{23}{83} \approx .28$. From table 3.5, we know that P2 will have this distribution $\frac{6}{65}$ times. When P1 has [99,44]|||[22], P2's adjusted distributions

**TABLE 3.6: P2's Adjusted [JJ,22]||[AK,AJ]||[KQ] Distribution When P1 Has JJ**

| HAND | COMBINATIONS |
|---|---|
| JJ | 0 |
| TT | 6 |
| 99 | 6 |
| 88 | 6 |
| 77 | 6 |
| 66 | 6 |
| 55 | 6 |
| 44 | 6 |
| 33 | 3 |
| 22 | 6 |
| AK | 8 |
| AQ | 8 |
| AJ | 0 |
| KQ | 16 |

*Total number of combinations = 83*

contain the same relative number of combinations of the winning hands, [AK,AJ]|||[33], as when P1 has TT (if you don't believe me, then as an active reader, you should verify it for yourself). Thus, when P1 has [99,44]|||[22], the probability that P2 has you beaten is also $\frac{3+8+8+4}{83} = \frac{23}{83} \approx .28$. From table 3.5, P1 has [99,44]|||[22] $\frac{42}{65}$ times.

The last case to address is when P1 has KQ. In that case, P2 has the distribution in table 3.8.

The probability that P2 has you beaten is $\frac{3+6+6+4}{77} = \frac{19}{77} \approx .25$. From Table 3.5, the probability that you are up against this distribution is $\frac{16}{65}$.

Given that P1 doesn't have you beaten, the probability that P2 has you beaten when the board is AA3 and you hold JJ is given by equation 3.3.

**TABLE 3.7: P2's Adjusted Distribution When P1 Has TT**

| HAND | COMBINATIONS |
|---|---|
| JJ | 1 |
| TT | 1 |
| 99 | 6 |
| 88 | 6 |
| 77 | 6 |
| 66 | 6 |
| 55 | 6 |
| 44 | 6 |
| 33 | 3 |
| 22 | 6 |
| AK | 8 |
| AQ | 8 |
| AJ | 4 |
| KQ | 16 |

*Total number of combinations = 83*

P1 has JJ  P1 has TT  P1 has [99,44]||[22]  P1 has KQ

$$\left(\tfrac{1}{65}\right)\left(\tfrac{19}{83}\right) + \left(\tfrac{6}{65}\right)\left(\tfrac{23}{83}\right) + \left(\tfrac{42}{65}\right)\left(\tfrac{23}{83}\right) + \left(\tfrac{16}{65}\right)\left(\tfrac{19}{77}\right) \approx .27 \quad (3.3)$$

Notice that this result is very close to .26. It so happens that in this case, considering P1's distribution didn't make much of a difference in considering P2's distribution. In other situations, though, you'll find more significant changes in the probabilities—we'll explore this issue more deeply in chapter 7.

Now that we have the probability that P2 has you beaten when P1 doesn't, we have all the numbers necessary to plug into equation 3.2 to find P(beaten).

$$(.26) + (.74)(.27) \approx .46 \quad (3.4)$$

**TABLE 3.8: P2's Distribution Given That P1 Has KQ**

| HAND | COMBINATIONS |
|---|---|
| JJ | 1 |
| TT | 6 |
| 99 | 6 |
| 88 | 6 |
| 77 | 6 |
| 66 | 6 |
| 55 | 6 |
| 44 | 6 |
| 33 | 3 |
| 22 | 6 |
| AK | 6 |
| AQ | 6 |
| AJ | 4 |
| KQ | 9 |

*Total number of combinations = 77*

Equation 3.4 shows that when you have 2 opponents on the [JJ,22]|||[AK,AJ]|||[KQ] distribution when you have JJ and the board is AA3, the probability that your are beaten is about .46.

I'm not going to do the precise analysis for the cases where you have 3 or more opponents, because as you can probably imagine, the precise calculations become quite cumbersome. As an approximation, though, if the probabilities were independent, we could say that the probability of your being beaten against $n$ opponents is:

$$P(beaten) \approx 1 - (1 - .26)^n = 1 - .74^n \qquad (3.5)$$

In most cases, the results from an *independence* approximation don't vary dramatically from the true probabilities until $n$ is about 4 or 5. The $(1 - .26)^n$ in equation 3.5 is from the fact that we first need to calculate P(not beaten); we then subtract that from 1 since P(beaten) is simply the complement of P(not beaten). Some people make the mistake of saying that *P(beaten)* ≈ .26". However, this is an approximation of the probability that *everyone* has you beaten. (Do you see how this is different from the probability of simply being beaten?) Situations like this are great for thinking in terms of complements. The results of equation 3.5 are given in table 3.9.

**TABLE 3.9: Approximate Probability That You Are Beaten When Against *N* Opponents on the [JJ,22] || [AK,AJ] || [KQ] Distribution When the Flop Is AA3 and You Hold JJ**

| OPPONENTS | P(BEATEN) |
|---|---|
| 1 | 0.26 |
| 2 | 0.45 |
| 3 | 0.59 |
| 4 | 0.70 |
| 5 | 0.78 |
| 6 | 0.84 |
| 7 | 0.88 |
| 8 | 0.91 |
| 9 | 0.93 |

Notice the .01 difference between the result for 2 opponents in table 3.9 and the exact answer we obtained in equation 3.4 for 2 opponents. The answers for larger values of *n* have more error associated with them; however, we don't need precise answers to know that you're in trouble when you have 3 or more opponents. Personally, when I have 2 opponents in a situation like this, I tend to bet the flop and then give up on the turn and the river if I get resistance. Occasionally, I'll bet again on the turn from position, hoping to get a free showdown on the river. In my experience, most players play *passively* on the river in this situation unless they have an ace here, meaning that I usually always get to showdown my better hand—I don't have to fold my hand if I'm never put to a decision to fold.

Now, some opponents are willing to play back at you—sometimes with two pair and other times as a pure bluff. The way they play back at you varies. Some raise you right away on the flop. Others might flat call on the flop and aggress on the turn or the river. When playing these more aggressive opponents, you'll need to adjust your strategy appropriately and not give up as often with two pair when you get resistance. The specific betting patterns for this strategy adjustment vary. When in early position, you can bet right out, you can check-raise, or you can check/call. After check/calling on the flop, you can either lead out on the turn or check with the intention of calling or raising. I tend toward the *stop-and-go,* meaning that I check/call the flop and bet out on the turn. When in late position, you can play either passively or aggressively. Against an opponent who likes to check-raise a lot on the flop, I may elect to check behind to keep the pot smaller on the turn and the river. Other times, I may decide to play more aggressively in position. The point to take away is that some players will not play paired boards passively, and you need to have some game plan so that you can take a lot of chips from them while, simultaneously, not getting stacked in the instances that these players actually do have you beaten.

Wow, that was a lot of work to dissect the AA3 flop! There was a lot of math there, and I hope you followed it. The big concept from the poker playing perspective is that when you have more than two opponents in a raised pot and you haven't hit a flop that has a paired face card, the general rule is that you should probably give up on the pot. Of course, I am putting forth a situational poker philosophy, so if your specific situation dictates continuing in the pot, by all means do so.

Let's now analyze the 553 flop under the same conditions that we analyzed the AA3 flop to see how much things change. The distribution for P1 is in table 3.10.

**TABLE 3.10: Distribution of 1 Opponent on [JJ,22] || [AK,AJ] || [KQ] with Respect to Combinations Given That You Hold JJ and the Flop Is 553**

| HAND | COMBINATIONS |
|---|---|
| JJ | 1 |
| TT | 6 |
| 99 | 6 |
| 88 | 6 |
| 77 | 6 |
| 66 | 6 |
| 55 | 1 |
| 44 | 6 |
| 33 | 3 |
| 22 | 6 |
| AK | 16 |
| AQ | 16 |
| AJ | 8 |
| KQ | 16 |

*Total number of combinations = 103*

The only hands that beat you are 55 and 33; therefore, the probability that P1 has you beaten is:

$$P(beaten\_by\_P1) = \frac{1+3}{103} = \frac{4}{103} \approx .04 \qquad (3.6)$$

P1's distribution of hands that lose to you changes the relative number of combinations in P2's winning distribution very slightly. Thus, it's acceptable to make the independence approximation used to obtain equation 3.5, acknowledging that the answers obtained for large numbers of players, *n*, may be unreliable. Using the independence approximation, we calculate the probability that you are beaten when against *n* opponents in equation 3.7.

$$P(beaten) \approx 1 - .96^n \tag{3.7}$$

Table 3.11 summarizes the results of this equation.

**TABLE 3.11: Approximate Probability That You Are Beaten When Against *N* Opponents on the [JJ,22]||[AK,AJ]||[KQ] Distribution When the Flop is 553 and You Hold JJ**

| OPPONENTS | P(BEATEN) |
|---|---|
| 1 | 0.04 |
| 2 | 0.08 |
| 3 | 0.12 |
| 4 | 0.15 |
| 5 | 0.18 |
| 6 | 0.21 |
| 7 | 0.25 |
| 8 | 0.28 |
| 9 | 0.31 |

Table 3.11 shows that flop 553 is much more favorable than the AA3 flop when all your opponents are on the [JJ,22]||[AK,AJ]||[KQ] distribution. I guess this doesn't come as a surprise, but it's always nice to know the actual numbers. Of course, the higher your overpair is in these situations, the better off you are. In this situation, I tend to bet if I have as many as three opponents. If you're in a pot containing three or more opponents on the flop, it's not very likely

that they're all on the [JJ,22]|||[AK,AJ]|||[KQ] distribution, so you need to be wary of the opponents with random hands that make trips. The reality is that in a raised pot with a flop like 553, P(beaten) is going to be somewhere between the results in table 3.3 and table 3.11. Unlike the AA3 flop, you'll usually be ahead when you get resistance. Like the AA3 flop, your decisions on the turn and the river will still be tricky when you do get resistance.

## Chapter Summary and Preview of What's to Come

We've just deeply studied the nature of unpaired flops and paired flops. The situations I use in this chapter involve your holding pocket pairs, but I hope you will see that the results I just derived have applications well outside the domain of playing pocket pairs. Regardless of whether or not you hold a pocket pair, it should be clear that you want top pair or better when you have 3 or more opponents on the flop, and that there are situations where you'll want top pair or better against only 2 opponents.

Now, if your full ring game has a lot of pots that are heads-up postflop or if you are in a game that is shorthanded, you need more tricks up your sleeve than hitting top pair or better. For those tougher games, I initially cite the results in chapter 1 involving continuation betting. However, we'll be going into much more detail about shorthanded play later. The reality is that if you are in a seven-plus-handed cash game where employing hit-to-win poker isn't good enough, get a table change, because hit-to-win games are prevalent at most stakes, and they are arguably the easiest games to beat, even if they are not always the most interesting to play.

The lesson to take away from playing paired flops is that

they present great bluffing opportunities against unwary opponents. Against opponents willing to resist your bets with ace high, you are then going to have some tricky pots to play, especially against those who choose to resist with aggression (passive opponents are much easier to deal with). This is even true when you have AA and the flop is something like 995.

## Problems

1. What is an independence approximation and why are independence approximations helpful in our analysis?

2. You hold 7♣6♥, and the board is Q♣Q♠3♦. You are in last position, and your three opponents have checked to you. What's the EV of a $\frac{2}{3}$ pot-sized bluff assuming that your opponents hold random hands and assuming that they will only call you if they have a queen. (Assume that you always lose the hand when you are called, which is a good assumption since the only ways you win when called are bluffing out trip queens or hitting a *runner-runner* straight.)

3. Suppose you have A7 in late position against three opponents and the flop is T72. Action is checked to you on the flop, and you check, adhering to the hit-to-win philosophy. The turn is a 3 and your opponents check to you. You don't have top pair and you have three opponents. Based on this limited information, do you think that you should check or bet?

## Answers to Problems

1. The independence approximation is the assumption that your opponents' hand distributions have no bearing on each other. As an example, if P1 and P2 are on [AA,JJ]|||[AK,AQ] and you know that your opponents will only call with [AA,KK], the independence approximation assumes that P1 folding [QQ,JJ]|||[AK,AQ] doesn't affect the probability of P2 having [AA,KK]. The independence approximation is helpful in our analysis because it easily enables us to estimate the probability that *n* players will fold behind since the probability of multiple independent events is simply the product of the individual probabilities. Doing the precise analysis and accounting for the entanglement of the hand distributions is much too time consuming for practical purposes. Note that the errors incurred by assuming independence in most cases don't become larger than about .05 until the number of players is about 4 or 5.

2. About +.6P.

   *Explanation:* From table 3.3, the probability of being against trips is about .24, meaning that the probability of everyone folding is about .76. The EV of a $\frac{2}{3}$pot bet is therefore $(.76)(+P) + (.24)(-\frac{2}{3}P) \approx +.6P$. This result indicates that paired boards present a unique bluffing opportunity. Opponents aware of this will not let you run them over (they will call you with an ace kicker), but against some tight opponents, paired boards are an invitation to steal the pot on the flop.

3. A bet is justifiable and probably the preferred play lacking any other information about the players at the table.

   *Explanation:* You are against three opponents, and you don't have top pair. From the work in this chapter, I suggested that you are playing hit-to-win poker when you have three or more opponents, meaning that if you took that advice blindly, you should shut down here. However, let's look at this situation more closely (no autopilot!). Very few players will check top pair on both the flop and the turn. As a result of the added information gained across two rounds of betting, it's reasonable to conclude that betting is the best play. Most likely, your opponents will fold, but even if you're called, it's likely that your opponent will check to you on the river, giving you the option to check behind for a cheap showdown (being in position is huge against passive opponents because of situations like this).

   Notice that if I changed this problem slightly by sticking you in early position, betting out from early position after the action is checked around on the flop is also a good play. The dynamics of play on the river are quite different, though. Knowing whether to bet the river, to check/call the river, or to check/fold the river is tricky when you are in early position after betting the turn. The best line of play relies heavily on observations that you have made throughout your session.

# 4

# HIT-TO-WIN POKER WITH POCKET PAIRS

♧♤♢♡

## Introduction

In the last chapter, we talked about the general importance of having top pair or better when you are in a pot with at least three opponents on the flop. In this chapter, we'll talk about the probabilities governing being in such a situation when you enter the pot with a pocket pair. Then, we'll talk about various lines of play that evolve when you flop top pair or better.

## Types of Flops on Which We Can Have a Set or Better

Let's first talk about the probability of flopping a set or better. After all, this flop is what we always hope for with our pocket pairs. We find many different textures of flops in which we flop a set or better, and in general, when you have such a hand, it is powerful. Before we continue, though, we should thoroughly investigate the types of flops we are happy with and which ones we may wish to disqualify. There are three variables to contend with:

1. Whether the board is unpaired, paired, or tripped* (Rank)

2. Whether the board creates straights and straight draws (Connectivity)

3. Whether the board creates flushes and flush draws (Suitedness)

In the next few sections, we'll investigate the impact that each variable has.

## The Impact of Rank

Let's see where you stand when you flop a set or better as a function of board rank. On an unpaired flop, you have a set. There may be some times that you'll have to be cautious with bottom set or even middle set (e.g., you hold KK, the flop is AKQ, and you have three opponents in a pot that was raised and reraised preflop before the action even got to you). In general, you are usually quite happy to have any set, though. If the flop is paired, you have either a full house or quads when you hit your hand. Your only real concern is that if you have something like 55 and the board is 5AA, the possibility exists that your opponent can draw to a higher full house. Suffice to say, you aren't *that* worried though—I'm just trying to address all possibilities here. The only case where there is

* I call a board "tripped" if it contains three cards of the same rank.

cause for concern is when the board is tripped. Of course, when the board is tripped, you have a full house. Against one opponent with random cards, $P(not\_against\_quads) = \left(\frac{46}{47}\right)\left(\frac{45}{46}\right) \approx .96$, meaning that the probability you are against quads is the complement, .04. However, if many players are in the hand, you must seriously consider the possibility that you are against quads. The probability that you are against quads when up against $n$ opponents with random hands is in table 4.1.

**TABLE 4.1: Probability of Quads Against *N* Opponents Holding Random Hands on a Tripped Board**

| OPPONENTS | P(AGAINST QUADS) |
|---|---|
| 1 | .04 |
| 2 | .09 |
| 3 | .13 |
| 4 | .17 |
| 5 | .21 |
| 6 | .26 |
| 7 | .30 |
| 8 | .34 |
| 9 | .38 |

These probabilities aren't too daunting. Of course, the rank of the trips on the board matters greatly with respect to your opponents' hand distributions, just as it did in chapter 3, when we considered the AA3 flop versus the 553 flop.

Besides being concerned about quads, if you have a low pocket pair, you must also be concerned about overcards falling on the turn or river. The probability of being against quads or a higher full house on the river if there's one overcard on the board and you are against one opponent with random cards is $1 - \left(\frac{41}{45}\right)\left(\frac{40}{44}\right) \approx .17$. The results of this calculation when you are against $n$ opponents are in table 4.2.

**TABLE 4.2: Probability That You Are Against Quads or a Higher Full House on the River When Against *N* Opponents Holding Random Hands on a Tripped Board and There's One Overcard to Your Pocket Pair**

| OPPONENTS | P(AGAINST QUADS) OR HIGHER BOAT |
|---|---|
| 1 | 0.17 |
| 2 | 0.32 |
| 3 | 0.45 |
| 4 | 0.56 |
| 5 | 0.65 |
| 6 | 0.73 |
| 7 | 0.79 |
| 8 | 0.84 |
| 9 | 0.88 |

The three additional outs for your opponents make play more difficult.

From this analysis of unpaired, paired, and *tripped boards*, we see that, in general, we are happy to hit a set or better on an unpaired board or a paired board. Whether or not you are happy having a full house with a tripped flop is a function of your pocket pair's rank, the number of opponents, your opponents' hand distributions, and the rank of the board cards.

## The Impact of Connectivity

Having analyzed the impact of the board rank, let's now address the connectivity of the flop. One classification system for the types of board connectivity is the following:

- No straight draws possible
- Inside straight draws possible
- Outside straight draws possible
- Made straights possible

Each of these categories can be divided into subcategories. For example, the flops 567 and 478 both make it possible for opponents to have straights. However, there are more combinations of hole cards that make a straight with a flop of 567 {34, 48, and 89} than with a flop of 478 {56}.

All the connectivity categories are possible for unpaired flops. On paired flops, it's impossible for opponents to have made straights, and on tripped flops there are no possible straight draws.

Of the connectivity categories, the only situation that we are possibly unhappy with is when a made straight is already possible. However, even if a made straight is possible, the probability that we are up against a straight is small. Let's examine the worst-case scenario, when you have a bottom set with 55 on a flop of 567, which has three possible straights. We are not considering flush draws yet, so assume that the flop has three distinct suits. Now, if you are in a pot with many limpers, the limpers in late position are likely on distributions such as the following:

[TT,22]|||[AJo,A9o]|||[AJs,A2s]|||[KQo,KTo]|||[KQs,K2s]|||
[QJo,QTo]|||[QJs,Q9s]|||[JT,43]|||[J9,53]

This distribution, in terms of combinations, is in table 4.3.

**TABLE 4.3: Number of Combinations for Each Hand When You Hold 55, the Board Is 567, and Your Opponent Is on a Distribution of [TT,22]||[AJo,A9o]||[AJs,A2s]||[KQo,KTo]||[KQs,K2s]||[QJo,QTo]||[QJs,Q9s]||[JT,43]||[J9,53]**

| HANDS | COMBINATIONS FOR EACH HAND | NUMBER OF HANDS | TOTAL COMBINATIONS |
|---|---|---|---|
| [TT,88]\|\|[44,22] | 6 | 6 | 36 |
| [77,66] | 3 | 2 | 6 |
| [55] | 0 | 1 | 0 |
| [AJo,A9o] | 12 | 3 | 36 |
| [AJs,A8s]\|\|[A4s,A2s] | 4 | 7 | 28 |
| [A7s,A6s] | 3 | 2 | 6 |
| [A5s] | 1 | 1 | 1 |
| [KQo,KTo] | 12 | 3 | 36 |
| [KQs,K8s]\|\|[K4s,K2s] | 4 | 8 | 32 |
| [K7s,K6s] | 3 | 2 | 6 |
| [K5s] | 1 | 1 | 1 |
| [QJo,QTo] | 12 | 2 | 24 |
| [QJs,Q9s] | 4 | 3 | 12 |
| [JT,98]\|\|[43] | 16 | 4 | 64 |
| [87] | 12 | 1 | 12 |
| [76] | 9 | 1 | 9 |
| [65] | 3 | 1 | 3 |
| [54] | 4 | 1 | 4 |
| [J9,T8] | 16 | 2 | 32 |
| [97,86] | 12 | 2 | 24 |
| [75] | 3 | 1 | 3 |
| [64] | 12 | 1 | 12 |
| [53] | 4 | 1 | 4 |
| | | **TOTAL** | 391 |

The only hands that beat your set of 5's are 77, 66, 98, 84, and 43. From table 4.3, we see that there are 6 + 6 + 16 + 0 + 16 = 44 combinations of hole cards out of 391 possible combinations. Thus, against one opponent, the probability that you are up against a straight or a higher set is $\frac{44}{391} \approx .11$. The probability that you are up against a straight is $\frac{32}{391} \approx .08$. Using the independence approximation, I computed table 4.4:

**TABLE 4.4: P(Beaten by Straight) and P(Beaten by Straight or Set) When You Hold 55, the Board Is 567, and Your Opponents Are on a Distribution of [TT,22] || [AJo,A9o] || [AJs,A2s] || [KQo,KTo] || [KQs,K2s] || [QJo,QTo] || [QJs,Q9s] || [JT,43] || [J9,53]**

| OPPONENTS | P(BEATEN BY STRAIGHT) | P(BEATEN BY STRAIGHT OR SET) |
|---|---|---|
| 1 | .08 | .11 |
| 2 | .15 | .21 |
| 3 | .22 | .30 |
| 4 | .28 | .38 |
| 5 | .34 | .45 |
| 6 | .39 | .51 |
| 7 | .44 | .57 |
| 8 | .49 | .62 |
| 9 | .53 | .66 |

From table 4.4, we see that you don't really have to worry about much until you're up against 4 or 5 opponents. However, keep in mind that even if you're beaten by a straight, you can draw to a full house or quads (more on this later). The moral of the story is that you shouldn't worry much when the board has three consecutive cards. Just be realistic—if there's a lot of raising and reraising, there's a decent chance that your hand is going to need to improve in order to win. Accept that fact, and only proceed if you're getting proper odds.

## The Impact of Suitedness

We've considered the impact of rank and connectivity when you flop a set or better. The final variable to consider is the flop's suitedness. If it's a rainbow flop, then the only time a flush beats you is a situation in which someone hits runner-runner. If the board has two of the same suit, then there may be flush draws to contend with, but you're well ahead in the hand. The only situation where the suitedness of a flop may cause concern is when it comes with three cards of the same suit. Consider the [TT,22]|||[AJo,A9o]|||[AJs,A2s]|||[KQo,KTo]||| [KQs,K2s]|||[QJo,QTo]|||[QJs,Q9s]|||[JT,43]|||[J9,53] distribution from before and the same 567 flop, except instead of it being a rainbow flop, it's now 5♠6♠7♠. Again, you hold 55. The hand distribution for an opponent here is the same as the distribution given in table 4.3.

The hands that your opponent can have a flush with are the following: {A♠J♠, A♠T♠, A♠9♠, A♠8♠, A♠4♠, A♠3♠, A♠2♠, K♠Q♠, K♠J♠, K♠T♠, K♠9♠, K♠8♠, K♠4♠, K♠3♠, K♠2♠, Q♠J♠, Q♠T♠, Q♠9♠, J♠T♠, T♠9♠, 9♠8♠, 4♠3♠, J♠9♠, T♠8♠}. In total, there are 24 flush combinations, two of which happen to be straight flushes. The probability that you are facing a flush when up against 1 opponent is $\frac{22}{391} \approx .06$. The probability that you are beaten by either a flush or a straight flush is $\frac{24}{391} \approx .06$. Using the independence assumption again, I calculated the probabilities of your being beaten by either a flush or a straight flush in table 4.5.

**TABLE 4.5: P(Beaten by Flush or Straight Flush) When the Board Is 5♠6♠7♠, You Have 55, and Your Opponents Are on a Distribution of [TT,22]||[AJo,A9o]||[AJs,A2s]||[KQo,KTo]||[KQs,K2s]||[QJo,QTo]||[QJs,Q9s]||[JT,43]||[J9,53]**

| OPPONENTS | P(BEATEN BY FLUSH OR STRAIGHT FLUSH) |
|---|---|
| 1 | 0.06 |
| 2 | 0.12 |
| 3 | 0.17 |
| 4 | 0.22 |
| 5 | 0.27 |
| 6 | 0.31 |
| 7 | 0.35 |
| 8 | 0.39 |
| 9 | 0.43 |

We see that you shouldn't be afraid of being up against a flush, and even if you're up against a flush, you can draw to a full house or quads. Even though you shouldn't be afraid, you should proceed with some caution, though, akin to the advice I gave regarding connected boards (see p. 102). Most of the time, a bet on the flop will take the pot down or get action from someone drawing to the nut flush or second nut flush. Sometimes you'll have more adventurous opponents as well. However, these adventurous types will usually flat call or put in a weak raise attempt. It's when you meet heavy resistance and betting action that you're going to need that board to pair to take down the pot. Accept that fact, and draw if the pot odds are good; else, fold without any regrets.

## Probability of Flopping a Set or Better

We started by assuming that the only flops we don't really want to see when we flop a set or better are those outlined in table 4.6.

**TABLE 4.6: Summary of "Bad" Flops for a Pocket Pair When You Flop a Set or Better**

| FLOP | RANK | CONNECTIVITY | SUITEDNESS |
|---|---|---|---|
| #1 | Unpaired | Made Straight Possible | Rainbow |
| #2 | Unpaired | Made Straight Possible | Two of the Same Suit |
| #3 | Unpaired | Made Straight Possible | Three of the Same Suit |
| #4 | Unpaired | No Made Straight Possible | Three of the Same Suit |
| #5 | Tripped | N/A | N/A |

We then showed that, in reality, the only flop that's close to being a disaster when you have a set or better is Flop #5. While we may have intuitively known this to be a truth, the work done so far in this chapter is significant in that it shows us roughly how many opponents we should be willing to bet into on these scary flops (3 or 4 at least). Of course, if there's very heavy betting action on Flops #1–#4, we need to be cautious so that we don't have to pay too high a price to draw to a full house or quads. If there's heavy betting action on Flop #5, you'll need to consider the rank of your pocket pair and the rank of the trips on the board in making your decision to continue with the hand. With these considerations in mind, let's actually look at the probability of flopping a set or better.

What we really want to do is calculate the probability of flopping a set or better *on a favorable board.* Whenever we analyze the probabilities of hitting hands, what we should really do is analyze the probabilities of hitting hands *on favorable boards.* Thus, besides sneaking in some postflop analysis, the past few sections are meant to set up our current calculation. Tripped flops are the only potential problem, but it's tough to generalize when they're favorable or unfavorable. Therefore, I'm going to calculate the probability of a favorable flop two times. First, I'll exclude tripped flops, treating them as bad flops. Second, I'll include tripped flops, treating them as favorable flops.

If we are counting tripped flops as bad flops, then what we are really calculating is the probability of flopping 1 or 2 cards of the same rank as your pocket pair. If you think back, you will recall that I already had you do this calculation (see p. 30, problem 5). I also provided a detailed explanation of how to do it in the answers. Citing my work from problem 5, the odds against a favorable flop, assuming that tripped flops are bad, are given by:

$$\frac{17296}{2304} \approx 7.51{:}1 \qquad (4.1)$$

Now, assume that tripped flops are okay. How many tripped flops are there? If you hold a specific pocket pair, there are 12 ranks of tripped flops that can appear. For instance, when you hold AA, the possible tripped flops are the following: {222, 333, 444, 555, 666, 777, 888, 999, TTT, JJJ, QQQ, KKK}. For each tripped flop, there are $\frac{4 \cdot 3 \cdot 2}{3!} = 4$ combinations since you are choosing 3 cards from a pool of 4. In total, there are $12 \cdot 4 = 48$ tripped flops. We can now adjust the odds from equation 4.1 by subtracting 48 from the numerator (the number of unfavorable flops) and adding it to the denominator (the number of favorable flops). Given that a tripped flop is acceptable, the odds against a favorable flop become:

$$\frac{17296-48}{2304+48} \approx 7.33{:}1 \tag{4.2}$$

.18 is a noticeable difference, but one that rarely impacts play.

When you have higher pocket pairs, you are not crippled by just having to hit a set or better. In the next section, we will examine the probability of flopping an overpair as a function of your particular pocket pair and go on to derive an approximate probability of getting a favorable flop for each pocket pair given that you are playing pure hit-to-win poker.

## Probability of Flopping an Overpair and Overall Probability of a Favorable Flop

Having calculated the odds against flopping a set or better, we must consider that hitting a set or better isn't the only way to win with a pocket pair. Any unimproved pocket pair can win shorthanded pots, and in particular, overpairs are very nice to have regardless of whether or not you're shorthanded. Since we're operating in the paradigm of hit-to-win poker, the next set of numbers to consider is the probabilities of, and odds against, flopping an overpair as a function of your pocket pair. Even though the analysis in chapter 3 suggests that paired boards aren't disastrous to your pocket pair, unpaired boards are more straightforward to play postflop; thus, in the first run of this calculation, let's calculate the probabilities of, and odds against, seeing three unpaired cards lower than the rank of your pocket pair. For AA, the probability that the first board card is lower than an ace is $\frac{48}{50}$.

The probability that the second card doesn't match the first card and is lower than an ace is $\frac{44}{49}$. Finally, the probability that the third card doesn't match either of the first two cards and is lower than an ace is $\frac{40}{48}$. The probability that the flop contains three unpaired cards below an ace, given that you hold AA, is $\left(\frac{48}{50}\right)\left(\frac{44}{49}\right)\left(\frac{40}{48}\right) \approx .72$. For KK, using the same thought process, the probability of flopping an overpair to an unpaired board is $\left(\frac{44}{50}\right)\left(\frac{40}{49}\right)\left(\frac{36}{48}\right) \approx .54$. Now that you see how the calculation works, the results for all 13 pocket pairs are in table 4.7.

**TABLE 4.7: Probability of Flopping an Overpair to an Unpaired Board**

| POCKET PAIR | P(UNPAIRED BOARD AND OVERPAIR) |
|---|---|
| AA | 0.72 |
| KK | 0.54 |
| QQ | 0.39 |
| JJ | 0.27 |
| TT | 0.18 |
| 99 | 0.11 |
| 88 | 0.07 |
| 77 | 0.03 |
| 66 | 0.01 |
| 55 | 0.003 |
| 44 | 0 |
| 33 | 0 |
| 22 | 0 |

Now, recall from our discussion about flopping a set or better that we were concerned about the type of flop with respect to connectivity and suitedness. Table 4.7 doesn't take connectivity or suitedness into account, and as we saw before, the probability that your opponents have made straights or flushes aren't that great unless you're in a family pot; however, because you're unlikely to improve your hand if you have an overpair on the flop, we should repeat our calculation, this time omitting Flops #1–#4 (table 4.6) from the pool of favorable flops.

A few remarks are in order before proceeding. If the flop contains three of a suit, and you have AA with a fourth of that suit, you have the nut flush draw. You may also be in good shape with KK for the king-high flush draw; however, it's usually not nearly as desirable to draw to the flush in that case—if you do hit, your implied odds are virtually nothing because your opponents will fear the four flush on board. Meanwhile, your reverse implied odds are considerable if you can't lay down to the ace-high flush. I'm *not* saying never to draw to the king-high flush in this case; if your opponent underbets and gives you 6:1 or 7:1 pot odds, it's an easy call. I'm just saying that this hand is not the great draw that overly optimistic players think it is. When calculating the percentage of a favorable flop for AA, I'm going to include flops containing three suited undercards where you have the nut flush draw. Another issue to consider is that if you flop connected undercards, you'll occasionally have a straight draw (e.g., you hold 77, and the flop is 456). Thus, ultimately, we're only "worried" about flops with connected undercards when you don't have a straight draw.

Now that we've established the parameters for the calculation, let's do it. Let's start with AA. There are 19,600 possible flops because we know two cards (AA). There are $\frac{48 \cdot 44 \cdot 40}{3!} =$ 14,080 total flops containing unpaired undercards. From these flops, we need to subtract the flops that are connected and the flops that contain three of a suit where we don't have the nut flush draw. Since there are flops that are both connected and suited, we need to avoid double counting. I will first count connected flops that are unsuited and then count all suited flops separately. The connected flops that we dislike are {234, 345, 456, 567, 678, 789, 89T, 9TJ}. TJQ and JQK are both acceptable flops since you have a straight draw with your ace.* In total, there are 8 types of connected flops that we want to discount. For each connected flop, there are 4•4•4 = 64 combinations. Four of those combinations contain three of the same suit. Therefore, there are 64 – 4 = 60 combinations of unsuited cards for each connected flop—note that doing the counting for this without complements is a lot tougher. Since there are 8 types of connected flops to discount, there are 8•60 = 480 connected flops that don't contain three of a suit. Now, we also need to subtract the flops that contain 3 of a suit where we don't hold the ace of that suit. For example, if we hold A♣A♠, we don't want any flops containing 3 diamonds or 3 hearts. Since we aren't counting the aces left in the deck, there are 12 cards left in each suit. The number or ways to choose 3 cards from a pool of 12 cards is $\frac{12 \cdot 11 \cdot 10}{3!} = 220$. Since there are two suits to consider, there are 2•220 = 440 combinations of undesirable suited flops. In total, there are 480 + 440 = 920 flops that are either connected, suited, or both. Therefore, there are 14,080 – 920 = 13,160 unpaired flops containing unconnected, unsuited undercards when you hold AA. The probability of getting a favorable flop where your AA is an overpair is $\frac{13{,}160}{19{,}600} \approx .67$. Table 4.8 reproduces table 4.7 with the addition

* TJQ and JQK may not be acceptable because these flops hit the following set of popular starting hands: [KK,TT]|||[KQ,KJ]|||[QJ,QT]|||[JT]. If you want to edit these numbers by considering T-J-Q and J-Q-K to be unfavorable flops, be my guest. The whole point of showing you all my work is so you can tweak it to fit the circumstances you find yourself in. My "hard and fast" rules may not apply to you for a wide variety of reasons. It's your responsibility as the reader to consider carefully everything that I present, take what helps you, and leave the rest behind.

of a third column displaying the results of the type of adjusted calculation I just did for AA.

**TABLE 4.8: Probability of Flopping an Overpair to an Unpaired Board and Probability of Flopping an Overpair to a Non-Dangerous Unpaired Board**

| POCKET PAIR | P(UNPAIRED BOARD AND OVERPAIR) | P(UNPAIRED, NONDANGEROUS BOARD) |
|---|---|---|
| AA | 0.72 | 0.67 |
| KK | 0.54 | 0.48 |
| QQ | 0.39 | 0.35 |
| JJ | 0.27 | 0.24 |
| TT | 0.18 | 0.16 |
| 99 | 0.11 | 0.10 |
| 88 | 0.07 | 0.06 |
| 77 | 0.03 | 0.03 |
| 66 | 0.01 | 0.01 |
| 55 | 0.003 | 0.003 |
| 44 | 0 | 0 |
| 33 | 0 | 0 |
| 22 | 0 | 0 |

Now, we could go ahead and add connected flops with *1-gaps*, such as 457. However, at that point, we are possibly getting a bit too conservative. Since the probabilities in table 4.8 are disjoint from the probability of flopping a set or better, you can combine the results from the second column in table 4.8 with the probability of flopping a set or better and get the results in table 4.9 (p. 112), which gives the probability of a favorable flop for each pocket pair. (Note that I deemed tripped flops as unacceptable when considering flopping a set or better.)

**TABLE 4.9: Probability of Getting a Favorable Flop with a Pocket Pair**

| POCKET PAIR | P(FAVORABLE FLOP) | APPROXIMATE ODDS AGAINST* |
|---|---|---|
| AA | .79 | 1:3.74 |
| KK | .60 | 1:1.51 |
| QQ | .47 | 1.14:1 |
| JJ | .36 | 1.78:1 |
| TT | .28 | 2.61:1 |
| 99 | .22 | 3.64:1 |
| 88 | .17 | 4.79:1 |
| 77 | .15 | 5.82:1 |
| 66 | .13 | 6.70:1 |
| 55 | .12 | 7.29:1 |
| 44 | .12 | 7.51:1 |
| 33 | .12 | 7.51:1 |
| 22 | .12 | 7.51:1 |

Table 4.9 is pretty close to a master table that should dictate your preflop play with pocket pairs if you are playing hit-to-win poker. The important thing to realize is the only pocket pairs that yield favorable flops more than 50 percent of the time are AA and KK. QQ is very close as well, being "safe" 47% of the time. Of course, we already know that the dangerous boards deemed unfavorable are not very dangerous when up against a small number of opponents; thus, QQ becomes safe over 50% of the time since most of the time, you will be raising with it preflop. JJ is a bit of a question mark. I tend to group it along with TT and sometimes 99, even though I play JJ more aggressively preflop. If we

* If the odds against are something like 1:3.74, it means that the odds in favor are 3.74:1.

make a broader definition of hit-to-win poker where it is acceptable not to have top pair when up against one or possibly two opponents, then JJ becomes an automatic raising hand, and when you can open in late position, TT becomes one as well (and possibly 99). There will be more to come when we analyze shorthanded play; however, to preview, the idea is that if an overcard (or two) falls in a shorthanded situation or if the board is paired, you aren't necessarily in trouble—against typical opponents, a bet will take down the pot. There are actually shorthanded games that can be beaten by raising preflop with virtually any two cards and then simply betting the flop. Shifting back to the hit-to-win mentality, I should mention that you should not expect to automatically cash in when you hit a favorable flop. For example, if you have an overpair, two pair or a set can still beat you. The probabilities of getting a favorable flop with 88 and below are close to the probabilities of flopping a set or better; therefore, it follows that they should only be played for sets or better under the hit-to-win paradigm. From table 4.9 and all the work leading up to it, we have an approximate idea of the postflop playability of all the pocket pairs in the hit-to-win model (even though these results have implications toward shorthanded play as well).

Now that we have a feel for how often you hit the flop with each pocket pair, let's proceed to some lines of play that develop when you do hit the flop. The numbers in table 4.9, combined with the rest of this chapter, will help you shape the approach you take with pocket pairs in the particular circumstances you find yourself in.

## Probability of Improving to a Full House or Quads with a Set

Even though we've seen how we aren't really in trouble when the flop is scary and we have a set, we should examine the situation where we flop a set and one of our opponents flops a straight or a flush. After all, there will be times when you know your opponent has hit a dangerous flop hard. If the guy who has folded his last fifty hands isn't backing down when the board is 6♥8♥Q♥, you need the board to pair if you're holding QQ so that you can get a full house or quads and beat his flush—there's no question that your set is no good here. To improve to a full house or quads when you flop a set, you have 7 outs on the turn. If you fail to make your hand on the turn, then you have 3 additional outs on the river (the cards that pair the turn card), meaning that you have 10 outs on the river. The probability of improving to a full house or quads, given that you flop a set, is therefore expressed in equation 4.3.

$$\left(\frac{7}{47}\right)\left(\frac{46}{46}\right) + \left(\frac{40}{47}\right)\left(\frac{10}{46}\right) = \frac{722}{2162} \approx .33. \qquad (4.3)$$

The first term reflects the case when you hit your draw on the turn. The second term reflects the case where you miss your draw on the turn but hit on the river. The result indicates that the odds against hitting a full house with two cards to come when you have a set are:

$$\frac{2{,}162 - 722}{722} = \frac{1{,}440}{722} \approx 1.99{:}1. \qquad (4.4)$$

On the turn, the probability of improving from a set is given by:

$$\frac{10}{46} \approx .22. \qquad (4.5)$$

On the turn, the odds against improving from your set on the river are therefore:

$$\frac{36}{10} \approx 3.6:1 \tag{4.6}$$

These numbers indicate that even if you have a set and your opponent has a straight or a flush, you are still in decent shape. If you're heads-up and your opponent bets the pot on the flop, you can make a slightly +EV call to draw to your full house or quads if you know for sure that your opponent won't bet on the turn (a pot-sized bet gives 2:1 odds, and you need 1.99:1 to call). It's very important to realize that to get 1.99:1 odds of getting a full house or quads with two cards to come, you must see both the turn and the river. If you know that your opponent has a straight or a flush and you call on the flop knowing that you will face a large bet on the turn, you really need to be getting $\frac{40}{7} \approx 5.71:1$ odds to call on the flop since you'll only see one card and not two. Of course, if your opponent makes a bet with Flops #1–#4 (see table 4.6), it doesn't mean that you are beaten. The important lesson is that Flops #1–#4 aren't really a problem when you have a set, because the probability that you're up against a straight or a flush isn't great, and even when you're up against a straight or a flush, your chances of improving are substantial.

## Flopping Top Set and Its Implications Toward Playing Middle and Bottom Set

Well, when you flop top set, you have flopped the best possible hand you can with a pocket pair on an unpaired board. However, having the best possible hand doesn't make life easy—very little is automatic in poker. If there are possible draws out, you need to figure out the best way to extract money while protecting your hand. If there are no possible draws out, you need to figure out how to maximize profit, given that you have the deck somewhat *crippled*. You also want to figure out whether to allow your opponents to have a free shot at picking up a straight draw or a flush draw on the turn. To go about rigorous analysis from the hand distribution perspective, we must first expand the flop categorizations from table 4.6. The possible flops you will encounter with your set are summarized in table 4.10:

**TABLE 4.10: Types of Flops You'll Encounter When You Flop a Set**

| FLOP | RANK | CONNECTIVITY | SUITEDNESS |
|---|---|---|---|
| #1 | Unpaired | None | Rainbow |
| #2 | Unpaired | Straight Draw Possible | Rainbow |
| #3 | Unpaired | Made Straight Possible | Rainbow |
| #4 | Unpaired | None | Two of the Same Suit |
| #5 | Unpaired | Straight Draw Possible | Two of the Same Suit |
| #6 | Unpaired | Made Straight Possible | Two of the Same Suit |
| #7 | Unpaired | None | Three of the Same Suit |
| #8 | Unpaired | Straight Draw Possible | Three of the Same Suit |
| #9 | Unpaired | Made Straight Possible | Three of the Same Suit |

At this point, though, any further analysis is impossible unless we come up with specific situations involving opponents. If you haven't gathered thus far, I'm a theoretic person, and I love to find answers to situations in general. In addition, I know that many people out there like general answers to be provided for them. However, as I've said before, grand, sweeping generalizations are tough to come by in poker analysis—I'm really providing a generalized machine through which information can be processed because as much as I like to think I'm Superman, the fact is that it's impossible for me to account for every nuanced situation my readership will encounter. Having established that, I'm going to apply my thinking to one situation where you flop top set. You'll find that the results will provide insight into other situations where you flop a set (the insight may tell you how to act or it may simply tell you how to think). If you have a specific situation that you want to analyze, you ultimately have to crank it through the machine yourself. With that in mind, check out the hand in table 4.11 (pp. 118–19).

Well, you are the cutoff (CO) and everyone has folded to you. The probability of getting a favorable flop with AA are so high that you definitely are not just playing to hit a set. You have the best preflop hand, and you want to make money with it. One mistake that some players make in tight games is just calling here, figuring that they want to trap the blinds in the hand and possibly get the button involved as well. The problem with this play is that you are definitely up against one random hand, the big blind, and possibly two others (depending on how the small blind and the button play). By limping, you place yourself at an information disadvantage on the flop. The benefit of raising preflop, and being the aggressor in general, is that it allows you to form more narrow distributions of most opponents' holdings. After all, if the flop comes 456 when you are against a random hand, and there is heavy betting action, how confidently can you carry on? With AA, you have a big edge, so

**Table 4.11: Hand Where You Flop Top Set**

**Game:** $200NL Hold'em
**Structure:** Small Blind: $1 Big Blind: $2
**Comments:** Home game with no rake, other than the $10 you paid to get in the door. You are P8 at a table where the players are generally tight-aggressive. The big blind, P2, is a skilled player who typically does well in very big games. In contrast to the other players, he is quite loose; however, he has lots of plays in his arsenal, including calling with absolutely nothing with the intent of bluffing based on perceived weakness. This game is a far cry from the rowdy, drunken home games that some of you are accustomed to—in the circles I run, the home games are tougher than almost any casino game out there. Given the following preflop action, what do you do?

| | 1(SB) XX | 2(BB) XX | 3 XX | 4 XX | 5 XX |
|---|---|---|---|---|---|
| **STACKS** | $350 | $500 | $150 | $250 | $100 |
| **PREFLOP** | b$1 | b$2 | >- | - | - |
| **STACKS** | | | | | |
| **FLOP** | | | | | |
| **STACKS** | | | | | |
| **TURN** | | | | | |
| **STACKS** | | | | | |
| **RIVER** | | | | | |
| **HOLE** | | | | | |

**Comments:** None.

**Legend:** SB = Small Blind; BB = Big Blind; B = Button; X = Unknown Hole Card; b = Blind or Straddle; > = Beginning of Betting Round Action; < = End of Betting Round Action; - = Fold; d = Action in the Dark; c = Call; r = Raise; E = Exposed Card; M = Main Pot; S = Side Pot; AI = All-In; R = Rake

| **6** | **7** | ***8*** | **9(B)** | **POT** |
|---|---|---|---|---|
| **XX** | **XX** | **A♥A♠** | **XX** | |
| $300 | $400 | $325 | $125 | |
| - | - | | | M = $3 |

you want to push it while, simultaneously, collecting information that will enable you to make the largest possible profit through well-informed postflop play.

Having established that a raise is in order, you have to figure out how much you should raise to. You'd like one or two callers because you have a big edge, but you don't want any more than that because you want your postflop decisions to be easy. Too large a raise will get no calls, unless someone mistakenly interprets the large raise as a pure blind steal attempt and decides to take a stand. A raise that is too small will leave you in a situation where you don't know what your opponents have, especially the big blind.

In my experience, a raise to 2.5BB–3.5BB is perfect here (except in unusual situations, I usually open for 3BB here). Why is 3BB a good raise here? It has to do with the pot odds that you are giving your opponents. Just like you should always think about your pot odds and implied pot odds when you call, whenever you make a bet or a raise, you should always think about the pot odds and implied odds that your opponents are getting. When you are ahead, you typically want to make the largest bet that your opponents will call, and to figure out the size of that bet, you need to know the odds your opponents are looking for.* Recall from chapter 1 (see p. 26) that if your opponent holds two unpaired cards, the probability, from his perspective, that he will hit one or more of his cards on the flop is about .32 (this doesn't account for flopping draws and a few other factors, but it's at least an approximation to start with). The odds against your opponent hitting the flop are therefore about $.68{:}.32 \approx 2.13{:}1$. Thus, to

* I had a friend help me with editing, and she initially replaced "looking for" with "need." I use "looking for" specially, though, because if you have opponents looking to make 2:1 calls for 5:1 shots, then by all means, you should bet the pot instead of one fourth of the pot.

make a +EV call in this model, your opponent needs at least \$2.13:\$1 odds to call. If you raise to 3BB (\$6), the total pot is \$9.

The big blind needs to call \$4 and is getting \$9:\$4 = \$2.25:\$1 to call. The SB is getting \$9:\$5 = \$1.80:\$1 odds to call. The call is +EV immediately for the BB, and the call is –EV for the small blind with respect to pot odds. Once implied odds are accounted for, along with the possibility of seeing the turn and the river for free, the SB may consider himself +EV on the call. The +EV is only marginal, and as a result of the reverse implied odds arising from the difficulty of playing most hands out of position postflop, the small blind will usually fold. Because of these reverse implied odds, the BB would be wise to fold most hands here, especially in a full ring game where there isn't pressure to play many hands. In this particular instance, a call from P2 is almost certain. This is good because you're extracting value out of your AA. Unfortunately, because of P2's looseness, you can't limit the set of hands he's in with. Against a loose BB, there's not really much more you can do except bet your good hands for value. As you can see the dynamics of optimal preflop play here are a complicated issue. All other considerations aside, I think you'll agree with me in saying that raising to \$6 is a pretty good move here. Table 4.12 shows the action after you raise to \$6.

Given how tight P1 and P9 are, you are surprised that they both call preflop. Since you opened for a raise in the CO, there's a chance that they might have put you on a steal and reduced their calling requirements. P2's call is not surprising here, given that he had \$20:\$4 = \$5:\$1 odds to call.

Let's assign hand distributions, starting with P1 and P9; they play similarly, so it's reasonable to assume that they're on approximately the same distributions. P1 and P9 would have most likely reraised with [AA,KK]. There's a chance that they would've also reraised with [QQ,TT]|||[AK,AQ] or some

**Table 4.12: Continuation of Hand Where You Flop Top Set**

**Game:** $200NL Hold'em
**Structure:** Small Blind: $1 Big Blind: $2
**Comments:** All three players behind you call your raise. The flop gives you top set, and there's a flush draw on the board. P1 and P2 check to you. It's your turn to act. What do you do?

| | 1(SB)<br>XX | 2(BB)<br>XX | 3<br>XX | 4<br>XX | 5<br>XX |
|---|---|---|---|---|---|
| **STACKS** | $350 | $500 | $150 | $250 | $100 |
| **PREFLOP** | b$1<br>$6 | b$2<br>$6< | >- | - | - |
| **STACKS** | $344 | $494 | | | |
| **FLOP**<br>**A♣9♣4♦** | >- | - | | | |
| **STACKS** | | | | | |
| **TURN** | | | | | |
| **STACKS** | | | | | |
| **RIVER** | | | | | |
| **HOLE** | | | | | |

**Comments:** None.

**Legend:** SB = Small Blind; BB = Big Blind; B = Button; X = Unknown Hole Card; b = Blind or Straddle; > = Beginning of Betting Round Action; < = End of Betting Round Action; - = Fold; d = Action in the Dark; c = Call; r = Raise; E = Exposed Card; M = Main Pot; S = Side Pot; AI = All-In; R = Rake

| 6 | 7 | *8* | 9(B) | POT |
|---|---|---|---|---|
| XX | XX | A♥A♠ | XX | |
| $300 | $400 | $325 | $125 | |
| - | - | $6 | $6 | M = $24 |
| | | $319 | $119 | |

subset of that distribution. One of the things about good players is that they play with a *mixed strategy*. In other words, sometimes, P1 might reraise with TT here. Other times he may call instead.* To treat this situation in the most analytic way possible, you have to assign probabilistic weights to each hand distribution based on your perceived notion of your opponents' mixed strategies. Of course, such an analysis can't be perfect unless you pick your opponents' strategies exactly. Hell, the HDM we've been doing against *fixed* strategies isn't perfect unless you can pin down the exact holdings of your opponents.† Our goal is to have a proper mental model of hold'em and a way to get results that are at least reasonable—with a proper mental model, your success in the game will be a large function of your ability to read your opponents properly.

We are going to assume that your opponents are employing fixed strategies in which it is fairly likely that they are reraising with QQ and possibly AK. Because P1 and P9 flat called and because they are tight players, they are probably on the following distribution: [JJ,22]|||[AQ,AJ]|||[KQ,KJ]. Realistically, P1 is more likely than P9 to have low pocket pairs like [55,22] because of the better odds he had on his call.

* You'll find that bad players also play with a mixed strategy, but it's a function of the fact that they don't know what they're doing. A good player employs a mixed strategy in an attempt to optimize his results. Unfortunately, the result of playing against a mixed strategy in either case is that evaluating the play of hands with HDM becomes more complicated.

† The strength of employing mixed strategy, then, is that it makes it even more difficult to derive profitable counter strategies. If you carry out a fixed strategy, it's fairly difficult for opponents to catch on. However, if you employ a mixed strategy, you've added a layer of complication that makes it virtually impossible for your opponents to catch on. Even if your opponents do catch on, the analysis can get so complicated that the only way to do it is with a paper and pencil, along with a calculator or computer or both.

In contrast to P1 and P9, P2 has a much wider distribution. I would say that he has any two *broadway cards*, any two suited cards, any connector, and any 1-gap. There's a chance that he may be in with any two cards, and I frankly wouldn't be surprised, but I'm going to assume that he has some starting requirements, as loose as they seem to be. Since he would've reraised with [AA,TT]|||[AK,AQ], we can discount those cards from P2's distribution. But everything else I just mentioned that isn't [AA,TT]|||[AK,AQ] is fair game.

Having considered your opponents' distributions, you then have the next task of optimizing your EV. If you bet, the only hands that P1 and P9 could possibly have that will give you action are the following: K♣Q♣, K♣J♣, 99, 44, AQ, or AJ. P2 will give you action with flush draws, 99, 44, AJ, A9, A4, and 94. He might give you some action with an ace with a kicker lower than a jack as well. He's loose, but skilled, so he'll probably be able to get away from such a hand, especially since you raised preflop and bet into three opponents on the flop. I also mentioned that P2 is capable of calling with the intent of bluffing, meaning that you'll get chips out of P2 that way, but I want to use the most conservative case possible to prove that even when facing the most conservative calling distributions, you're better off betting than slowplaying. From here, we need to know the probabilities of your opponents having these hands. Tables 4.13 and 4.14 (next page) are their distributions in terms of combinations.

Wow, P2's distribution is intense! I'll be honest—there was so much to keep track of that I forgot some flush drawing possibilities for P2 the first time I did these tables. Anyway, now that we have all this information, let's use it to find the probability of everyone folding when you bet. I'm going to use the independence approximation to simplify the math.

P9 and P1 have the same distribution, so let's just consider P9 for now. P9 gives you action with flush draws

**TABLE 4.13: Distribution for P1 and P9**

| STARTING HAND | COMBINATIONS | STARTING HAND | COMBINATIONS |
|---|---|---|---|
| JJ | 6 | 33 | 6 |
| TT | 6 | 22 | 6 |
| 99 | 3 | AQ | 4 |
| 88 | 6 | AJ | 4 |
| 77 | 6 | KQ (not K♣Q♣) | 15 |
| 66 | 6 | K♣Q♣ | 1 |
| 55 | 6 | KJ (not K♣J♣) | 15 |
| 44 | 3 | K♣J♣ | 1 |

*Total number of combinations = 94*

**TABLE 4.14: Distribution for P2**

| STARTING HAND | COMBINATIONS | STARTING HAND | COMBINATIONS |
|---|---|---|---|
| 99 | 3 | J♣4♣ | 1 |
| 88 | 6 | J3s (not J♣3♣) | 3 |
| 77 | 6 | J♣3♣ | 1 |
| 66 | 6 | J2s (not J♣2♣) | 3 |
| 55 | 6 | J♣2♣ | 1 |
| 44 | 3 | T9 | 12 |
| 33 | 6 | T8 (not T♣8♣) | 15 |
| 22 | 6 | T♣8♣ | 1 |
| AJ | 4 | T7s (not T♣7♣) | 3 |
| AT | 4 | T♣7♣ | 1 |
| A9s | 1 | T6s (not T♣6♣) | 3 |
| A8s | 1 | T♣6♣ | 1 |
| A7s | 1 | T5s (not T♣5♣) | 3 |
| A6s | 1 | T♣5♣ | 1 |
| A5s | 1 | T4s (not T♣4♣) | 2 |
| A4s | 0 | T♣4♣ | 1 |

| STARTING HAND | COMBINATIONS | STARTING HAND | COMBINATIONS |
|---|---|---|---|
| A3s | 1 | T3s (not T♣3♣) | 3 |
| A2s | 1 | T♣3♣ | 1 |
| KQ (not K♣Q♣) | 15 | T2s (not T♣2♣) | 3 |
| K♣Q♣ | 1 | T♣2♣ | 1 |
| KJ (not K♣J♣) | 15 | 98 | 12 |
| K♣J♣ | 1 | 97 | 12 |
| KT (not K♣T♣) | 15 | 96s | 3 |
| K♣T♣ | 1 | 95s | 3 |
| K9s | 3 | 94s | 2 |
| K8s (not K♣8♣) | 3 | 93s | 3 |
| K♣8♣ | 1 | 92s | 3 |
| K7s (not K♣7♣) | 3 | 87 (not 8♣7♣) | 15 |
| K♣7♣ | 1 | 8♣7♣ | 1 |
| K6s (not K♣6♣) | 3 | 86 (not 8♣6♣) | 15 |
| K♣6♣ | 1 | 8♣6♣ | 1 |
| K5s (not K♣5♣) | 3 | 85s (not 8♣5♣) | 3 |
| K♣5♣ | 1 | 8♣5♣ | 1 |
| K4s (not K♣4♣) | 2 | 84s (not 8♣4♣) | 2 |
| K♣4♣ | 1 | 8♣4♣ | 1 |
| K3s (not K♣3♣) | 3 | 83s (not 8♣3♣) | 3 |
| K♣3♣ | 1 | 8♣3♣ | 1 |
| K2s (not K♣2♣) | 3 | 82s (not 8♣2♣) | 3 |
| K♣2♣ | 1 | 8♣2♣ | 1 |
| QJ (not Q♣J♣) | 15 | 76 (not 7♣6♣) | 15 |
| Q♣J♣ | 1 | 7♣6♣ | 1 |
| QT (not Q♣T♣) | 15 | 75 (not 7♣5♣) | 15 |
| Q♣T♣ | 1 | 7♣5♣ | 1 |
| Q9s | 3 | 74s (not 7♣4♣) | 2 |
| Q8s (not Q♣8♣) | 3 | 7♣4♣ | 1 |
| Q♣8♣ | 1 | 73s (not 7♣3♣) | 3 |
| Q7s (not Q♣7♣) | 3 | 7♣3♣ | 1 |
| Q♣7♣ | 1 | 72s (not 7♣2♣) | 3 |
| Q6s (not Q♣6♣) | 3 | 7♣2♣ | 1 |
| Q♣6♣ | 1 | 65 (not 6♣5♣) | 15 |
| Q5s (not Q♣5♣) | 3 | 6♣5♣ | 1 |
| Q♣5♣ | 1 | 64 (not 6♣4♣) | 11 |

| STARTING HAND | COMBINATIONS | STARTING HAND | COMBINATIONS |
|---|---|---|---|
| Q4s (not Q♣4♣) | 2 | 6♣4♣ | 1 |
| Q♣4♣ | 1 | 63s (not 6♣3♣) | 3 |
| Q3s (not Q♣3♣) | 3 | 6♣3♣ | 1 |
| Q♣3♣ | 1 | 62s (not 6♣2♣) | 3 |
| Q2s (not Q♣2♣) | 3 | 6♣2♣ | 1 |
| Q♣2♣ | 1 | 54 (not 5♣4♣) | 11 |
| JT (not J♣T♣) | 15 | 5♣4♣ | 1 |
| J♣T♣ | 1 | 53 (not 5♣3♣) | 15 |
| J9 | 12 | 5♣3♣ | 1 |
| J8s (not J♣8♣) | 3 | 52s (not 5♣2♣) | 3 |
| J♣8♣ | 1 | 5♣2♣ | 1 |
| J7s (not J♣7♣) | 3 | 43 (not 4♣3♣) | 11 |
| J♣7♣ | 1 | 4♣3♣ | 1 |
| J6s (not J♣6♣) | 3 | 42 (not 4♣2♣) | 11 |
| J♣6♣ | 1 | 4♣2♣ | 1 |
| J5s (not J♣5♣) | 3 | 32 (not 3♣2♣) | 15 |
| J♣5♣ | 1 | 3♣2♣ | 1 |
| J4s (not J♣4♣) | 2 | | |

*Total number of combinations = 539*

(K♣Q♣, K♣J♣), 99, 44, AQ, or AJ. From the numbers in table 4.13, the probability that P9 has a flush draw is $\frac{2}{94}$, the probability that he has a set is $\frac{6}{94}$, and the probability that he has a pair of aces is $\frac{8}{94}$. The probability that P9 does not have any of these hands and will fold to a bet is $\frac{78}{94}$.

Let's first consider the lines of play when you bet the flop. The times when P9 doesn't have a flush draw, a pair of aces, or a set are the easiest—he folds to your bet. Now, for the other three cases, the tree diagrams branch out very quickly. When accounting for P9's various hole cards [(down to the level of differentiating between AQ♣ and AQ(not ♣)] along with the categories of cards that fall on the turn and the river, my precise analysis yielded a tree diagram with forty outcomes, and I hadn't even accounted for different patterns of betting that could have occurred! We desire to perform precise analysis, but we must acknowledge that we don't possess precise knowledge of the betting patterns along every conceivable branch anyway. For an analogy, suppose you are trying to find the 0–60 time for your car. You can spend $100,000 for the most accurate timepiece ever built, but measuring the time to the nearest billionth of a second doesn't mean a damn thing if you're using the arrow on your speedometer to indicate when you hit 60 mph. Your calculations are only as precise as your least precise measurement. In that spirit, I scrapped my monster tree diagram, realizing that the most efficient way of getting meaningful results is to consider simplified breakdowns of each scenario.

In the spirit of breaking down each situation, let's first consider the cases where you lead out on the flop. The pot is $24, so a nice bet here is $16. Figure 4.1 suggests what happens when P9 has a flush draw (K♣Q♣ or K♣J♣).

**Figure 4.1: Tree Diagram When P9 Has K♣Q♣ or K♣J♣**

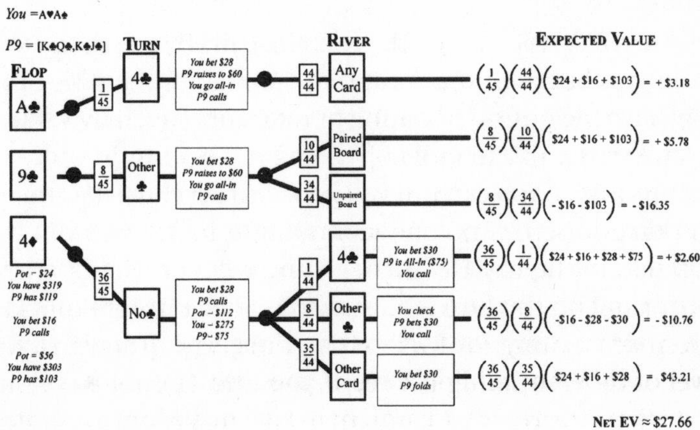

We see that the EV from this line of play is about $27.66. Since the probability of P9 having K♣Q♣ or K♣J♣ is $\frac{2}{94}$, the contribution of this line of play to the total EV is $(\frac{2}{94})$ ($27.66) ≈ $0.59. Figure 4.2 suggests lines of play evolving from when P9 has a set.

**Figure 4.2: Tree Diagram When P9 Has a Set (99 or 44)**

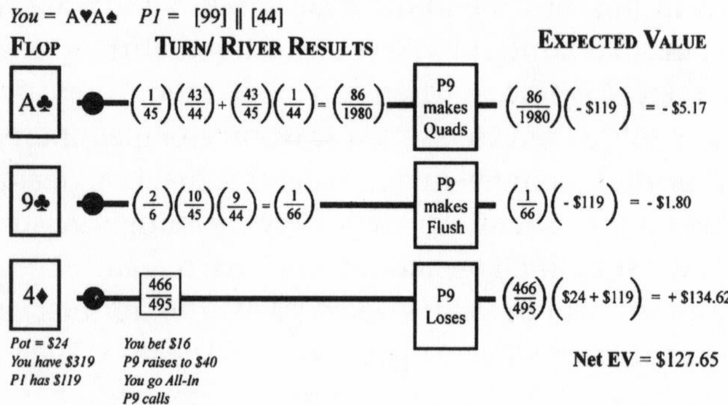


We see that the EV from this line of play is about $127.65. Since the probability of P9 having 99 or 44 is $\frac{6}{94}$, the contribution of this line of play to your total EV is $(\frac{6}{94})$($127.65) ≈ $8.15.

When P9 has AQ or AJ, he's most likely going to raise when you bet the flop. A raise to $40 seems plausible. You now have the option of calling or reraising. Given P9's stack, if you reraise, you're probably going to go all-in in order to put him all-in. You can just call here, but if a club falls and P9 isn't on a flush draw, your action might be killed. Even if a club doesn't fall on the turn, calling a bet on the flop and betting out on the turn is a suspicious play; P9 might not fall into your trap anyway. Given that, I'm going to say that you reraise all-in on the flop here. If you aren't going to get action from P9 anyway, you might as well make him pay if he's drawing. After raising all-in, P9 folds AQ or AJ here. You win the \$24 in the pot preflop plus the \$40 that you get out of P9 on the flop: \$24 + \$40 = \$64. P9 has AQ or AJ $\frac{8}{94}$ times, meaning that the EV from this line of play is $(\frac{8}{94})(\$64) \approx \$5.45$.

The final line of play is when P9 doesn't have anything. The $\frac{78}{94}$ times that this happens, you win \$24, meaning that the EV of this line of play is $(\frac{78}{94})(\$24) \approx \$19.91$. Your total EV for when you bet \$16 on the flop in this situation is therefore \$0.59 + \$8.15 + \$5.45 + \$19.91 = \$34.10. Now that we have the EV associated with betting \$16, let's trace through all the possibilities when you check.

When P9 has K♣Q♣, he's most likely going to check behind. Some players may choose to semi-bluff here, but given your raise and the preflop interest, P9, a tight player, is probably the type who doesn't want to get trapped by a check-raise in a pot like this. Given that P9 checks behind, figure 4.3 gives the line of play when P9 has a flush draw.

**Figure 4.3: Tree Diagram When P9 Has K♣Q♣ or K♣J♣**

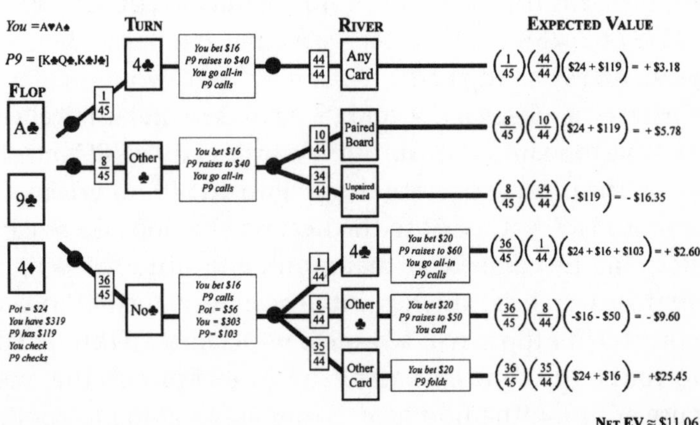

We see that the EV for this line of play is \$11.06. P9 has a flush draw $\frac{2}{94}$ times, meaning that the contribution of this line of play to the total EV is $(\frac{2}{94})(\$11.06) \approx \$0.24$. Figure 4.4 outlines what happens when P9 has a set.

### Figure 4.4: Tree Diagram When P9 Has 99 or 44

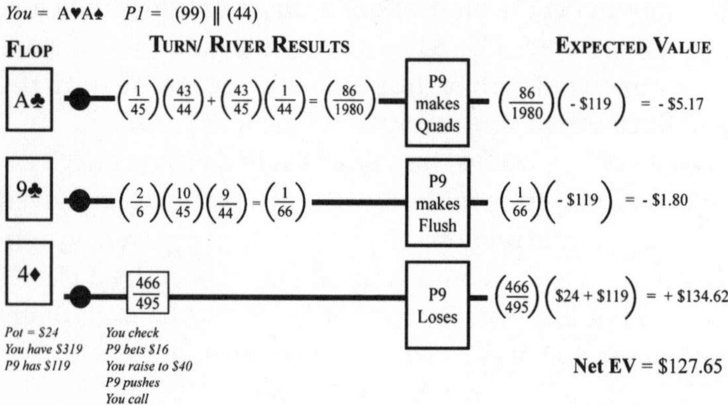


We see that all the chips end up in the middle anyway, and the EV for this line of play is \$127.65. Since P9 has a set $\frac{6}{94}$ times, the contribution of this line of play to the total EV is $(\frac{6}{94})(\$127.65) \approx \$8.15$. Now, let's see what happens when we check and P9 has top pair.

When you check to P9, and P9 has AQ or AJ, he's likely to bet something like \$16. You don't want a club to kill your action on the turn, so you're going to raise to \$40. As before, P9 is going to fold AQ or AJ to the heat on the flop. There isn't much that he can beat at that point, and since he's a tight player, he won't see much point in going any further. When P9 has AQ or AJ, you win \$24 + \$16 = \$40. Since P9 has AQ or AJ $\frac{8}{94}$ times, the contribution of this line of play to the total EV is $(\frac{8}{94})(\$40) \approx \$3.40$.

The final line of play occurs when P9 has a pocket pair that misses the flop, KQ (not K♣Q♣), or KJ (not K♣J♣). The whole theory behind slow playing is to allow one of these hands to catch up so that you can get action from them on later betting rounds. Unfortunately, there's no way you're going to get action from KQ or KJ, unless P9 happens to have K♣ and hits a fourth club on the turn for which you give him proper odds to draw (since you are betting $\frac{1}{2}$ to $\frac{2}{3}$ pot, that's not happening). Thus, you're hoping that P9 hits a set on the turn with a pocket pair. The lines of play evolving from checking to P9 when he didn't hit the flop are outlined in figure 4.5.

## Figure 4.5: Tree Diagram for Slowplaying When P9 Missed the Flop

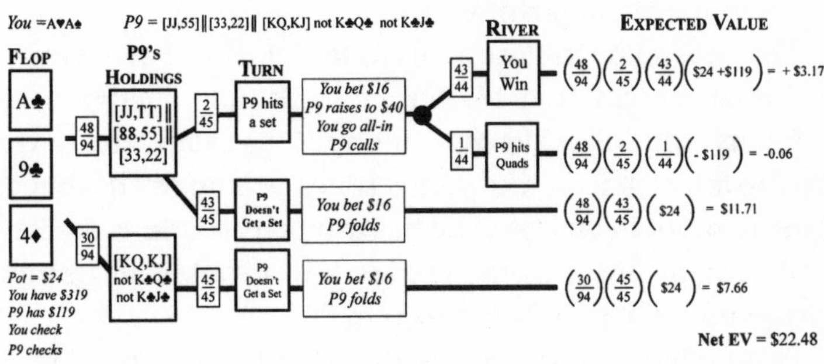


The EV for this line of play is \$22.48. Notice that the probability of each situation (pocket pair, KQ, or KJ) was already taken into account. Thus, \$22.48 is the total EV contribution from this line of play. Now that we've accounted for all possibilities when we check the flop, the net EV of checking the flop is \$0.24 + \$8.15 + \$3.40 + \$22.48 = \$34.27. This is an improvement of \$0.17 from when you bet on the flop, given that the lines of play I outlined are what you can expect to happen.

This calculation illustrates that against tight opponents like P9 and P1, slowplaying may marginally increase your EV in a heads-up situation. However, since there's so much room to play around with the numbers and possibly even the hand distributions, you shouldn't rely on this result. There are some major benefits to betting here, especially when up against opponents apt to overplay top pair. It's best to try to get the chips in on the flop against such opponents, before a scare card falls that kills all your action. Now, if we consider that you aren't actually heads-up in this hand, you should have more motivation to bet. There's a chance that P1 or P2 checked with the intention of check-raising (especially P2 who is very aggressive, but we'll get to him in a second). You know you're ahead in the hand now, so get as much money in as possible.

That was some intense analysis for P9. The analysis for P1 is similar, except that his bigger stack may change some numbers. You will make more money if he catches up to you on the turn, but at the same time, you may be able to squeeze more from him if he has top pair or a flush draw by playing aggressively from the start. We've looked at the tight players enough, so let's move on to P2.

From table 4.14, the probability that P2 has a flush draw is $\frac{55}{539}$; the probability that he has a set is $\frac{6}{539}$; the probability that he has a pair of aces is $\frac{14}{539}$; and the probability that he has two pair is $\frac{3}{539}$. The probability that he has nothing is therefore $\frac{461}{539} \approx .86$. If you give P2 a free card, the probability that he improves to a set is $\left(\frac{36}{539}\right)\left(\frac{2}{45}\right) \approx .003$. The probability of P2 improving is so small because he has so many possible hands. Because his chance of improving is so small, betting against him appears to be the best line of play if you were playing against P2 heads-up, and because you are against multiple opponents, you generally shouldn't slowplay your top set on this board with a possible draw.

All this talk has been about a sample hand where you flop top set. When you have middle set or bottom set, there is a greater probability that your opponents have top pair, a hand that will generally give you action. It therefore makes sense that you generally do not want to be slowplaying middle or bottom set.

## Do You Want to Shut Out Flush Draws from the Start?

We've analyzed betting proportionately and slowplaying. Now, let's shift gears—let's talk about betting in a fashion so that you completely shut out draws from the start. The way to accomplish this is to overbet the pot—bet twice the size of the pot or so. There are three main lines of play now: you can either overbet the flop, you can bet normally on the flop and overbet the turn, or you can bet normally on the flop and the turn. Let's see which line of betting leads to the greatest profit against a flush draw. We will continue talking about the case from the last section where you flop top set; however, this analysis is applicable in a wide range of situations where you have made hands versus drawing hands.

Suppose you are against P1. You are now sure he has K♣Q♣. There is $24 in the pot. You bet $100, a bet that pretty much any player won't call with a flush draw, especially if the player is tight like P1. With this bet, your EV is $24. There is a 100% chance that you win the pot since your tight opponent will fold. Figure 4.6 outlines what happens when you bet proportionately with respect to the pot on both the flop and the turn, allowing P1 to draw both betting rounds.

**Figure 4.6: Tree Diagram for Flopping Top Set Against a Draw and No Overbetting**

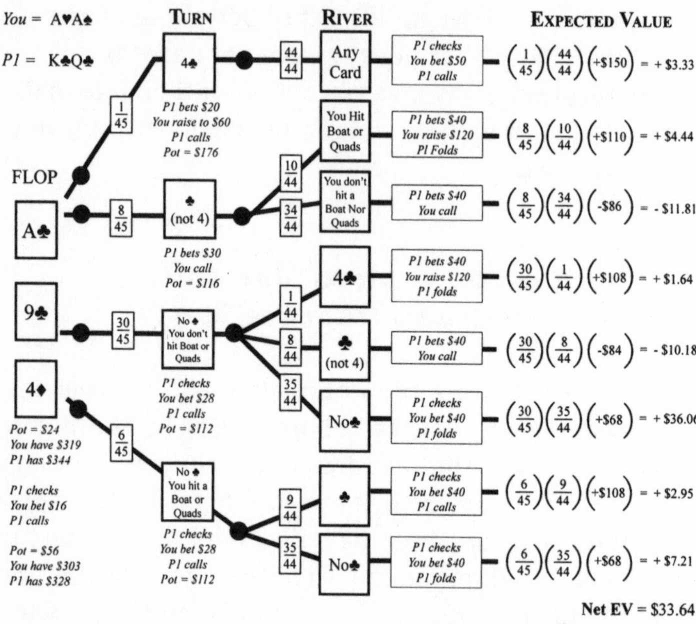


The basic idea behind this line of play is that you bet $\frac{2}{3}$ pot on the flop, and if the third club doesn't hit, you bet again. The total EV for this line of play comes out to +$33.64. Now, instead of betting $\frac{2}{3}$ pot on the turn, assume you overbet the turn when a third club hasn't fallen and you still just have a set. The new tree diagram for that situation is in figure 4.7.

The total EV of this line of play is +$32.79, which is only marginally worse than when you do not overbet the turn given that your opponent is on a flush draw. The results from the three lines of play are summarized in table 4.15.

## Figure 4.7: Tree Diagram for Flopping Top Set Against a Draw and Overbetting the Turn After Betting $\frac{2}{3}$ Pot on the Flop

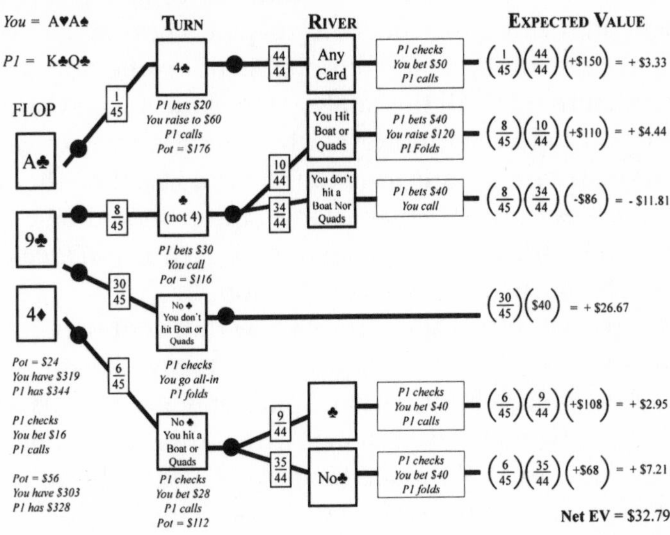


### TABLE 4.15: Lines of Play When You Have a Set Against P1's Flush Draw

| FLOP ACTION | TURN ACTION | EV |
|---|---|---|
| Overbet | N/A | +$24.00 |
| Bet $\frac{2}{3}$ Pot | Overbet | +$32.79 |
| Bet $\frac{2}{3}$ Pot | Bet $\frac{2}{3}$ Pot | +$33.64 |

Comparing the three lines of play, the best way to play against a flush draw in this case appears to be betting in a fashion that tempts P1 to draw on the flop and the turn. Note that the EV from allowing P1 to draw on both rounds is only marginally higher than the EV from allowing P1 to draw only on the flop. Because many assumptions were made in this analysis, the error involved is probably higher than the $0.85 difference in EV. Thus, shutting out your opponent on the turn may not be a bad play. The one clear-cut thing is that shutting out your opponent on the flop costs you substantial EV. All this analysis was done in an example where you have a set; however, these results carry over to when you have anything from top pair to a straight—the absolute values of the EV may change, but it should be clear that against straightforward opponents like P1, you are better off not shutting them out on the flop.

Notice that in this analysis we knew that your opponent was drawing to a flush. When you're actually playing, you don't have precise information. Your opponent may have a flush draw, he may have top pair with a weak kicker, or he may be slowplaying a made hand. Whenever you overbet the turn, you're going to get action from a monster hand (a set or better); however, weaker hands will fold. These weaker hands may normally give you action if you bet more proportionately with respect to the pot. Thus, even though the EV from betting the flop and the turn normally is marginally different in comparison to when you bet the flop normally and overbet the turn, these added considerations for actual play indicate that you lose valuable EV by shutting out your opponent on the turn.

When taking this recommended line of play, just keep the following in mind: if you bet in a fashion that allows your opponents to draw on the flop and the turn, it's imperative that you don't do anything crazy if the flush draw possibly hits—don't give your opponents big implied odds. If you aren't skilled in that art, then your EV will go way down by taking my recommended line of play, and the line of play that you should probably take is the one where you bet the flop normally and then overbet the turn.*

## Playing a Set Against Known Made Hands

Our analysis of when you flop a set is just about done. The last thing to consider is what happens when an opponent also has a made hand. When your opponent has a made hand, you are going to get action on the flop, the turn, and the river, unless your opponent eventually figures out that he's beaten. If you slowplay on the flop, you will possibly get action for two betting rounds, but you will miss out on the opportunity to get money across all three betting rounds. You also give your opponent one less opportunity to make a big mistake, like going over the top of your bet. The moral of the story is, once again, to come out betting on the flop when you have top set against another made hand.

We know you're going to make money from an opponent with top pair. It makes sense to reason that there's really no point slowplaying middle or bottom set when it's checked to you. It's also clear that there's no point slowplaying any set when there's a draw on the board. Having said that, the one case where slowplaying a set *may be* an acceptable play is if there are no draws on the flop. By letting a free card fall on the turn, you increase the chance that your opponents will

* I have really only been addressing cash game situations so far, even though the EV result can be applied to your *chip EV* in tournaments. Intournaments, if I have a short medium stack, I usually elect to shut out the flush draw on the turn (if I'm really hurting, I shut it out immediately on the flop). I'd rather sacrifice 2–3BB in EV to be guaranteed a stack of 15 + BB—at that point, it doesn't matter too much if you have 15BB or 17BB.

catch a hand that they'll give you action with. Personally, I make many continuation bets when I play, so I usually don't slowplay.* The whole point of my continuation betting is to set myself up for a big payout when my opponent plays back at the wrong time, and by slowplaying, I'm deviating from this primary strategy. We've spent a long time talking about how to play your sets. Let's now turn to what happens when you flop an overpair.

## Flopping an Overpair, Showing Aggression in Late Position, Blocking Bets from Early Position, and Learning Even More About Flopping Sets

The play when you flop a set is relatively straightforward. You are aggressive until a scare card comes out, and at that point, you usually call down provided that the bets are reasonably sized with respect to the pot. An overbet may be a bluff, but it also may be a feigned bluff. In the games I typically play online, an overbet on the turn or the river usually seems to be a made hand. This play is popular because weak players seem to process the overbet instantly as a bluff attempt. Some people, recognizing this, have become wise and have started using it as a value bet attempt. The problem is that these days, only weak players typically succumb to this line of play, and, indeed, it seems to be less effective now than it was about a year ago. Just keep in mind that when you face a large bet on the turn or the river, your opponent

* The only slowplay that I employ is check-raising in situations where I know that I'm going to trap a lot of money in the hand between the initial bettor and myself. The key to pulling this play off is having a good sense of where the bet on the flop is going to come from.

will typically have the goods until you have evidence proving the contrary.

Betting in a way that doesn't shut your opponent out is only profitable when you don't give your opponents big implied odds. Part of not offering huge implied odds is getting away when betting becomes disproportionate with respect to the pot. Sometimes, you'll find yourself in games where overbetting is routine and done with a large range of holdings. In that case, get ready for some high EV and some high swings in your bankroll—in these types of games, you're more than happy to go to war with your set when a potential flush draw or straight draw hits. Typically, though, you want something close to the nuts when facing overbettors on the turn or the river.

Now, because more hands can beat you, playing an overpair is trickier than playing a set. Don't get me wrong, an overpair is a good hand. At the same time, don't fall in love with it; an overpair is good, but it's vulnerable. In addition to straights and flushes, you now also have to worry about two pair and sets. Furthermore, when you're behind in the hand, you don't have good odds to improve. The key with overpairs, therefore, is to extract maximum value when you are ahead, while, simultaneously, not dumping away a bunch of chips when you're beaten. Table 4.16 (pp. 142–43) is a classic example with KK. I include the entire hand from both players' perspectives because there's a lot of interesting play from both players.

Preflop, P3 makes a standard raise UTG with TT in a six-handed game. I personally oscillate between limping UTG with TT and raising UTG with TT in shorthanded games. If my opponents are aggressive, I tend to limp more, looking to take down a big pot when I catch a set. If my opponents are passive, I raise more, with the intention of taking down the pot heads-up on the flop by betting (we'll do more analysis

**Table 4.16: Play of an Overpair from Late Position When Opponent Flops a Set**

**Game:** Shorthanded $400NL Hold'em
**Structure:** Small Blind: $2 Big Blind: $4
**Comments:** Game where a reraise implies [AA,KK] and where people will sometimes call a reraise with AA instead of going back over the top in an attempt to trap the reraiser. This is an online game where the rake is very small with respect to the pot.

| | 1(SB) | 2(BB) | 3 | 4 | 5 |
|---|---|---|---|---|---|
| | XX | XX | T♣T♥ | XX | K♣K♠ |
| **STACKS** | $700 | $500 | $1,500 | $400 | $1,000 |
| **PREFLOP** | b$2 | b$4 | >$12 | - | $36 |
| | - | - | $36< | | |
| **STACKS** | | | $1,464 | | $964 |
| **FLOP** | | | >$40 | | $100 |
| **T♠5♣2♥** | | | $100< | | |
| **STACKS** | | | $1,364 | | $864 |
| **TURN** | | | >$125 | | $300 |
| **J♦** | | | $300< | | |
| **STACKS** | | | $1,064 | | $564 |
| **RIVER** | | | >$300 | | - |
| **7♠** | | | | | |
| **HOLE** | | | | | |

**Comments:** P3 wins the pot without a showdown when P5 folds on the river.

**Legend:** SB = Small Blind; BB = Big Blind; B = Button; X = Unknown Hole Card; b = Blind or Straddle; > = Beginning of Betting Round Action; < = End of Betting Round Action; - = Fold; d = Action in the Dark; c = Call; r = Raise; E = Exposed Card; M = Main Pot; S = Side Pot; AI = All-In; R = Rake

| 6 XX | POT |
| --- | --- |
| $800 | |
| - | M = $78 |
| | |
| | M = $278 |
| | |
| | M = $878 |
| | |
| | |

in chapter 6, which is devoted to shorthanded play, but remember from our initial work back in chapter 1 how profitable continuation bets can be). After P3 makes a standard raise, P5 reraises. This reraise sounds the [AA,KK] alarm. The conditions I described regarding a reraise signaling [AA,KK] are very accurate for many games (even shorthanded ones), and it creates a fascinating dynamic. P5 wants to get good value from his hand, and he would like to get the raiser heads-up in a pot, but by doing so, he announces his hand to the table. P3 now has two paths in this hand. If P5 is the type of player who can't get away from a high pocket pair, P3 can trap P5 for a lot of chips when he hits a set. In other words, he's getting proper implied odds to continue in the hand.

On the other end of the spectrum, if P5 is aware that he announced [AA,KK], then he may be exposing himself to a huge bluff. If P3 is tricky and courageous, he can pull a fancy bluff, advertising that he flopped a set when he didn't. In addition, if there's a draw on the board, P3 has the option of acting like he's on a draw in an effort to steal the pot if the supposed draw actually falls on the board. Of course, P5 has to be capable of laying down an overpair for this bluff to succeed. If P5 is aware of this bluffing opportunity available to P3, he may be more apt to overplay his hand when P3 has a set. The actual playing dynamics ultimately depend (the proverbial answer to any poker question is "it depends") on the particular opponent you are facing.

One additional possibility to keep in mind is that some players in P3's position, if they have AA, will trap you by calling your reraise instead of reraising again. To avoid these tricky dynamics, I tend to reraise with a wider distribution of hands to keep my opponents off guard. I also reraise with a wider distribution of hands because, in my experience, most of my opponents aren't nearly as tricky as they could be; usually, when I reraise preflop, I take down the pot very easily with a continuation bet on the flop. I continually think about this problem because there are some tricky players out there, but I don't know if there's a great solution to it, other than to be aware of all the possibilities.

With the dynamics for the hand in place, the flop comes ten high with no draws. P3 hits top set, and he knows that P5 probably has a big overpair. Some players check here, intending simply to call P5's probable bet. P3 takes a better line of play—he actually bets into P5. This is a great play because P5 is most likely going to raise and build a larger pot for later betting rounds. By building the pot here, P3 guarantees a bigger payout should there be action on the turn and the river.* Sure enough, after P3 bets, P5 raises. P3 now has some interesting lines of play. He can call here with the intention of checking the turn, he can call here with the intention of immediately betting out on the turn, or he can go back over the top. Each of these lines of play has its merit, and the EV of each line of play changes dramatically as a function of the opponent you are up against (JV and I say it constantly—pay attention!). Let's consider each line of play for P3.

What happens when P3 calls the raise here and checks the turn? Some players in P5's shoes may bet. Different motivations exist for this bet. Some players would assign P3 to a hand such as AT or JJ and assume that the check on the turn implies weakness; they think their KK is ahead, and they naturally bet to get value from what they perceive to be the best hand. Other players use a bet on the turn to protect themselves. Suppose that after P3 checks, P5 becomes suspi-

* This book is pretty much just covering NL situations, but this idea of building the pot is really important when you are playing pot-limit (PL) games. If you've noticed, since my maximum raise is usually the size of the pot, or just under the size of the pot, many of my results are at least somewhat applicable to the world of PL hold'em.

cious. After the flop, the pot is $278. If he checks the turn, P3 may bet $200 on the river, a bet that P5 may be forced to call. Instead of having to call $200 on the river, P5 can bet in position on the turn, say $150. If he gets called and bet into on the river, he can be fairly confident in folding unless he's up against the type of foe who calls bets on the flop and the turn with the intention of bluffing on the river (a great, sophisticated play to toss in your arsenal, but if you overuse it and your opponents catch on, you will be in a lot of trouble).

By betting $150 on the turn and folding to either a bet on the river or a check-raise on the turn, P5 actually saves money with this bet ($50 in this case) provided that P3 is relatively straightforward. If P3 checks to P5 on the river, P5 simply checks behind unless he is fortunate to river a king. This bet in position on the turn is meant to preserve a showdown. The other great thing about this line of play is that if P3 is on top pair, there is a chance that he might be looking to check/call the turn with the intention of checking on the river. By checking the turn, you are losing $150 by not getting P3's money in on the turn. Thus, even if P3's river bet is only around $150 when P5 checks behind, P5 is better off betting this same amount of money on the turn to get money from a worse hand; by playing passively, P5's chances of extracting money from a worse hand are greatly reduced.

We can conclude that betting in position on the turn accomplishes two major tasks—it saves you money when you are behind *and* it extracts value when you are ahead. For that reason, if I am P5, I love betting in position on the turn here when checked to. Meanwhile, from P3's perspective, he makes $150 on the turn when he is up against a P5 who will bet in position. With the $100 he makes on the flop, calling the raise on the flop and check/calling on the turn will, therefore, make about $250 against P5 who will bet in position (assume P5 puts no additional money in on the river). If P3 is, instead, up against P5 who checks behind on the turn with the intention of calling a bet on the river, P3 makes between $75 and $200 on the river, depending on his chosen bet size. P5's bet in position is meant to protect against players who will bet a larger percentage of the pot, but that does not mean that every opponent will bet $200 into a $278 pot here—a $100–$150 is much more likely to be called and is probably the most likely bet. In total, P3 makes somewhere in the range of $200–$250 by calling the raise on the flop and checking the turn to P5 who checks behind on the turn and calls the river.

While checking behind on the turn loses less money for P5, the problem is that it leaves him open to bluff attempts on the river. If P3 bets the pot on the river, is he bluffing or not? You simply do not know. Again, players are less apt to bet into someone who shows aggression on the turn, and in addition, when you have better hands, you need to extract value. So in most games, against most opponents, I stand by my original claim that betting in position on the turn is the favorable play if you are P5 and P3 bets into you.

Now, instead of calling the raise on the flop and checking the turn, suppose that P3 elects to use a stop-and-go, meaning that he calls the raise on the flop in early position and then bets out from early position on the turn. (He'll probably bet around half the size of the pot on the turn—he bets $125 in this example.) There are a few possibilities. P5 may be really suspicious of P3 and simply fold. In that case, P3 only makes $100 from the flop. P5 may call the bet on the turn, with the intention of either folding or calling a bet on the river. P5 calls on the turn with the intention of folding on the river if he assumes that his call will signal to P3 that he has a legitimate hand. Thus, if P3 bets the river, P5 assumes his overpair is no good.

This line of reasoning is similar to that used in betting the turn in position. Personally, I hate this line of play. In my experience, calling the turn doesn't really slow down an early position aggressor. The early position aggressor is going to call most likely on the river anyway, so many times, he's simply going to fire on the river. This leaves P5 open to folding his overpair when it is, in fact, the best hand. If you find an opponent who often checks in early position after getting called on the turn, calling in position is a good play, but against most players, you'll find that you just wind up in trouble. When P5 calls on the turn with the intention of folding on the river, P3 makes about $225–$250, depending on the size of his bet on the turn. Meanwhile, if P5 also calls on the river, P3 makes about $450, assuming a river bet of $200 into a pot of about $500.

The final possibility for P5, the one that we see here, is that P5 actually raises in position. The reason that he raises in position here is the same reason that he bets in position when checked to; if P3 is behind, he will usually just call the raise and check the river—P3 will typically only show aggression in response to P5's aggression if he has P5's overpair beaten. As we just saw, if P5 calls on the turn with the intention of calling on the river, he loses $200 on the river—he loses a total of about $325 across the turn and the river. By raising to $300, P5 actually saves himself $25 (possibly more, depending on the size of P3's river bet). Against P5 in this hand, P3 made $400 on the flop and the turn.

The final possibility on the flop is for P3 simply to go back over the top. In this case, P5 will probably go all-in or fold. The relative frequencies of those actions will give the EV of going back over the top. Against weak players who can't fold a napkin, I push all the chips in on the flop if I'm P3. If they have KK and an ace falls on the turn, I may not get any more money in the pot, so I might as well get the money in now if P5 is weak. Strong players are capable of folding the overpair though (which is why I opened this section talking about this potential bluffing opportunity against a reraiser). If P5 is a strong player, which seems to be the case from this hand, I think that P3 took the best line of play. Incidentally, I think the numbers show that P5 also took the best line of play, given that he doesn't know for sure that he's up against a set. He limited his losses while, simultaneously, giving players with inferior holdings the opportunity to call.

The different lines of postflop play that I just described in analyzing this problem are typical of the lines of play that I encounter on a daily basis. From my work with the numbers and my piece-by-piece dissection of various lines of play, I think it's clearer that it pays to lead out with your monster hands. It should also be clear that, when you are in position, you want to be aggressive with decent holdings, such as overpairs, that aren't monsters. Betting in position with such hands allows you to extract money from weaker holdings while, simultaneously, allowing you to save money against players who make bets that are around $\frac{1}{2}$ to $\frac{2}{3}$ pot. The only issue I didn't really get to is what happens when your opponent will bet about $\frac{1}{3}$ pot on both the turn and the river. In that case, calling down may be the best route, especially if raising the turn will drive out inferior holdings. In general, though, when you're the driver in NL hold'em, you have a much better idea of where you're going. We've explored the lines of play that develop from having an overpair in position. Now, let's take the same hand, except this time, I'm going to swap the relative positions of the players holding KK and TT (I put P5 in the BB because it's a natural way to get the reraise to happen). This situation is displayed in table 4.17 (pp. 150–51).

## Table 4.17: Play of an Overpair from Early Position When Opponent Flops a Set

**Game:** Shorthanded $400NL Hold'em
**Structure:** Small Blind: $2 Big Blind: $4
**Comments:** Game where a reraise implies [AA,KK] and where people will sometimes call a reraise with AA instead of going back over the top in an attempt to trap the reraiser. This is an online game where the rake is very small with respect to the pot.

| | 1(SB) | 2(BB) | 3 | 4 | 5 |
|---|---|---|---|---|---|
| | XX | K♣K♠ | T♣T♥ | XX | XX |
| **STACKS** | $700 | $1,000 | $1,500 | $400 | $500 |
| **PREFLOP** | b$2 | b$4 | >$12 | - | - |
| | - | $36 | $36< | | |
| **STACKS** | | $964 | $1,464 | | |
| **FLOP** | | >$40 | $40< | | |
| **T♠5♣2♥** | | | | | |
| **STACKS** | | $924 | $1,424 | | |
| **TURN** | | >$100 | $100< | | |
| **J♦** | | | | | |
| **STACKS** | | $824 | $1,324 | | |
| **RIVER** | | >$125 | <$350 | | - |
| **7♠** | | - | | | |
| **HOLE** | | | | | |

**Comments:** P3 wins the pot without a showdown when P2 folds on the river.

**Legend:** SB = Small Blind; BB = Big Blind; B = Button; X = Unknown Hole Card; b = Blind or Straddle; > = Beginning of Betting Round Action; < = End of Betting Round Action; - = Fold; d = Action in the Dark; c = Call; r = Raise; E = Exposed Card; M = Main Pot; S = Side Pot; AI = All-In; R = Rake

| 6<br>XX | POT |
|---|---|
| $800 | |
| - | M = $74 |
| | |
| | M = $154 |
| | |
| | M = $354 |
| | |
| | |

This hand exemplifies the advantage of position in NL hold'em against a typical opponent in this situation. In the last hand, P3 played quite well, extracting the most money possible from P5. Many opponents slowplay their sets, meaning that P5 would have gotten away losing a lot less money (probably around $200 or $250). In this hand, however, P2 is forced to lose money on the flop, the turn, and the river should P3 choose to call instead of raising. I should clarify something here. All this time that I've been referring to slowplaying, I've been referring to the type of slowplay where you check when everyone else checks. If someone bets ahead of you, the texture of play changes considerably. Raises have much more meaning than bets, so P3 might be best served by calling on the flop. Calling here is also a slowplay, but it's a different type of slowplay than checking after everyone else has checked.

Now, against some opponents, P3 makes more money by raising. Thus, it really boils down to the proverbial "it depends." Whether P3 should raise in position on the turn is also debatable. Being that I raise in position with top pair to preserve the showdown, I prefer to raise in position on the turn with a set as well in order to add deception to my play. If my opponents were to think that I only raise in position on the turn with top pair, I'd be screwed—especially when they see me check down with top pair, and sometimes two pair. I need to be caught raising in position with monsters if raising in position on the turn is to work successfully. People tend to play passively when they are uncertain. By instilling uncertainty in my opponents, I can read my opponents more easily.

Now that we've looked at P3's play of his set in position, let's look at P2's play of his pair out of position. The bet on the flop is standard. P2 reraised preflop and is therefore going to follow with a bet on the flop. When P3 calls, P2 is thinking that P3 has a marginal hand or a monster. He doesn't know which; therefore, on the turn, P2 bets again. If P3 is on a monster, he'll most likely announce it here. If P3 is tricky, though, he may raise on the turn as a bluff or with a marginal hand, trying to sell a set. P3 only calls here (another tricky play). Now, at this point, if P2 checks on the river, he's pretty sure that P3 will bet with a good hand and check a marginal hand. The number of good hands that P3 bets with that P2 beats is uncertain, but as long as the bet is reasonably sized (about half the pot), P2 is probably forced to call. If P3 bets a larger amount, P2 might be moved off his hand, and, in fact, the problem with P2 checking here is exactly that. By checking, he's giving P3 more of an invitation to move him off his hand.

To get a call from worse hands and to prevent him from being moved off his hand, P2 is forced to bet out of position here. This bet on the river is known as a blocking bet. The idea behind it is that if P3 has a worse hand, he cannot raise, but he can call (again, he'll raise if he's tricky though, but until you see evidence to the contrary, assume your opponents are straightforward). If P3 has a better hand, he'll make it known by raising. By betting $125 on the river here, P2 actually saves money, because if he checks to P3, there's a good chance that P3 might bet $175 or so, expecting a call from someone who advertised either AA or KK preflop.

We see that P2 is forced to bet the flop, the turn, and the river when his opponent doesn't play back, and in total, P2 can't avoid losing less than $265 here. Unless he picks up a read on P3's betting patterns, there's pretty much nothing else he can do. By playing passively, he's opening himself up to losing more against better hands and he's not extracting maximum value from marginal hands that'll check behind. The moral of the story is that when you're in early position, just like in late position, you need to be aggressive. Acting first, betting into unknown territory, is the primary reason that being out of position is considered a disadvantage. In chapter 6, about shorthanded play, I'll actually talk about an "early aggressor" advantage that exists against tight-passive opponents, but for now, let's just say that the positional disadvantage is the reason that you should avoid playing marginal hands from early position (including the blinds).

## Chapter Summary and Preview of What's to Come

Wow, what a chapter! I covered a lot of important material, using pocket pairs as the driving force. Early in the chapter, we studied the probabilities of hitting various types of flops, and from there, we formed a model of how to play hit-to-win poker with pocket pairs. We then looked at how postflop play evolves when you hit a monster or a decent hand with some vulnerability (overpair). Even though this chapter used pocket pairs as the driving force, the section about playing top set is applicable when you flop any type of big hand (e.g., straights and flushes), and the section about playing overpairs is applicable when you flop top pair. The only situation not covered in gross detail is the situation where you flop two pair. I'll say that flopping two pair lies closer to the situation where you have a set, but you have to be aware that your hand isn't as powerful—you don't have great redrawing possibilities against straight and flush draws.

One big lesson imparted is that when you flop a monster and it's checked to you, you typically want to bet. I hope that you've also discovered the merits of being aggressive regardless of your position. You've learned about raising in position on the turn to preserve a showdown, and you've also learned about blocking bets. Both of these plays are successful against nontricky players because they extract maximum value from worse hands while allowing you to save money against better hands. These plays are also useful against tricky players, but you have to be aware of how the playing dynamics change when your opponents aren't straightforward. This is going to be a function of the particular opponents that you find yourself against.

I hope that you've become comfortable with HDM. It's a very powerful way of looking at hold'em, even if it's not possible to have perfect information to pump through it. We've spent a lot of time talking about what happens when you've made hands. Besides completely missing the flop, the other situation that occurs in hold'em is flopping a draw. In the next chapter, we'll explore probabilities involving drawing hands and then proceed to look at various lines of play. First, though, let's do some problems.

## Problems

1. Consider the following hand:

**Table 4.18: Problem 1a.**

**Game:** $100NL Hold'em
**Structure:** Small Blind: $2 Big Blind: $3
**Comments:** Casino game with a $3 rake and $1 jackpot rake (only in L.A. can you find a game where people have no problem with 80 percent of the blinds going into the table, never to be seen again—this is a big reason why I spend most of my time playing online). You are P4 at a table that has been quite lively. UTG just limped, and you are holding 77.

| | 1(SB) | 2(BB) | 3 | *4* | 5 |
|---|---|---|---|---|---|
| | XX | XX | XX | 7♣7♥ | XX |
| **STACKS** | $60 | $175 | $120 | $135 | $360 |
| **PREFLOP** | b$2 | b$3 | >$3 | | |
| **STACKS** | | | | | |
| **FLOP** | | | | | |
| **STACKS** | | | | | |
| **TURN** | | | | | |
| **STACKS** | | | | | |
| **RIVER** | | | | | |
| **HOLE** | | | | | |

**Comments:** None.

**Legend:** SB = Small Blind; BB = Big Blind; B = Button; X = Unknown Hole Card; b = Blind or Straddle; > = Beginning of Betting Round Action; < = End of Betting Round Action; - = Fold; d = Action in the Dark; c = Call; r = Raise; E = Exposed Card; M = Main Pot; S = Side Pot; AI = All-In; R = Rake

a. What's your decision here?

b. You end up limping, and action proceeds as described in table 4.19 (pp. 158–59). What do you do?

| 6 | 7 | 8 | 9(B) | POT |
|---|---|---|---|---|
| XX | XX | XX | XX | |
| $200 | $40 | $120 | $500 | |
| | | | | M = $4<br>Rake = $4 |
| | | | | |
| | | | | |
| | | | | |
| | | | | |

## Table 4.19: Problem 1b.

**Game:** $100NL Hold'em
**Structure:** Small Blind: $2 Big Blind: $3
**Comments:** After you limp, there's a raise and a bunch of callers.

| | 1(SB) | 2(BB) | 3 | *4* | 5 |
|---|---|---|---|---|---|
| | XX | XX | XX | 7♣7♥ | XX |
| **STACKS** | $60 | $175 | $120 | $135 | $360 |
| **PREFLOP** | b$2 | b$3 | >$3 | $3 | $15 |
| | - | - | $15 | | |
| **STACKS** | | | | | |
| **FLOP** | | | | | |
| **STACKS** | | | | | |
| **TURN** | | | | | |
| **STACKS** | | | | | |
| **RIVER** | | | | | |
| **HOLE** | | | | | |

**Comments:** None.

**Legend:** SB = Small Blind; BB = Big Blind; B = Button; X = Unknown Hole Card; b = Blind or Straddle; > = Beginning of Betting Round Action; < = End of Betting Round Action; - = Fold; d = Action in the Dark; c = Call; r = Raise; E = Exposed Card; M = Main Pot; S = Side Pot; AI = All-In; R = Rake

| 6 | 7 | 8 | 9(B) | POT |
|---|---|---|---|---|
| XX | XX | XX | XX | |
| $200 | $40 | $120 | $500 | |
| $15 | - | $15 | - | M = $76<br>Rake = $4 |
| $185 | | $105 | | |
| | | | | M = $96<br>Rake = $4 |
| | | | | |
| | | | | |
| | | | | |

d. Action proceeds as in table 4.21 (pp. 162–63). What now?

**Table 4.21: Problem 1d.**

**Game:** $100NL Hold'em
**Structure:** Small Blind: $2 Big Blind: $3
**Comments:** You decided to call, and after 4 opponents saw the turn with you, a third spade came on the turn. In addition, there is the possiblity that an opponent holding 98 just made a straight. P3 bets $85 into a $176, and there are 3 players remaining.

| | 1(SB) | 2(BB) | 3 | *4* | 5 |
|---|---|---|---|---|---|
| | XX | XX | XX | 7♣7♥ | XX |
| **STACKS** | $60 | $175 | $120 | $135 | $360 |
| **PREFLOP** | b$2 | b$3 | >$3 | $3 | $15 |
| | - | - | $15 | $15< | |
| **STACKS** | | | $105 | $120 | $345 |
| **FLOP** | | | >$20 | $20 | $20 |
| **T♠7♠3♦** | | | | | |
| **STACKS** | | | $85 | $100 | $325 |
| **TURN** | | | >$85 | | |
| **J♠** | | | | | |
| **STACKS** | | | | | |
| **RIVER** | | | | | |
| **HOLE** | | | | | |

**Comments:** None.

**Legend:** SB = Small Blind; BB = Big Blind; B = Button; X = Unknown Hole Card; b = Blind or Straddle; > = Beginning of Betting Round Action; < = End of Betting Round Action; - = Fold; d = Action in the Dark; c = Call; r = Raise; E = Exposed Card; M = Main Pot; S = Side Pot; AI = All-In; R = Rake

| 6<br>XX | 7<br>XX | 8<br>XX | 9(B)<br>XX | POT |
|---|---|---|---|---|
| $200 | $40 | $120 | $500 | |
| $15 | - | $15 | - | M = $76<br>Rake = $4 |
| $185 | | $105 | | |
| $20 | | $20< | | M = $176<br>Rake = $4 |
| $165 | | $85 | | |

2. a. You are now in the hand in table 4.22. What's your decision?

**Table 4.22: Problem 2a.**

**Game:** $50NL Hold'em
**Structure:** Small Blind: $.25 Big Blind: $.50
**Comments:** Online game with a negligible rake. You are P8 at a table that you've just joined. This is your fourth hand, and you haven't seen anything unusual yet; you have virtually no data about your opponents.

| | **1(SB)**<br>**XX** | **2(BB)**<br>**XX** | **3**<br>**XX** | **4**<br>**XX** | **5**<br>**XX** |
|---|---|---|---|---|---|
| **STACKS** | $60 | $175 | $120 | $30 | $60 |
| **PREFLOP** | b$.25 | b$.50 | >- | $0.50 | $0.50 |
| **STACKS** | | | | | |
| **FLOP** | | | | | |
| **STACKS** | | | | | |
| **TURN** | | | | | |
| **STACKS** | | | | | |
| **RIVER** | | | | | |
| **HOLE** | | | | | |

**Comments:** None.

**Legend:** SB = Small Blind; BB = Big Blind; B = Button; X = Unknown Hole Card; b = Blind or Straddle; > = Beginning of Betting Round Action; < = End of Betting Round Action; - = Fold; d = Action in the Dark; c = Call; r = Raise; E = Exposed Card; M = Main Pot; S = Side Pot; AI = All-In; R = Rake

| 6 | 7 | *8* | 9(B) | POT |
|---|---|---|---|---|
| XX | XX | 5♥5♠ | XX | |
| $10 | $25 | $100 | $65 | |
| - | $2 | | | M = $3.75 |

b. You call the raise, and the action occurs as in table 4.23 (pp. 166–67). What do you do?

Table 4.23: Problem 2b.

**Game:** $50NL Hold'em
**Structure:** Small Blind: $.25 Big Blind: $.50
**Comments:** What's your decision now?

| | 1(SB) | 2(BB) | 3 | 4 | 5 |
|---|---|---|---|---|---|
| | XX | XX | XX | XX | XX |
| **STACKS** | $60 | $175 | $120 | $30 | $60 |
| **PREFLOP** | b$.25 | b$.50 | >- | $0.50 | $0.50 |
| | $6 | $6 | | $6 | - |
| **STACKS** | | | | | |
| **FLOP** | | | | | |
| **STACKS** | | | | | |
| **TURN** | | | | | |
| **STACKS** | | | | | |
| **RIVER** | | | | | |
| **HOLE** | | | | | |

**Comments:** None.

**Legend:** SB = Small Blind; BB = Big Blind; B = Button; X = Unknown Hole Card; b = Blind or Straddle; > = Beginning of Betting Round Action; < = End of Betting Round Action; - = Fold; d = Action in the Dark; c = Call; r = Raise; E = Exposed Card; M = Main Pot; S = Side Pot; AI = All-In; R = Rake

| 6 | 7 | *8* | 9(B) | POT |
|---|---|---|---|---|
| XX | XX | 5♥5♠ | XX | |
| $10 | $25 | $100 | $65 | |
| - | $2<br>$10 | $2 | $6 | M = $36.50 |

3. You hold Q♥Q♠. The board is 8♣7♣2♠4♦3♠. Your opponent is on [AA,77]|||[A♣K♣,A♣Q♣]. The pot is currently $200. You are in EP. If you bet $75, your opponent will raise with a set or [AA,QQ] (you'll fold to the raise), he will call with [JJ,TT], and he will fold anything else. If you check, your opponent will bet $100 with a set or [AA,JJ]—he will check everything else.

   a. If you check, is calling the $100 bet +EV?

   b. What's the better line of play against this opponent: making a $75 blocking bet or checking?

## Answers to Problems

1a. You should limp.

*Explanation:* The probability of an unpaired, non-dangerous flop is pretty low (.15 according to table 4.9). If you are playing this hand at a nine-handed table, you are playing it primarily to flop a set or better. Recall that you are about a 7.5:1 underdog to get such a flop, thus, you would like to see a few additional callers preflop. In addition, you want to know that your opponents will put in a lot of money if you hit your flop. You want huge implied odds; you do not want to just get 7.5 big blinds in the pot because you need to consider the reverse implied odds associated with hitting a set and losing to a higher set, a straight, or a flush. In general, I like to have at least 15 big blinds in my stack, and I like my opponents to have the same.* You want

* Of course, if I'm in a cash game, I have the maximum allowed buy-in in front of me at all times. If you are +EV against your opponents, there's

to make at least 15–20 big blinds in a big hand to make up for the four or five pots where you hit a set or better but only end up making 3 or 4 big blinds. You have many big blinds in front of you, and you have many opponents at a lively table with the same; thus, a limp is in order here. There is one note about the word "lively" that may be worth noting, though. If the table is lively because there are lots of *big* raises, I would elect to fold here—you will not get the proper price to call a big raise, so why waste $3 in early position with lots of eager overbettors remaining to act. If it is a typical lively table, there is usually reasonably sized preflop raising accompanied by many callers and aggressive postflop play.

1b. You should call.

*Explanation:* You're faced with a $12 call into a pot of $64.* You're already getting about 5.33:1 odds. The very favorable implied odds accompanying your

---

no reason not to. If I'm in a no-max buy-in game, I buy in for at least 100 big blinds (usually 200–300 big blinds and sometimes even more—I've bought in for $1,000 at $1–$2 blind games with a no-max buy-in). If you think your competition is too tough, you should move to a different table (unless you are consciously trying to improve your game), and if you aren't comfortable with losing 200–300 big blinds on a single hand, then you should be playing for lower stakes. It's very rare that I ever have to put in more than 150 big blinds into a pot, but it does happen. It happens when I have *the* goods, and when I have *the* goods, I want to make as much money as possible.

* Notice how I subtract the rake right away. When you are playing and counting the pot, you should always know how much the rake is so you can make appropriate adjustments. Most of the time, when you are playing online or in high stakes casino games, the rake will be small with respect to the pot or will be in the form of a timed collection, so you don't have to worry about it. However, in low-medium limit casino games, the rake can dramatically affect decisions, especially when you are in late position and everyone has folded to you.

5.33:1 pot odds mean that you will expect to make much more than just 7.5 big blinds on average when you hit your flop. The implied odds are favorable for two reasons: First, you'll have four lively opponents going into the flop. There's a good chance that at least one of them will hit the flop. The first reason is good enough, but second, there was a raise preflop, and whenever there's a preflop raise, the probability of heavy postflop action increases. Besides the favorable pot odds and implied odds, a final, extremely important point to be considered here is that your call closes the betting action. It's impossible for there to be a reraise that may push you out of the pot. For all the reasons cited in this paragraph, you should enthusiastically call.

1c. I'm not at the table, and there's not any nuanced information in the hand description, but with the information given, I'd raise to $50.

*Explanation: Ka-chingaling!* You flopped a set. Furthermore, P3 has already shown interest in the flop. The preflop raiser has yet to act, so one line of play is to call P3's bet, expecting P5, the preflop raiser, to raise on the flop. To estimate the likelihood of P5 raising, assume that he's on the following hand distribution: [AA,TT]|||[AK,AJ]|||[KQ], which may actually be too tight of a distribution given my description of the game. Table 4.24 gives hand distribution in terms of combinations.

Assume that P5 raises with an overpair or a flush draw (he'll also raise with a set, in which case your set is crushed since the only set P5 can have with the assigned distribution is a set of tens). Given his distribution, the probability that P5 raises behind you

**TABLE 4.24: P5's Hand Distribution for Problem 1c.**

| HAND | COMBINATIONS |
|---|---|
| AA | 6 |
| KK | 6 |
| QQ | 6 |
| JJ | 6 |
| TT | 3 |
| AK (no A♠K♠) | 15 |
| A♠K♠ | 1 |
| AQ (no A♠Q♠) | 15 |
| A♠Q♠ | 1 |
| AJ (no A♠J♠) | 15 |
| A♠J♠ | 1 |
| KQ (no K♠Q♠) | 15 |
| K♠Q♠ | 1 |

*Total number of combinations = 91*

with a hand you can beat is $\frac{28}{91} \approx .31$. By calling here, you open yourself up to letting a bunch of callers in cheaply with flush draws or straight draws. Remember that the way to make money against these hands is to make them pay a premium price. I think that raising to $50 here is the play of choice. If your stack is deeper, I'd raise to $60 or $70, but you have to make a decently sized bet on the turn.

1d. Fold.

*Explanation:* Well, you ended up doing what I argued against doing in my answer to 1c, and the worst possible result happened. Everyone called, and a spade fell. Not only is it a spade, but it's the J♠, meaning that 89 made a straight as well. Did P3 just hit a draw? Did someone behind you hit a draw? Who the hell knows? This is one of those situations where I'm inclined to think that a set is no good, though. Given that, you need to see if you have odds to stay in. The pot is currently $261, and you are faced with an $85 bet. With one card to come, you are theoretically a 36:10 = 3.6 underdog to improve your hand. With all the callers, there is a decent chance that at least one of your T's is dead, though, meaning that you might actually be something like a 36:9 (about 4:1) or a 36:8 (4.5:1) underdog to improve. Notice how you can use information about your opponents' holdings to adjust the number of outs you have.

At the moment, you are getting $261:$85 ≈ $3.07:$1. If P3 was not on a draw, then you probably know for sure that at least one person behind you will call, meaning that you are getting $346:$85 ≈ $4.07:1 to call. If P3 was on a draw, who knows whether you will get action behind you. Given that you are probably 4:1 or 4.5:1 against improving, you really need two callers behind you. Because of this, I think that the correct play here is to fold. You went from being somewhere around a 75 percent favorite on the flop to being bet out of the pot on the turn. This is why I advocate jamming the pot with your made hands while you have a known statistical advantage.

2a. If P4 and P5 are both going to call, then you can call. If at least one of them will fold, though, then you should fold. You do not know much about the table yet, so, I would be inclined to fold.

*Explanation:* There is currently $3.75 in the pot, so you are getting $3.75:$2 to call. You have 55, so you are looking to play this hand to flop a set or better.

You need $7.5:$1 odds after accounting for implied odds and reverse implied odds, so the question is whether you are getting proper implied odds to play. To determine that, you need to know something about P4 and P5. Some players will call any reasonably sized raise with any two cards after they have already invested money in the pot. Others will fold to raises, even minimum raises, after limping.

If P4 and P5 both typically fold to raises after they have limped, folding is probably in order here. P7, the preflop raiser, only has $23 left in his stack, meaning that the times that you do get involved in heavy postflop action after flopping your set or better, you won't be winning enough compared to the times that there's no heavy betting action. Now, suppose that either P4 or P5 is the type who'll call here simply because he's already limped. If one of them calls, then an additional $1.50 is going into the pot, meaning that you're now getting $5.25:$2 odds to call. When you are up against two opponents, there's a better chance that you'll have an opponent who hits the flop so that you'll get heavy betting action, but many bets still need to go into the pot. P5 is deeply stacked, but P4 isn't. Thus, if only one of them is guaranteed to call, then I would elect to fold here.

If both P4 and P5 are guaranteed to call, you're then getting $6.75:$2 odds to call. At this point, you have three opponents, and there's a decent chance of enough bets going into the pot postflop when you hit your hand. This is the only situation where I'd call the raise. Typically, I like to be in against at least three other players when entering a pot with a small pocket pair when looking to hit a set. If the stack sizes are really deep (50 or more BB), then I am willing to limp with just two opponents if at least one of them is fairly aggressive postflop. Since you don't know much about the table yet, I'd be inclined to fold.

2b. You should fold.

*Explanation:* Wow! Look at all that action. You are getting $36.50:$8 ≈ $4.56:$1 odds, and if P9 just calls, you are getting $40.50:$8 ≈ $5.06:1 odds. With all this action, you are sure to have the implied odds necessary to continue even after accounting for reverse implied odds. There is one major problem here, though. What's the chance that P9 is just going to call here? In problem 1, your call closed the betting action. In this problem, your call doesn't close the betting action. In the betting pattern where there's only one preflop raise and a bunch of limpers are remaining to act behind you, you can be fairly confident that there won't be a reraise, and you can confidently call if you're getting proper odds. In this case, though, there's a reraiser remaining to act. Reraisers are much more likely than limpers to raise, meaning that you'll be forced to another preflop decision. The pot is large enough so that P9 might simply go all-in, completely shutting you out of the pot. Thus, the play here is to fold, unless you somehow pick up an amazing tell indicating that P9 will call. How you pick up such a tell when playing online is anybody's guess, but perhaps you've seen this betting pattern a lot at this table, and P9 has always called—this would be the only possible time that you could possibly justify calling here.

3a. Calling is +EV against your opponent's betting distribution.

*Explanation:* The first task, as always, is to break down your opponent's hand distribution with respect to combinations. For convenience, I've highlighted the results corresponding to each of your opponent's holdings in table 4.25 if you call the $100 bet.

**TABLE 4.25: Opponent's Holdings for Problem 3**

| HAND | COMBINATIONS | RESULT |
|---|---|---|
| AA | 6 | -$100 |
| KK | 6 | -$100 |
| QQ | 1 | $100 |
| JJ | 6 | $300 |
| TT | 6 | $200 |
| 99 | 6 | $200 |
| 88 | 3 | -$100 |
| 77 | 3 | -$100 |
| A♣K♣ | 1 | $200 |
| A♣Q♣ | 1 | $200 |

*Total number of combinations = 39*

Your EV for calling is therefore:

$$\left(\tfrac{6}{25}\right)(-\$100) + \left(\tfrac{6}{25}\right)(-\$100) + \left(\tfrac{1}{25}\right)(+\$100) + \left(\tfrac{6}{25}\right)(+\$300) +$$
$$\left(\tfrac{3}{25}\right)(-\$100) + \left(\tfrac{3}{25}\right)(-\$100) = +\$4.00 \qquad (4.7)$$

Calling here is slightly +EV, meaning that you should call the $100 bet after checking.

3b. The $75 blocking bet is better.

*Explanation:* Table 4.26 outlines your payouts for the $75 blocking bet.

**TABLE 4.26: Payouts for a $75 Blocking Bet for Problem 3**

| HAND | COMBINATIONS | RESULT |
|---|---|---|
| AA | 6 | -$75 |
| KK | 6 | -$75 |
| QQ | 1 | -$75 |
| JJ | 6 | $275 |
| TT | 6 | $275 |
| 99 | 6 | $200 |
| 88 | 3 | -$75 |
| 77 | 3 | -$75 |
| A♣K♣ | 1 | $200 |
| A♣Q♣ | 1 | $200 |

*Total number of combinations = 39*

From this table of payouts, the EV of the $75 blocking bet is therefore:

$$\left(\tfrac{6}{39}\right)(-\$75) + \left(\tfrac{6}{39}\right)(-\$75) + \left(\tfrac{1}{39}\right)(-\$75) + \left(\tfrac{6}{39}\right)(+\$275) + \left(\tfrac{6}{39}\right)(+\$275) + \left(\tfrac{6}{39}\right)(+\$200) + \left(\tfrac{3}{39}\right)(-\$75) + \left(\tfrac{3}{39}\right)(-\$75) + \left(\tfrac{1}{39}\right)(+\$200) + \left(\tfrac{1}{39}\right)(+\$200) \approx +\$89.10. \qquad (4.8)$$

Your payouts from checking, meanwhile, are:

$$\left(\tfrac{6}{39}\right)(-\$100) + \left(\tfrac{6}{39}\right)(-\$100) + \left(\tfrac{1}{39}\right)(+\$100) + \left(\tfrac{6}{39}\right)(+\$300) + \left(\tfrac{6}{39}\right)(+\$200) + \left(\tfrac{6}{39}\right)(+\$200) + \left(\tfrac{3}{39}\right)(-\$100) + \left(\tfrac{3}{39}\right)(-\$100) + \left(\tfrac{1}{39}\right)(+\$200) + \left(\tfrac{1}{39}\right)(+\$200) \approx +\$74.36. \qquad (4.9)$$

Your EV is higher when you make the $75 blocking bet, thus, the $75 blocking bet is the better line of play.

# 5

# DRAWING HANDS

♧♤♢♡

## Introduction

The last chapter dissected the play of made hands. This chapter focuses on the other side of hold'em: playing draws. Many types of draws exist in NL hold'em. Preflop, when you hold unpaired cards, you are drawing to a pair, two pair, trips, a full house, or quads. If your unpaired cards happen to be suited, you are drawing to a flush, and if your unpaired cards happen to be connected, you are drawing to a straight. In addition to these draws, we already encountered a drawing situation in the last chapter where we examined the play of low pocket pairs. Recall that when playing low pocket pairs, you are usually drawing to a set or better on the flop, and when your set is beaten, you are drawing from a set to a full house or quads. With all these drawing situations that occur in hold'em, it is vital to know the probabilities of completing each of them and then to see how these probabilities dictate our optimal lines of play.

## Probability of Flopping One Pair or Better with Unpaired, Unsuited, Unconnected Hole Cards

If you hold unpaired, unsuited, unconnected hole cards like A9, you're looking to flop one pair or better. For now, let's not restrict ourselves to flopping top pair, and let's not restrict ourselves to unpaired, unconnected, unsuited flops. The probability of missing the flop entirely is:

$$\left(\tfrac{44}{50}\right)\left(\tfrac{43}{49}\right)\left(\tfrac{42}{48}\right) \approx .68 \qquad (5.1)$$

The probability of flopping one of your cards is given by equation 5.2.

$$3\left(\tfrac{6}{50}\right)\left(\tfrac{44}{49}\right)\left(\tfrac{43}{48}\right) \approx .29 \qquad (5.2)$$

The probability of flopping two of your cards is given by equation 5.3.

$$3\left(\tfrac{6}{50}\right)\left(\tfrac{5}{49}\right)\left(\tfrac{44}{48}\right) \approx .03 \qquad (5.3)$$

Finally, the probability of flopping three of your cards is given by equation 5.4.

$$\left(\tfrac{6}{50}\right)\left(\tfrac{5}{49}\right)\left(\tfrac{4}{48}\right) \approx .001 \qquad (5.4)$$

We've discussed the .68 obtained from equation 5.1 Let's now focus on equations 5.3 and 5.4. For those of you who love to call with junk like 83o from the SB, hoping to flop two pair or better, the exact answers from equations 5.3 and 5.4 tell us that the odds against hitting such a flop are 27.82:1. When are you going to have proper odds, accounting for implied odds and reverse implied odds, to play a hand like 83o? You'll virtually never have odds to call with junk, even from the small blind. So, our first lesson about starting hands is not to play random junk from the blinds. Just making this adjustment to your game alone will dramatically improve your results (if you play one hundred hands at a ten-handed table, you will save up to five big blinds, which is actually quite a bit).

## Probabilities of Hitting a Straight or a Flush with Five Cards to Come

Now, instead of considering random junk, let's consider connectors and suited cards. Suppose that you hold unsuited connectors in the following range: [JT,54]—in other words, the connectors that can make the most possible straights (four). With five cards to come, let's figure out the probability of getting a straight. For this initial calculation, assume that all straights using both hole cards are considered good, despite the rank, connectivity, or suitedness of the flop. However, idiot straights, or even worse, cases like where you have 45 and the board comes 6789T, won't be counted as straights. In that case, for a hand like JT, the available straights are {789TJ, 89TJQ, 9TJQK, TJQKA}. For a specific straight, like 789TJ, there are 4•4•4 = 64 combinations (789 in this case). After considering 789, there are two board cards remaining. Forty-seven cards are left in the deck after counting your JT and the 789 on the board, meaning that $\frac{47 \cdot 46}{2!} = 1{,}081$ combinations remain for the last two board cards. Out of a deck of fifty cards, $\frac{50 \cdot 49 \cdot 48 \cdot 47 \cdot 46}{5!} = 2{,}118{,}760$ combinations of five cards exist. Thus, the probability of getting a particular straight with five cards to come is $\frac{(64)(1081)}{2{,}118{,}760} = \frac{69{,}184}{2{,}118{,}760}$. Since there are four total possible straights, the overall probability of getting a straight with five cards to come is given by equation 5.5:

$$(4)\left(\frac{69{,}184}{2{,}118{,}760}\right) = \frac{276{,}736}{2{,}118{,}760} \approx .13 \qquad (5.5)$$

If you hold connected hole cards, your odds against hitting a straight with five cards to come are given by equation 5.6.

$$\frac{2{,}118{,}760 - 276{,}736}{276{,}736} \approx 6.66{:}1 \tag{5.6}$$

Now, we could make an adjustment so that we ignore boards with four or five to a suit and boards that have three of a kind, but equation 5.6 at least gives us an idea as to the approximate odds needed preflop to justify going for a straight.

Now, instead of having an unsuited connector, suppose you have two suited cards, (e.g., AXs). What's the probability that you make a flush with five cards to come? I had you do this in a chapter 1 problem, so I'll just quickly recap the analysis. With five cards to come, the probability of getting a flush where three board cards are of your suit is given by equation 5.7.

$$\frac{\left(\frac{11\cdot10\cdot9}{3!}\right)\left(\frac{39\cdot38}{2!}\right)}{2{,}118{,}760} = \frac{122{,}265}{2{,}118{,}760} \approx .06 \tag{5.7}$$

Equation 5.8 gives the probability of getting a flush with four board cards of your suit.

$$\frac{\left(\frac{11\cdot10\cdot9\cdot8}{4!}\right)(39)}{2{,}118{,}760} = \frac{12{,}870}{2{,}118{,}760} \approx .006 \tag{5.8}$$

Equation 5.9 gives the probability of getting a flush where all five board cards are of your suit.

$$\frac{\left(\frac{11\cdot10\cdot9\cdot8\cdot7}{5!}\right)}{2{,}118{,}760} = \frac{462}{2{,}118{,}760} \approx .0002 \tag{5.9}$$

We see that the total probability of getting a flush with five cards to come is $\frac{122{,}265 + 12{,}870 + 462}{2{,}118{,}760} = \frac{135{,}597}{2{,}118{,}760} \approx .06$. In other words, the contributions from boards with four or five of the same suit aren't large. The only flushes that you really want are flushes where the board has three of a suit anyway. Equation 5.10 gives the odds against hitting any flush with five cards to come when your hole cards are suited.

$$\frac{2{,}118{,}760 - 135{,}597}{135{,}597} \approx 14.63. \tag{5.10}$$

Equation 5.11 gives the odds against hitting a flush where exactly three board cards are of your suit.

$$\frac{2{,}118{,}760-122{,}265}{122{,}265} \approx 16.33:1 \qquad (5.11)$$

Connectors and suited cards have been considered separately. Now, what if you have a suited connector, like 78s? The chance of getting a straight is $\frac{276{,}736}{2{,}118{,}760}$, and the chance of getting a flush is $\frac{135{,}597}{2{,}118{,}760}$. We can't just add these two probabilities together to get the chance of getting a straight or a flush, though, because we'd be double counting the times you have a straight and a flush. Therefore, we need to find how many boards give a straight and a flush so that we can subtract them from the sum once to kill the double counts.

Consider a board where you've made a straight. Table 5.1 outlines the possibilities for the specific case where you hold 7♣8♣ and you make a straight with 456 on the board.

**TABLE 5.1: Combinations for Getting a Straight and a Flush with 7♣8♣**

| BOARD CARDS | COMBINATIONS FOR STRAIGHT CARDS | COMBINATIONS FOR XX | TOTAL COMBINATIONS |
|---|---|---|---|
| 4♣5♣6♣xx | 1 | $\frac{47\cdot 46}{2!} = 1{,}081$ | 1,081 |
| 456(2clubs)xx (1club) | 3•3 = 9 | 9•38 = 342 | 3,078 |
| 456(2 clubs)xx (2clubs) | 3•3 = 9 | $\frac{9\cdot 8}{2!} = 36$ | 324 |
| 456(1club)xx (2clubs) | 3•3•3 = 27 | $\frac{10\cdot 9}{2!} = 45$ | 1,215 |

Thus, there are 1,081 + 3,078 + 324 + 1,215 = 5,698 boards that contain both straights and flushes when the board is 456. Since there are 4 total possible straights, you have

4•5,698 = 22,792 total combinations that yield both straights and flushes. There are then 276,736 + 135,597 − 22,792 = 389,541 boards that give you a straight, a flush, or both. The probability of getting a straight or a flush with five cards to come with [JTs,54s] is given by equation 5.12.

$$\frac{389{,}541}{2{,}118{,}760} \approx .18 \tag{5.12}$$

The odds against getting a straight or a flush with five cards to come is given by:

$$\frac{2{,}118{,}760 - 389{,}541}{389{,}541} \approx 4.44{:}1 \tag{5.13}$$

The results that I've calculated thus far are summarized in table 5.2.

**TABLE 5.2: Summary of Odds Involving Getting Straights and Flushes with Five Cards to Come**

| TYPE OF HAND HELD | APPROXIMATE ODDS AGAINST HITTING DRAW WITH FIVE CARDS TO COME |
|---|---|
| Unsuited, Connected | 6.66:1 |
| Suited, Not Connected | 14.63:1 |
| Suited, Connected | 4.44:1 |

Table 5.2 is a good launching point for determining the playability of drawing hands. From this table, we see that under most playing conditions, you need bets to go into the pot postflop to get proper odds to draw (the exception is suited connectors in pots with three or more limpers). Because of the odds involved, we want to play these hands in situations similar to those where we played low pocket pairs. The big difference with low pocket pairs, though, is that with low pocket pairs, play was simply based on whether we

hit the flop. When we hit the flop with a low pocket pair, we have a huge hand. When we hit the flop with a connector or a suited hand, most of the time, we will end up flopping a *draw* as opposed to a made hand—we'll need to hit a card on the turn or river to complete our draw and win the hand. This means that we'd like to be involved in pots with a low potential for huge action on the flop. From that perspective, we don't really want to be playing these hands in raised pots. We want to see the flop cheaply and make a good chunk of profit from implied odds.

## Playing on the Flop When You Flop a Drawing Hand

When you play drawing hands like suited cards and connectors, you don't usually hit your big hand on the flop. If you hold two suited cards, your most likely playable flop is when you flop two of your suit, giving you 9 outs. With connectors, your most likely playable flops are when you flop an outside straight draw or a *double gutshot straight draw*—draws where you have 8 outs.

On the flop, you have two cards to come. Let's say you have an outside straight draw on the flop. You have 8 outs to complete on the flop, and you have 8 outs to hit on the turn if you don't hit on the flop. Some people think that they effectively have 16 outs with which they can win, and with two cards to come, they assume that the odds against hitting are 31:16. Admittedly, this approximation isn't horribly off, but it's still off. With one card to come, thinking of odds is very straightforward. With two cards to come, though, thinking about odds is tricky. Personally, when I'm dealing with multiple events, I like to think in terms of probabilities and then transform the probabilities to odds afterward.

If you have 8 outs on the flop, there's an $\frac{8}{47}$ probability that you'll hit your draw on the turn. In the $\frac{39}{47}$ times that you don't hit your draw on the turn, there's an $\frac{8}{46}$ probability that you'll hit your draw on the river. Thus, the probability of hitting your draw with two cards to come is $\frac{8}{47} + \left(\frac{39}{47}\right)\left(\frac{8}{46}\right) = \frac{340}{1081} \approx .31$. The odds against hitting your draw with two cards to come are therefore $\frac{1081-340}{340} \approx 2.18{:}1$. Notice how these odds are worse than the odds you get by simply adding your outs from the turn and the river. The probabilities of, and odds against, hitting a draw with two cards to come as function of the number of outs you have are given in table 5.3.

**TABLE 5.3: Probability of, and Odds Against, Hitting a Draw with Two Cards to Come**

| NUMER OF OUTS ON THE FLOP | P(COMPLETE DRAW WITH 2 CARDS TO COME) | ODDS AGAINST HITTING DRAW WITH 2 CARDS TO COME |
|---|---|---|
| 1 | .04 | 22.50:1 |
| 2 | .08 | 10.88:1 |
| 3 | .12 | 7.00:1 |
| 4 | .16 | 5.07:1 |
| 5 | .20 | 3.91:1 |
| 6 | .24 | 3.14:1 |
| 7 | .28 | 2.59:1 |
| 8 | .31 | 2.18:1 |
| 9 | .35 | 1.86:1 |
| 10 | .38 | 1.60:1 |
| 11 | .42 | 1.40:1 |
| 12 | .45 | 1.22:1 |
| 13 | .48 | 1.08:1 |
| 14 | .51 | .95:1 |
| 15 | .54 | .85:1 |
| 16 | .57 | .75:1 |

| NUMER OF OUTS ON THE FLOP | P(COMPLETE DRAW WITH 2 CARDS TO COME) | ODDS AGAINST HITTING DRAW WITH 2 CARDS TO COME |
|---|---|---|
| 17 | .60 | .67:1 |
| 18 | .62 | .60:1 |
| 19 | .65 | .54:1 |
| 20 | .68 | .48:1 |
| 21 | .70 | .43:1 |

This table indicates that once you have 14 or more outs, your probability of hitting your draw is greater than 50 percent. When you have 8 or 9 outs, you will hit your draw about one-third of the time. The best way to have these numbers available when you are playing is simply to memorize this table; there are discernable patterns in the probabilities that make memorizing them quite easy. When you have between 1 and 7 outs, the probability of hitting one of your outs with 2 cards to come is given by taking the number of outs and multiplying by .04. When you have between 8 and 17 outs, the probabilities change by an average of about .035, meaning that every two outs past 7 adds another .07. When you have past 17 outs, you are a nice favorite in the hand. The actual probabilities don't matter much at that point—you just need to figure out how to get the most value out of your draw. If you are wondering how you can possibly have 21 outs, think of when you have an outside straight flush draw with two overcards (e.g., you hold K♣Q♣ and the board is J♣T♣5♦). On such a board, you have 6 overcard outs, 9 flush outs, and 6 straight outs that don't complete a flush, giving you a total of 21 outs.

The numbers in table 5.3 are essential knowledge; however, we need to address three issues: First, these are the probabilities of hitting your draw given that you're seeing the turn *and* the river. If you're just going to end up seeing the turn, then you must consider your probability of winning with only one card to come. For example, if you have 9 outs on the flop, the probability of hitting your draw on the turn is $\frac{9}{47} \approx .19$. Contrast this .19 to the .35 probability of hitting your draw with two cards to come. Second, table 5.3 doesn't help you count your outs correctly. Suppose you have A♣2♣ and the flop is J♣7♣5♦. There are 9 clubs that complete your flush. These outs are all certainly good (unless you happen to be drawing against someone with a hand like 8♣9♣—in this case, T♣ is no longer an out since your opponent makes a royal flush with it). There are also 3 aces left in the deck that give you an overpair to the flop, meaning that you potentially have 12 outs. You have to be careful, though. Are the aces *clean outs*? What if you are up against AJ? Hitting an ace in that case is a disaster.

A valuable lesson is that your overcard outs aren't always clean outs—your effective number of outs is somewhere between 9 and 12, and considering that you may have to include flush draws in your opponents' hand distributions, your effective number of outs is really somewhere between 7 and 12. Analytically finding the exact number of effective outs requires that you have your opponents on precise distributions, but as an estimate, you can probably say that you effectively have 9–10 outs. In chapter 1, I talked about being overly optimistic about implied odds. In the same way, many players are overly optimistic when counting their outs. Be a realist; don't be an optimist! Realists leave the poker table with full racks, while optimists leave the poker table with empty racks.

The last issue regarding table 5.3 is that it does not account for redrawing possibilities. Once again, you have A♣2♣ and the flop is J♣7♣5♦; only this time, instead of having AJ, your opponent has a set with 77. Now, you have 9 outs (actually, only 8, because the 5♣ is no longer an out). However, even if you hit your flush, your opponent can still improve to a full house. The table says that the probability of hitting your draw is .31, but the actual probability of winning the hand, according to Poker Stove, is about .2556, changing the pot odds needed from 2.18:1 to 2.91:1. This shows that redrawing possibilities can be significant.

When you are away from the poker table, you can sit around all day and compute such redrawing scenarios exactly. However, computing every situation you'll find yourself in is pretty much impossible. A few common situations where draws face redraws do occur, though. Table 5.4 (pp. 188–89) summarizes the results for these situations.

The drawing hand probabilities in table 5.4 were calculated using Poker Stove. It should be noted that in case #2, there's an approximately 10% chance of a tie. (Tying doesn't really matter in the other cases, though.) Table 5.4 shows that for an initial venture into the numbers, the only case drastically affecting things is a situation where you're drawing against a set.* Outside of being against a set, you don't really have too much to worry about regarding redraws. It's hard to account for redraws on the spot; however, cases #4 and #7 indicate that the odds against winning when drawing against a set to a straight or a flush are about 3:1, where, without the redraw possibilities, the odds against winning are about 2:1.

We've examined the probabilities of hitting straight draws and flush draws. With that knowledge in hand, it's now time to investigate the best ways to play them.

* P(win) for an outside straight draw against two pair is affected by .05, but since P(win) is still about .5 in that case, the change doesn't really mean much.

**Table 5.4: Representative Drawing Situations Involving Opponents with Redraws**

| | CLASS OF DRAW/REDRAW SITUATION | DRAWING HOLE CARDS | REDRAWING HOLE CARDS |
|---|---|---|---|
| #1 | Outside straight draw vs. flush draw with an overcard | 5♣6♠ | K♥2♥ |
| #2 | Outside straight draw vs. flush draw without an overcard | 5♣6♠ | 2♥3♥ |
| #3 | Outside straight draw vs. two pair | 5♣6♠ | Q♣8♠ |
| #4 | Outside straight draw vs. a set | 5♣6♠ | 7♣7♦ |
| #5 | Flush draw with overcard vs. pair with higher overcard | K♥2♥ | A♣Q♦ |
| #6 | Flush draw vs. two pair | A♥2♥ | Q♣8♠ |
| #7 | Flush draw vs. a set | A♥2♥ | 7♣7♦ |
| #8 | Outside straight flush draw vs. two pair | 7♣8♣ | Q♥6♦ |
| #9 | Outside straight flush draw vs. a set | 7♣8♣ | 6♦6♠ |

| FLOP | DRAWING HAND WINNING PROBABILITY | DIFFERENCE FROM SITUATION WITHOUT REDRAWS |
|---|---|---|
| 7♥8♥3♠ | .30 | –.01 |
| 7♥8♥Q♠ | .31 | .00 |
| 7♥8♥Q♠ | .30 | –.01 |
| 7♥8♥Q♠ | .26 | –.05 |
| 7♥8♥Q♠ | .45 | –.03 |
| 7♥8♥Q♠ | .32 | –.03 |
| 7♥8♥Q♠ | .25 | –.10 |
| 5♣6♣Q♠ | .49 | –.05 |
| 5♣6♣Q♠ | .42 | –.12 |

## Playing Draws (Less Than 14 Outers) from Early Position

When you have a draw in early position, you have three options on the flop. You can check with the intention of calling if you are getting proper odds, you can check with the intention of raising as a semi-bluff, or you can simply bet. When we talked about playing made hands, I talked about betting around $\frac{2}{3}$ pot. In working through each line of play, I'm going to operate in a world where all bets are $\frac{2}{3}$ pot. Realize that the analysis I do can be tweaked to talk about any bet size you wish—again, the power of being able to do your own analysis is priceless.

Suppose that you check your draw with the intention of calling if you get proper odds. Assuming that the standard bet on the flop is $\frac{2}{3}$ pot, you are getting

$$\frac{P+\frac{2}{3}P}{\frac{2}{3}P}=\frac{\frac{5}{3}P}{\frac{2}{3}P}=\frac{5P}{2P}=\frac{5}{2}=2.5:1 \text{ odds to call.}$$

With two cards to come, you are getting proper odds to draw to an 8 outer or better (recall that an outside straight draw is an 8 outer and a flush draw is a 9 outer). With one card to come, you are getting odds to draw to a 14 outer or better. Given implied odds and the good chance that you will be drawing to two cards anyway, a $\frac{2}{3}$ pot bet usually warrants a call.

Having seen this situation from the perspective of the drawing player, I hope you now realize why $\frac{2}{3}$ pot is my bet size of choice on the flop—against most opponents on draws, this is about the borderline bet size to illicit a call. Some opponents on draws are willing to call much larger bets (I'm sure you've seen people call bets twice the size of the pot with flush draws). If you're up against such opponents, make them pay the price! On the other end of the poker-playing spectrum, there are players against whom you'll need to tweak this bet to about half the pot to extract maximum value from your hands. The key, once again, is to know whom you're up against and to make them pay accordingly.

Let's return to where you are drawing. Given that you call a $\frac{2}{3}$ pot bet on the flop, you will most likely face a $\frac{1}{2}$ pot bet on the turn. A $\frac{1}{2}$ pot bet gives pot odds of 3:1. An 8-outer (like an outside straight draw) on the turn needs $\frac{38}{8}$ = 4.75:1 odds to call. A 9-outer (like a flush draw) on the turn needs $\frac{37}{9}$ $\approx$4.11:1 odds to call. Against weaker players, you can call these bets and make a marginal profit from implied odds, but if you are against solid players who might not necessarily give you implied odds with hands as good as two pair (or even a set), then you will lose money.

Having examined the betting rounds separately, we should now examine the total odds across this line of play where you check/call $\frac{2}{3}$ pot on the flop and check/call $\frac{1}{2}$ pot on the turn when you miss the turn (assume a heads-up situation). Suppose the pot is $12 on the flop, meaning that you call an $8 bet on the flop. On the turn the pot is $12 + $8 + $8 = $28. You have to call a half-pot bet of $14. Thus, you're paying $8 + $14 = $22 to draw for a profit $12 + $8 + $14 = $34. Ouch. Looking at the hand as a whole, you are getting $34:$22 ≈ $1.55:$1 odds. Without considering implied odds, this is +EV for an 11 outer or better. Including implied odds, you're probably marginally +EV with a flush draw or an outside straight draw against an opponent who bets like that. Of course, we aren't considering the cases where you hit your draw on the turn, but in those cases, it's a reasonable assumption that the most you'll get out of your opponent on the turn will be $14—the big question is whether you'll get additional money on the river. Again, it depends on your opponent.

It seems reasonable that the check/call, check/call line of play lays you $1.55:$1 regardless of when you hit your draw and before we account for implied odds on the river when you hit. (Recall that I'm covering drawing in a heads-up scenario—the numbers will be much more in your favor if we include even just one more caller.)

Having examined the check/call, check/call line of play, I think it would be nice to find a cheaper way to draw. Granted, not all opponents will bet as intelligently with respect to the pot. Some opponents may severely underbet the pot, and if so, the check/call, check/call line of play will usually be best (I say it repeatedly—know your opponents!). However, against the type of bettor I've described, the stop-and-go, or simply leading out in early position on the flop and the turn is sometimes a better way to draw. Let's examine the stop-and-go first.

Suppose the pot is $12 again. You check the flop, your opponent bets $8, and you call. On the turn, the pot is $28. If you check, your opponent will bet $14, so instead of check/calling $14, why not put out a blocking bet of $10? Fine, if you are raised, you will be paying more to draw, and you may even be shut out of the pot if the raise is large enough. However, most opponents won't raise the turn unless they have a monster, and even then, many players will slowplay hands like sets on the turn (recall the extensive discussion in chapter 4 about the play of overpairs). The result is that most of the time your blocking bet will result in your paying $10 as opposed to $14. Let's see the difference in drawing odds across the flop and the turn. You are now paying $8 + $10 = $18 in an attempt to make $12 + $8 + $10 = $30. You are now getting $30:$18 ≈ $1.67:$1 odds.

What if you decide to use a $14 blocking bet instead? You are back to getting $1:55:$1 odds, but your chances of winning the hand have improved because of your added *fold eq-*

*uity*. Not only can you win the hand by hitting your draw, but you can also win the hand now if your opponent folds. Your opponent can't fold if you check to him! Also, my opinion is that you increase your implied odds on the river by throwing out a blocking bet on the turn. Some opponents won't put you on a draw when you bet out on the turn from early position. To determine which variation of the stop-and-go is optimal, or even applicable, you need to weigh the percentage of times your opponent will raise, call, or fold. The lower the raising percentage is, the more apt you should be to use the stop-and-go. The only factor not considered is if you are up against an opponent who will often check the turn after you check. If you are up against such an opponent, the $10 blocking bet is not as good as taking a free card by checking (unless you have huge fold equity).

As opposed to using the stop-and-go, you can also simply bet out on the flop and the turn. Suppose you're against an opponent who won't raise you on the flop often. Furthermore, assume that your standard bet on the flop is $\frac{2}{3}$ pot and that your standard bet on the turn is $\frac{1}{2}$ pot, but your opponent isn't very observant and won't notice that you lead for $\frac{1}{2}$ pot on the flop and $\frac{2}{5}$ pot on the turn with draws. If these conditions are met, then the following analysis holds. Starting with the same $12 as before, you are betting $6 on the flop, meaning that the pot will become $24. On the turn, 40% of the pot is $9.60, but in reality, you'd probably bet $10. Thus, you bet $10 on the turn. You're paying $16 total for a profit of $12 + $6 + $10 = $28, meaning that you're getting $1.75:$1 odds to draw. If you're up against such an opponent, this line of play is awesome because you can now profitably draw to a 10 outer without worrying about implied odds, and you aren't far off from profitably drawing to a flush without implied odds (1.86:1 needed).

Against observant opponents, you can't change your bet

sizes so obviously. In those cases, you have two options: First, you can use a mixed strategy with your made hands, occasionally betting less with them as you'd like to bet your draws. Second, you can use mixed strategy with your draws, betting them like your made hands, meaning that you won't be saving money on your draws, but you'll be getting added fold equity. Honestly, both approaches are valid, and you'll probably be better off using a mixture of both. The best approach will, of course, depend on your opposition. In casinos, and especially online, players aren't very attentive, though. I usually get away with betting a smaller fraction of the pot in early position with draws without anyone noticing. Some online players, especially on one popular site, like to employ a minimum bet from early position to draw really cheaply. I don't recommend that play because it's obvious and everyone does it—I raise that minimum bet by overbetting the pot with any two cards, and I virtually always end up taking the pot. Then again, if your opponents are really willing to let you draw by betting $\frac{1}{10}$ pot or less by early position, you might as well take advantage of the situation. Be a poker chameleon and adapt to your surroundings.

The final line of play when drawing in early position is check-raising on the flop. After check-raising, play on the turn is awkward. Do you check the turn or bet the turn? Either way, you are paying more money to make your draw than with the other lines of play (you've put more money in on the flop, and since the pot on the turn is bigger, you'll be paying more on the turn as well). By putting in the most money, it follows that you are getting the worst odds. As a result, I personally dislike check-raising with my draws. However, there are no absolutes, and there may be times to check-raise your draws. One potential merit of check-raising is that your fold equity on the flop is greater from check-raising than it is from immediately betting out. This fold equity is often negated by the bad odds you are getting to draw when you are called, but we should acknowledge it. Another benefit to consider, is that if opponents see you check-raise with draws, you are more likely to receive action on future hands when you actually have the goods. Check-raising the flop with draws is an interesting play to throw in once in a while as part of a mixed strategy or when you are up against an opponent who mostly folds to check-raises. In general, though, this line costs a fair chunk of change if you use it too often or predictably.

In this section, we've discussed the dynamics of playing drawing hands such as straight draws and flush draws in early position. Really, the analysis extends to any draw for which you aren't a favorite to win with two cards to come (e.g., take a 12 outer like a flush draw with a live overcard). Summarizing the results, the best ways to draw in early position are to bet out on the flop and the turn or to employ the stop-and-go, provided that your opponent will usually bet when checked to but will usually just call when bet into. If your opponent is likely to raise your preemptive bets, then you're better off check/calling, and if your opponent is likely to check behind, then you may be better off checking as well, unless your fold equity is high enough. The line of play that's best will, therefore, depend on your opponent. Our discussion of playing draws from early position is finished; let's now see how to handle draws (less than 14 outers) from late position.

## Playing Draws (Less Than 14 Outers) from Late Position

On the flop, you have two options when drawing in late position: you either can play passively (check or call) or aggressively (bet or raise). The option you choose is largely determined by your opponent(s). Let's first examine passively playing draws.

When you are in late position, your opponents will either check to you or bet into you. When up against one opponent who bets $\frac{2}{3}$ pot on the flop and $\frac{1}{2}$ pot on the turn, we know from the previous section that you are getting \$1.55:\$1 odds across the hand (excluding implied odds and reverse implied odds on the river). Meanwhile, if your opponent checks the flop and you also check, you may face a $\frac{1}{2}$ pot bet on the turn. If the pot is \$12 and your opponent bets \$6, you are getting \$3:\$1 odds for your draw across play on the flop and the turn—very favorable odds allowing you a +EV draw to a 7 outer or better. The following is an obvious statement, but for completeness, if your opponent checks the flop and the turn, you are getting infinite odds to draw. The more passive your early position opponent is, the more inclined you should be to check behind unless you have overwhelming fold equity (especially on the flop).

Let's now examine aggressively playing draws in position. Suppose it is checked to you on the flop. To keep your betting consistent, you bet $\frac{2}{3}$ pot. Your opponent(s) may fold, but if you get called, most opponents will check to you on the turn. This play is commonly referred to as a "free-card play" because you are getting the option of seeing the river without having to put money in on the turn. If your fold equity is high, foregoing the free card and betting the turn might be best. Many opponents who call the flop are apt to call the turn, though. Thus, taking the free card is usually desirable. If you are betting in position on the flop and taking the free card on the turn, your odds work as follows: Suppose, again, that the pot is \$12, and you bet \$8. Your opponent calls, meaning that you are getting \$20:\$8 = \$2.5:\$1 to draw two cards—notice that this is +EV for an 8 outer.

Granted, it is not as good as the 3:1 you get versus an opponent apt to bet $\frac{1}{2}$pot on the turn when you check; however, you have added fold equity and deception with this line of play. Additionally, the 3:1 you have to pay on the turn is not sufficient to call a straight or flush draw if your opponent won't give you implied odds.

If the amount you bet with your semi-bluffs and your made hands is identical, you make it very difficult for your opponents to make optimum decisions—you are effectively playing a type of mixed strategy. If you are playing against opponents who allow you to bet less with your semi-bluffs (say 40 percent of the pot) without being aware and without fighting back, you have a ridiculous advantage—you are getting fold equity and you are getting to draw for the cheapest price possible with the exception of when your opponent gives you infinite odds by also checking to you on the turn. When I first sit at a table, I try to test the texture of the table by seeing if my opponents respond differently to different betting amounts. If they do, then I change gears and always bet the same amount with my made hands and my semi-bluffs. If my opponents allow me to semi-bluff cheaply, though, I take full advantage of it.*

We've covered aggressive play when your opponent checks to you. Now, what will happen if your opponent bets into you on the flop? In that case, the aggressive line of play is raising. Once again, the pot is $12. Your opponent bets $8, meaning that a standard raise is to around $24. Suppose you raise to $24 and your opponent calls. Most opponents will check the turn here, giving you a free card (albeit a more ex-

* An interesting note is that against some opponents, smaller bets will actually have more fold equity. By betting smaller in relation to the pot, some opponents will think that you are trying to trap them. If you can draw for less and simultaneously increase your fold equity, then you are getting the best of both worlds!

pensive one than the free card you got when your opponent checked and you bet). Against an opponent who will gracefully check the turn for you, you are paying \$24 in an effort to win \$12 + \$24 = \$36. You get \$36:\$24 = \$1.5:\$1 odds to draw by raising in position, slightly worse than the \$1.55:\$1 you get when you call the flop and your opponent bets $\frac{1}{2}$ pot on the turn, but slightly better than the \$1.45:\$1 you get when your opponent bets $\frac{2}{3}$ pot on the flop and the turn. You also open yourself up to a reraise on the flop, and if your opponent pulls a stop-and-go, you have to pay a very high price to draw. Being the victim of a reraise on the flop or a stop-and-go on the turn is probably balanced out by the fold equity you get. Of course, this is a function of your opponent's distribution and how he plays—there's no way I can make a sweeping generalization.

One benefit to raising on the flop is that it adds deception to your play—if you are caught semi-bluffing a few times, you increase the likelihood of getting action when you have a substantial holding. To get better odds, consider raising to \$20 (2.5 times the amount of the original bet). In that case, you pay \$20 to win \$32 for \$32:\$20 ≈ \$1.6:\$1 odds, and you still have decent fold equity. If you are really stingy and want to get even better odds, you can attempt a minimum raise. However, your fold equity will be pretty much shot. You also have to think about disguising your play against observant opponents. How would you raise in position with a made hand? If you raise to \$16, your opponent is getting $\frac{\$12+\$8+\$16}{\$8}$ = \$4.5:\$1 odds to call. You are giving opponents willing to bet their draws in early position great odds to call. As a result, when raising in position with draws to get free cards, it seems desirable to raise to between 2.5 and 3 times what your opponent bets. Do not forget what I said about inattentive opponents, though. If your opponents are not paying attention to patterns in your relative betting and raising amounts, by all means use the minimum raise in position to get the cheapest free card possible.

Well, we've covered the basic lines of play for playing draws (less than 14 outers) in position. In general, calculated aggression is the way to go. The exception is a situation where you face calling stations who seldom bet; against such opponents, you get the best odds to draw by checking or simply calling in the rare instances they do bet.

One last issue to be considered is the dynamic of having multiple opponents. A common situation is that you are in last position with two or three opponents. Suppose you have three opponents. The first two players check and the third player bets. What do you do now? Do you call, or do you raise to try to get a free card? If the two players who checked are apt to call if you just call, but will fold if you raise, then playing the hand passively becomes the preferred route since you will be getting much better odds to draw. If the two players who checked are apt to fold even if you just call, then you may as well treat the hand as if it is heads-up and semi-bluff. And if the two players who checked are apt to call when you semi-bluff, then semi-bluffing becomes the desired route—getting a free card in this betting pattern is almost guaranteed from my experience, meaning that you are getting great odds to draw. In fact, if you raise and get three callers, you are getting \$3:\$1 on your raise in a circumstance where you are either 2.18:1 or 1.86:1. The raise itself is +EV, meaning that you have successfully raised your draw for value! In the next section, we will discuss this in more detail in addition to handling 14+ outers on the flop.

## Raising for Value Against Multiple Opponents and with 14+ Outers

We've considered the dynamics of trying to save money when you are drawing against one opponent, and we have briefly discussed drawing against multiple opponents. Now, consider a situation where you have a flush draw against three opponents and where you are last to act. The early position opponent bets the flop, and your other two opponents call. It is now your turn to act. Assume the pot was $20 and the bet was $10. If you raise to $40, you are getting an additional $90 in the pot (assuming everyone not only stays in but just calls—big assumption for a NL game). You are investing $30 extra to get $90 more in the pot, meaning that you are getting $3:$1 on that money. Meanwhile, with two cards to come, the odds against you hitting your flush are 1.86:1. Not only are you most likely getting a free card, but the raise itself is +EV! Just to reiterate from the last section, when you do this, you are raising for value.

Now that we've acquainted ourselves with this idea of raising draws for value, I should say that in a typical NL game, with a 13 outer or less, this raise in position would most likely not be a raise for value. It's only truly a value raise if you *expect* people to call; if you *just happen* to get enough callers, which is the more likely case in a NL game, then just be happy that you incidentally pulled off an immediately +EV free-card play. This idea of raising draws for value is a line of thought that I've carried over from limit hold'em. In limit hold'em, the concept of raising for value (on the flop *and* the turn) is huge for two reasons: First, opponents who enter pots rarely fold to raises. Second, if you are reraised, the raising amounts are fixed, meaning that your overall drawing odds are still quite favorable when you are reraised.

In NL hold'em, it's tough to get everyone to call a standard raise like the one just described, even if they've already put money in the pot. Also, when you're reraised, you end up paying a high price for your draw. The size of the raise will probably force you to call, but when you look at the overall line of play, you're getting horrible odds. Thus, raising a draw (13 outer or less) for value in NL hold'em is something that you rarely get to do—when you raise in position with draws, it's typically just for the free-card play as previously described. Just be aware of those rare opportunities in NL hold'em where you may be able to raise for value, and if you ever hit the limit hold'em tables, really look for ways to make your unwary opponents pay!*

All this time, I have been talking about draws where you have 13 or less outs. Now, what if you have 14 or more outs on the flop? Assuming that your opponents have no big redraws, you are over 50% to win the hand. In that case, even when you are heads-up, you are raising for value. Furthermore, if you have an opponent with a big redraw, but you have two or more opponents, your raise with your 14+ outer on the flop will also be a huge raise for value. It is very important that you truly have a 14+ outer on the flop. Remember what I said earlier about not being optimistic with your perceived outs. Nothing is worse than thinking you have 15 outs with a straight flush draw, only to be up against a higher

* My favorite play in limit hold'em (and possibly poker in general) is a specific type of check-raise for value. I have a 15 outer in late position. It's the turn, I have 4 or more opponents, and I know that the only guy left to act behind me is going to bet (I love chip-loading tells in live play). Sure enough, I check, and he bets. Lo and behold—everyone calls. What do I do? I put in a check-raise for value from late position! I usually don't get reraised, so I end up getting \$4:\$1 (or more) on a 31:15 $\approx$ 2.07 : 1 shot! Not only am I getting huge +EV on this hand, but my opponents get the idea that I'm reckless since I check-raised and turn with a draw—huge +EV for later hands with the increased action I'll get with my made hands.

flush draw and realizing that your supposed 15 outer is really only an 8 outer (6 straight outs and 2 straight flush outs) after jamming the pot and getting all-in on the flop. When you genuinely think you have a 14+ outer, then, and only then, go in the pot with "all guns a blazin'."

## Chapter Summary and Preview of What's to Come

In this chapter, we first established that entering a pot with any two cards, hoping to hit two pair or better, is not profitable, even from the small blind. To be profitable, you need implied odds on the order of 10+ big blinds, and even more than that after accounting for the reverse implied odds associated with situations like being beaten by a higher two pair and being beaten by trips with a higher kicker. We then discussed hole cards conducive toward drawing—connectors, suited cards, and suited connectors—and examined the overall probabilities of hitting straights and flushes with them. Acknowledging that most postflop play with these hands will involve drawing to straights or flushes, we then looked at the probabilities of hitting draws with one or two cards to come. We also explored the effect of your opponents' redraws, and we determined that, as an approximation, redraws only have to be seriously considered when drawing to a straight or a flush against a set. From there, we examined lines of play that minimize drawing costs when you have less than 14 outs on the flop, and we determined that your opponents' styles of play are going to determine the best lines of play to take. For the instances where you have 14+ outs, we discussed the idea of raising for value.

Up until now, we've been operating mostly in the realm of hit-to-win poker, the realm that most people associate mathematical analysis with. By now, though, you've seen that I've applied math to a wide range of situations in poker not normally handled mathematically. In the next chapter, I introduce you to the world of shorthanded NL hold'em. It's possible to beat some shorthanded games by playing hit-to-win, but if you're going to maximize your profits and beat heads-up and three-handed games, you need to operate outside the hit-to-win realm. Topics to be covered include the probability of flops hitting opponents (something we've already touched on quite a bit), prime bluffing opportunities, and the use of your opponents' betting frequencies to unlock their primary strategies. The chapter will conclude with a very important section on why you should never buy in for 20BB or less and play heads-up in a cash game against someone with 200 + BB (or even just 100 + BB).

## Problems

1. a. What's the probability of getting a straight using both hole cards with five cards to come if you have a 1-gap?

   b. What's the probability of getting a straight using both hole cards with five cards to come if you have a 2-gap?

   c. What's the probability of getting a straight using both hole cards with five cards to come if you have a 3-gap?

2. a. What's the probability of getting a straight using both hole cards or a flush with five cards to come if you have a suited 1-gap?

   b. What's the probability of getting a straight using both hole cards or a flush with five cards to come if you have a suited 2-gap?

c. What's the probability of getting a straight using both hole cards or a flush with five cards to come if you have a suited 3-gap?

3. You have 7♣6♣, and the flop is T♣9♣2♦.

   a. How many outs do you have?

**Table 5.5: Hand for Problem 4a.**

**Game:** $2,000NL Hold'em
**Structure:** Small Blind: $10 Big Blind: $20
**Comments:** Shorthanded online game with a negligible rake. P1 is loose-aggressive when there's no preflop raiser, but when there's a raise, he's fairly tight. You are P5, and action has been recorded until you're check-raised on the flop.

| | 1(SB) | 2(BB) | 3 | 4 | *5(B)* |
|---|---|---|---|---|---|
| | XX | XX | XX | XX | A♦K♦ |
| **STACKS** | $5,000 | $1,700 | $2,500 | $12,400 | $5,000 |
| **PREFLOP** | b$10 | b$20 | >$20 | $20 | $100 |
| | $100 | - | - | $100< | |
| **STACKS** | $4,900 | | | $12,300 | $4,900 |
| **FLOP** | >$0 | | | $0 | $200 |
| **Q♦J♦5♣** | $600 | | | - | |
| **STACKS** | | | | | |
| **TURN** | | | | | |
| **STACKS** | | | | | |
| **RIVER** | | | | | |
| **HOLE** | | | | | |

**Comments:** None.

**Legend:** SB = Small Blind; BB = Big Blind; B = Button; X = Unknown Hole Card; b = Blind or Straddle; > = Beginning of Betting Round Action; < = End of Betting Round Action; - = Fold; d = Action in the Dark; c = Call; r = Raise; E = Exposed Card; M = Main Pot; S = Side Pot; AI = All-In; R = Rake

b. What are the odds against you hitting your draw with two cards to come?

4. a. You are in the hand described in table 5.5. What do you do?

| | |
|---|---|
| | **POT** |
| | |
| | M = $340 |
| | |
| | M = $1,140 |
| | |
| | |
| | |

b. You call and action proceeds as in table 5.6. What do you do?

**Table 5.6: Hand for Problem 4b.**

**Game:** $2,000NL Hold'em
**Structure:** Small Blind: $10 Big Blind: $20
**Comments:** Shorthanded online game with a negligible rake. P1 is loose-aggressive when there's no preflop raiser, but when there's a raise, he's fairly tight. Postflop, P1 is tricky, but not necessarily reckless. You're P5, and action has been recorded until the turn, where P1 has bet $1,200 into you.

| | 1(SB) | 2(BB) | 3 | 4 | *5(B)* |
|---|---|---|---|---|---|
| | XX | XX | XX | XX | A♦K♦ |
| **STACKS** | $5,000 | $1,700 | $2,500 | $12,400 | $5,000 |
| **PREFLOP** | b$10 | b$20 | >$20 | $20 | $100 |
| | $100 | - | - | $100< | |
| **STACKS** | $4,900 | | | $12,300 | $4,900 |
| **FLOP** | >$0 | | | $0 | $200 |
| **Q♦J♦5♣** | $600 | | | - | $600< |
| **STACKS** | $4,300 | | | | $4,300 |
| **TURN** | >$1,200 | | | | |
| **A♠** | | | | | |
| **STACKS** | | | | | |
| **RIVER** | | | | | |
| **HOLE** | | | | | |

**Comments:** None.

**Legend:** SB = Small Blind; BB = Big Blind; B = Button; X = Unknown Hole Card; b = Blind or Straddle; > = Beginning of Betting Round Action; < = End of Betting Round Action; - = Fold; d = Action in the Dark; c = Call; r = Raise; E = Exposed Card; M = Main Pot; S = Side Pot; AI = All-In; R = Rake

| | POT |
|---|---|
| | |
| | M = $340 |
| | |
| | M = $1,540 |
| | |
| | |
| | |

c. You call, and action proceeds as in table 5.7. Do you call, go all-in, or fold?

**Table 5.7: Hand for Problem 4c.**

**Game:** $2,000NL Hold'em
**Structure:** Small Blind: $10 Big Blind: $20
**Comments:** Shorthanded online game with a negligible rake. P1 is loose-aggressive when there's no preflop raiser, but when there's a raise, he's fairly tight. Postflop, P1 is tricky, but not necessarily reckless. You're P5, and action has been recorded until the river, where you're faced with an interesting decision.

| | 1(SB) | 2(BB) | 3 | 4 | *5(B)* |
|---|---|---|---|---|---|
| | XX | XX | XX | XX | A♦K♦ |
| **STACKS** | $5,000 | $1,700 | $2,500 | $12,400 | $5,000 |
| **PREFLOP** | b$10 | b$20 | >$20 | $20 | $100 |
| | $100 | - | - | $100< | |
| **STACKS** | $4,900 | | | $12,300 | $4,900 |
| **FLOP** | >$0 | | | $0 | $200 |
| **Q♦J♦5♣** | $600 | | | - | $600< |
| **STACKS** | $4,300 | | | | $4,300 |
| **TURN** | >$1,200 | | | | $1200< |
| **A♠** | | | | | |
| **STACKS** | $3,100 | | | | $2,600 |
| **RIVER** | >$1,250 | | | | |
| **A♣** | | | | | |
| **HOLE** | | | | | |

**Comments:** None.

**Legend:** SB = Small Blind; BB = Big Blind; B = Button; X = Unknown Hole Card; b = Blind or Straddle; > = Beginning of Betting Round Action; < = End of Betting Round Action; - = Fold; d = Action in the Dark; c = Call; r = Raise; E = Exposed Card; M = Main Pot; S = Side Pot; AI = All-In; R = Rake

| POT |
| --- |
| M = $340 |
| M = $1,540 |
| M = $3,940 |

## Answers to Problems

1a. *P(straight)* ≈ .10.

*Explanation:* Suppose you hold a specific 1-gap, like J9. You can make 3 types of straights involving both hole cards: {789TJ, 89TJQ, and 9TJQK}. There are $4 \cdot 4 \cdot 4 \cdot \left(\frac{47 \cdot 46}{2!}\right) = 69{,}184$ combinations for each, meaning that there are (3)(69,184) = 207,552 total combinations. There are 2,118,760 total combinations of 5 cards, meaning that the probability of getting a straight with a 1-gap like J9 is $\left(\frac{207{,}552}{2{,}118{,}760}\right) \approx .10$.

1b. *P(straight)* ≈ .07

*Explanation:* Suppose you hold a specific 2-gap, like J8. In that case, you can make 2 types of straights using both hole cards: {789TJ and 89TJQ}. For each of these straights, there are 69,184 combinations, meaning that there are (2)(69,184) = 138,368 total combinations. Since there are 2,118,760 total combinations of 5-card boards, the probability of getting a straight with a 2-gap like J8 is $\left(\frac{138{,}368}{2{,}118{,}760}\right) \approx .07$.

1c. *P(straight)* ≈ .03

*Explanation:* Suppose you hold a specific 3-gap, like T6. In that case, you can make only 1 type of straight using both hole cards: {6789T}. There are 69,184 combinations for this type of straight. There are 2,118,760 total combinations of 5-card boards. Therefore, the probability of getting a straight with a 3-gap like T6 is $\left(\frac{69{,}184}{2{,}118{,}760}\right) \approx .03$.

2a. *P(straight_or_flush)* ≈ .15

*Explanation:* Consider 7♣9♣. From previous work in this chapter, we know that there are 135,597 combinations of flushes. From the answer to 1a, we know that there are 207,552 combinations of straights. If we add these two numbers together, we get 343,149 combinations. From this, we need to subtract the double counts; in other words, the instances where you simultaneously hit a straight and a flush. Table 5.8 shows the combinations for which you have a straight and a flush for a particular straight combination, 56**789**.

**TABLE 5.8: Combinations of a Straight and a Flush for a 1-Gap**

| CASE | BOARD CARDS | COMBINATIONS FOR STRAIGHT CARDS | COMBINATIONS FOR XX | TOTAL COMBINATIONS |
|---|---|---|---|---|
| #1 | 5♣6♣8♣xx | 1 | $\frac{47 \cdot 46}{2!} = 1{,}081$ | 1,081 |
| #2 | 568(2clubs)xx (1club) | 3•3 = 9 | 9•38 = 342 | 3,078 |
| #3 | 568(2clubs)xx (2clubs) | 3•3 = 9 | $\frac{9 \cdot 8}{2!} = 36$ | 324 |
| #4 | 568(1club)xx (2clubs) | 3•3•3 = 27 | $\frac{10 \cdot 9}{2!} = 45$ | 1,215 |

From this table, we see 1,081 + 3,078 + 324 + 1,215 = 5,698 combinations that need to be subtracted for a particular straight. There are 3 possible straights, so, in total, (3)(5,698) = 17,094 combinations should be subtracted. We therefore conclude that there are 343,149 – 17,094 = 326,055 combinations of straights and flushes. Since there are 2,118,760 boards containing five cards, the probability of making a straight or a flush with a suited 1-gap is $\frac{326{,}055}{2{,}118{,}760} \approx .15$. The odds against this happening are $\frac{2{,}118{,}760-326{,}055}{326{,}055} \approx 5.50{:}1$.

2b. *P(straight_or_flush)* ≈ .12.

*Explanation:* Consider 6♣9♣. From previous work in this chapter (see p. 180), we know that there are 135,597 combinations of flushes. From the answer to 1b, we know that there are 138,368 combinations of straights. If we add these two numbers, we get 273,965 combinations. From these, we need to subtract the double counts, in other words, the instances where you simultaneously hit a straight and a flush. Table 5.9 shows the combinations for which you have a straight and a flush for a particular straight combination, 5**6**78**9**:

**TABLE 5.9: Combinations of a Straight and a Flush for a 2-Gap**

| CASE | BOARD CARDS | COMBINATIONS FOR STRAIGHT CARDS | COMBINATIONS FOR XX | TOTAL COMBINATIONS |
|---|---|---|---|---|
| #1 | 5♣7♣8♣xx | 1 | $\frac{47 \cdot 46}{2!} = 1{,}081$ | 1,081 |
| #2 | 578(2clubs)xx (1club) | 3•3 = 9 | 9•38 = 342 | 3,078 |
| #3 | 578(2clubs)xx (2clubs) | 3•3 = 9 | $\frac{9 \cdot 8}{2!} = 36$ | 324 |
| #4 | 578(1club)xx (2clubs) | 3•3•3 = 27 | $\frac{10 \cdot 9}{2!} = 45$ | 1,215 |

From Table 5.9, we see that there are 1,081 + 3,078 + 324 + 1,215 = 5,698 combinations that need to be subtracted for a particular straight. There are 2 possible straights, so, in total, (2)(5,698) = 11,396 combinations should be subtracted. We therefore conclude that there are 273,965 – 11,396 = 262,569 combinations of straights and flushes. Since there are 2,118,760 boards containing 5 cards, the probability of making a straight or a flush with a suited 2-gap is $\frac{262,569}{2,118,760} \approx .12$. The odds against this happening are $\frac{2,118,760-262,569}{262,569} \approx 7.07{:}1$.

2c. *P(straight_or_flush)* ≈ .12

*Explanation:* Consider 5♣9♣. From previous work in this chapter, we know that there are 135,597 combinations of flushes. From the answer to 1c, we know that there are 69,184 combinations of straights. If we add these two numbers, we get 204,781 combinations. From these, we need to subtract the double counts, in other words, the instances where you simultaneously hit a straight and a flush. Table 5.10 shows the combinations for which you have a straight and a flush for a particular straight combination, **5**678**9**.

**TABLE 5.10: Combinations of a Straight and a Flush for a 3-Gap**

| CASE | BOARD CARDS | COMBINATIONS FOR STRAIGHT CARDS | COMBINATIONS FOR XX | TOTAL COMBINATIONS |
|---|---|---|---|---|
| #1 | 6♣7♣8♣xx | 1 | $\frac{47 \cdot 46}{2!} = 1{,}081$ | 1,081 |
| #2 | 678(2clubs)xx (1club) | 3•3 = 9 | 9•38 = 342 | 3,078 |
| #3 | 678(2clubs)xx (2clubs) | 3•3 = 9 | $\frac{9 \cdot 8}{2!} = 36$ | 324 |
| #4 | 678(1club)xx (2clubs) | 3•3•3 = 27 | $\frac{10 \cdot 9}{2!} = 45$ | 1,215 |

From this table, we see that there are 1,081 + 3,078 + 324 + 1,215 = 5,698 combinations that need to be subtracted for a particular straight, and there is only 1 type of straight. We therefore conclude that there are combinations of straights and flushes. Since there are 2,118,760 boards containing 5 cards, the probability of making a straight or a flush with a suited 3-gap is $\frac{199{,}083}{2{,}118{,}760} \approx .09$. The odds against this happening are $\frac{2{,}118{,}760 - 199{,}083}{199{,}083} \approx 9.64{:}1$.

3a. Question can't be answered.

*Explanation:* You may have answered "12 outs" since you have 9 flush outs and an additional 3 outs with which you can make a straight. However, with the lack of information I gave you, how do you know whether all your outs are good? How many people are in the hand? What has the betting action been? Are you possibly up against a higher flush draw? Are you possibly up against QJ, meaning that your straight draw is no longer good? In all seriousness, you *usually* aren't afraid of being against better draws because the probability isn't that high. However, that *doesn't* mean that you should ignore the possibility of better draws existing. The difference between great players and mediocre players is that great players have such keen awareness of their opponents and that they know when they are drawing dead with a hand like this. I purposefully posed a bad question here—I hope you learned the lesson I tried to teach.

3b. You don't know how many outs you really have, so how can you know your odds against hitting your draw?

*Explanation:* Assuming you have 12 outs, your

odds against completing your draw with two cards to come are 1.22:1. However, I'm going to flog the dead horse here and say that you don't know whether or not you have 12 outs. You may have 9 outs, you may have 3 outs, or you may be drawing completely dead. If we were to compute a long-term average over every situation you encounter, I'd guess that it would average out to something like 11.5 or so outs, but who knows for sure.

4a. You should call.

*Explanation:* There is $1,140 in the pot, and you are faced with a $400 decision. You are getting $1,140:$400 = $2.85:$1 odds to call. You currently have a flush draw and an inside straight draw, giving you at least 12 outs. Hey, you also have two overcards, meaning that you have 6 additional outs, right? Wrong. Let's examine the betting action. P1 is loose when he has the opportunity to be the primary aggressor, but he really tightens up when someone else takes the lead in the hand. This is how I play five-to-six handed games, and from my Poker Tracker stats, most of the other top shorthanded NL players online play like this as well. The key is realizing that P1 has a good hand here. Even though he's tricky and is predisposed toward aggressive play, his aggressive play is calculated, and since he is in after you raised, he has good hole cards. I had myself in mind when I talked about P1, so I am just going to say that P1's hand distribution is [AK,AQ]|||[QQ,TT]. If a loose player raised, I would include AJ and KQ in the distribution, but in most cases, I avoid those hands in raised pots until the game is only three or four handed. There are times that I reraise with AK and

QQ here as part of a mixed strategy, but I call with those hands a fair amount of the time as well.

From P1's distribution, you can see that your overcard outs are rarely good. There is a chance that P1 check-raised as a pure bluff, but most likely, P1's holdings can be narrowed to [AQ]||[QQ,JJ], meaning that he has top pair or a set. There are 9 combinations of AQ and 3 combinations each of QQ and JJ, meaning that 60% of the time you are up against top pair and that 40% of the time you are up against a set. The additional 3 king outs you pick up 60% of the time are roughly cancelled out by the adverse effect that the set redraws have on your flush and straight outs. According to Poker Stove, you win this hand .4591 times, tie .0054 times, and lose .5355 times. The odds against you winning the hand with two cards to come are about 1.18:1, which is just slightly better than the 1.22:1 odds against hitting a 12 outer (as I said before, the times that you are against redraws and the times that you have additional king outs cancel each other out).

From the odds, you are easily +EV to call if you think that you won't be shut out of the pot on the turn. If you think you're going to be shut out of the pot, you need $\left(\frac{47-12}{12}\right) \approx \$2.92:\$1$ odds to call. Since you're getting \$2.85:\$1 here, a call is +EV. I guess P1 isn't exactly like me, since I wouldn't give you such good odds to draw. As a matter of fact, I wouldn't have even check-raised here—I would've bet right out, in hopes that you raise with a drawing hand or with an overpair.

We've determined that you should call. Should you reraise to try to get a free card? 60% of the time, you'll get him to fold AQ, but the other 40 % of the time, you're cruising for a bruising—P1 is going to push all-in with his set. By raising, you aren't going to get a free card. However, the EV of reraising is very interesting. Suppose you decide to raise to $1,500. 60% of the time, you win $1,140, and 40% of the time, P1 pushes all-in with QQ or JJ. When P1 pushes all-in, you're put to the decision seen in table 5.11 (pp. 218–19).

The pot contains $6,740, and you are faced with a call of $3,400. You are getting about $1.98:$1 odds to call. Against [QQ,JJ], Poker Stove states that you win .3384 times and never tie, meaning that you need $1.96:$1 odds to call. You are just barely getting proper odds to call at this point, meaning that you must call. When you are up against [QQ,JJ], your EV for the line of play is (.3384)(+$5440) + (.6616)($4,700) = –$1268.62. 60% of the time, you are +$1140, and 40% of the time, you are –$1268.62, meaning that your overall EV for reraising here is (.60)(+$1140) + (.40)(–$1268.62) = +$176.55. Despite the initial appearance that this is a bad play, you are actually +EV here. If you were –EV, our analysis would be complete. However, now we have to delve deeper into the situation where you call so that we can compare EVs and ultimately choose the line of play with the highest EV.

You are 1.18:1 against winning with two cards to come. Assume that if you call, P1 will bet $1,000 on the turn no matter what falls. If you've hit your draw, you have big +EV going into the river. If you miss your draw, you call the $1,000, meaning that across the flop and the turn, you've paid $400 + $1,000 = $1,400 in an attempt to win $1,140 + $1,000 = $2,140. Your pot odds across the flop and the turn are

**Table 5.11: You Reraise and P1 Pushes All-In**

**Game:** $2,000NL Hold'em
**Structure:** Small Blind: $10 Big Blind: $20
**Comments:** Shorthanded online game with a negligible rake. P1 is loose-aggressive when there's no preflop raiser, but when there's a raise, he's fairly tight. You are P5, and action has been recorded assuming that you reraise P1's check-raise on the flop.

| | 1(SB) XX | 2(BB) XX | 3 XX | 4 XX | *5(B)* A♦K♦ |
|---|---|---|---|---|---|
| **STACKS** | $5,000 | $1,700 | $2,500 | $12,400 | $5,000 |
| **PREFLOP** | b$10<br>$100 | b$20<br>- | >$20<br>- | $20<br>$100< | $100 |
| **STACKS** | $4,900 | | | $12,300 | $4,900 |
| **FLOP** Q♦J♦5♣ | >$0<br>$600<br>$4,900 | | | $0<br>- | $200<br>$1,500 |
| **STACKS** | | | | | |
| **TURN** | | | | | |
| **STACKS** | | | | | |
| **RIVER** | | | | | |
| **HOLE** | | | | | |

**Comments:** None.

**Legend:** SB = Small Blind; BB = Big Blind; B = Button; X = Unknown Hole Card; b = Blind or Straddle; > = Beginning of Betting Round Action; < = End of Betting Round Action; - = Fold; d = Action in the Dark; c = Call; r = Raise; E = Exposed Card; M = Main Pot; S = Side Pot; AI = All-In; R = Rake

| | POT |
|---|---|
| | |
| | M = $340 |
| | |
| | M = $6,740 |

\$2,140: \$1,400, meaning that every 2.18 hands, you're making \$2,140(1):\$1400(1.18) = \$2,140:\$1652. For every 2.18 hands, you're making \$2,140 – \$1652 = \$488. Your EV across the flop and the turn when you have to draw on both rounds is therefore $\frac{\$488}{2.18} \approx$ +\$223.85. Now, provided that you aren't conceding huge reverse implied odds in those cases where your flush or straight wins, we see that the EV of calling is higher than the EV where you reraise. Both plays are +EV, but our goal in poker isn't just to be EV. Our goal in poker is to optimize EV.

4b. Call.

*Explanation:* Well, we have P1 on [AQ]|||[QQ,JJ], but the relative frequencies of the hands in that distribution have changed with the appearance of the ace on the turn. There are still 3 combinations each of QQ and JJ. However, there are now only 6 combinations of AQ. Thus, you are drawing to a 15 outer 50% of the time and to an 11 outer the other 50% of the time. Averaging these numbers, we get that you have (.5)(15) + (.5)(11) = 13 outs. The odds against you winning are therefore $\left(\frac{44-13}{13}\right) \approx 2.38:1$, which agree with the results obtained from Poker Stove.

P1 has bet \$1,200 into a pot of \$1,540, meaning that you are getting \$2,740:\$1,200 ≈ 2.28:1 odds. You are slightly –EV with respect to strict pot odds, but after taking implied odds and reverse implied odds into account, calling is a +EV play here.

4c. Fold.

*Explanation:* Every hand that you put P1 on ([AQ]|||[QQ,JJ]) gives him a full house. As a result, you must fold your trip aces here, even though you have the best kicker. If you are going to be a top player, you need to be willing to lay down hands like this. Play properly with respect to your reads. If you are making bad decisions, the only thing to blame at that point are your reads, and you need to make appropriate adjustments to how you read your opponents.

# 6

# SHORTHANDED PLAY

♧♤◇♡

## Introduction

When I play live poker, the extent to which I participate in table banter varies depending on my perception of the most profitable image for the table I'm at. When the conversation turns to online poker, I occasionally tell people the truth about how I simultaneously play four to six tables of medium-stakes, shorthanded NL hold'em. Most of the time I'm in a full-handed casino game, I play a small percentage of hands (10%–15%). My nickname among my circle of Caltech poker playing friends is "Too Tight Tony (TTT)," and they also refer to me as "Knish" (for those who don't know, Joey Knish is a character in the movie *Rounders* who shrewdly and unadventurously "grinds it out on his leather ass"). Because I'm so tight in full-handed ring games, my foes are shocked, and they say things like, "You are way too tight to play short-handed—you should stick to full-handed games." This response reveals much information about my opponents. People saying this assume that their opponents never change strategies, and because I get this response a lot, it seems reasonable to say that most players think like this. If you do change gears, your opponents will eventually notice, but it'll certainly take them some time. Reciprocally, players making such remarks are probably incapable of changing gears themselves. My experience at the tables, and probably yours, indicates that except for small changes in calling and raising requirements, people are generally incapable of changing gears.*

The reason I play so tightly in most full ring games has a lot to do with the numbers we've discussed up until now. In most ring games, at least three players see the flop. As a result, you need to play hit-to-win poker. Some plays allow you to raise more liberally to narrow the field, but if you pull these plays off too often, they will no longer narrow the field, and you'll end up leaking a bunch of money away. The people observing me play my full-handed hit-to-win game don't realize that I can shift gears faster than a NASCAR driver. To thrive in shorthanded games, you must become a poker chameleon who can readily adapt to the circumstances you find yourself in. You must constantly change colors, shifting back and forth between loose-aggressive and tight-aggressive play.

Even though you must constantly change gears, most shorthanded poker is won by taking a large number of small pots by betting the flop (usually after having raised preflop). The rake ends up being a huge factor. If you are paying rake on a per hand basis, a lot of these +EV bets into small pots become marginally +EV or even –EV. If the rake is high enough where these bets are –EV, you are screwed, and the

* Why people are incapable is another question entirely. Some people are scared. Others are simply stubborn and unwilling. Figuring out the underlying reasons may unlock important weaknesses that you should take full advantage of.

game is going to be unbeatable in most circumstances. This is why I play most of my shorthanded poker online. If I play live shorthanded poker, it has to be in a game with a timed collection, and if I am in a game with a timed collection, I actually prefer it to be shorthanded since I get to play many more hands per hour.

So, what exactly is a shorthanded game? Most people consider six-handed games to be shorthanded, and, indeed, most of the ideas presented in this chapter will apply to games with six or less players (including yourself). In fact, some ideas will cross over into other situations as well. Other ideas may be more suitable for games with five or less players. Instead of just classifying games as full handed or shorthanded, I actually have a more specific classification system:

- 7+ Players: Full-handed
- 6 Players: Not quite full handed
- 5 Players: Shorthanded
- 4–3 Players: Really shorthanded
- 2 Players: Heads-up

I do not consider games with six players to be truly shorthanded because there is a notion of preflop early position play. When you are UTG in most six-handed games, you have to exercise somewhat tighter hand selection than when you are in the other positions. This consideration pretty much disappears when five-handed, which is why I consider five-handed games to be where true shorthanded poker begins.

The key to beating shorthanded games is versatility. When you are no longer in the hit-to-win realm, the notion of counterstrategies implemented across multiple hands becomes extremely important. Some shorthanded games contain opponents who are overly loose and aggressive, and the key to beating those games will be a slightly looser version of your bread-and-butter hit-to-win game (the more shorthanded you are, the looser you will have to be). However, most of the time, you need to take advantage of the fact that the flop and usually the turn help no one. Continuation bets and semi-bluffs are necessary weapons in shorthanded hold'em. Ultimately, the adjustments you make will be how often to use these tools and what bet sizes to use when you do employ them.

Some opponents will let you raise them preflop and continuation bet all day without putting up a fight. Other opponents will reraise you constantly and fight back with tricky bluffs. Shorthanded play requires a very disciplined sort of aggression. People will play back at you, and you need to know when to pull the trigger on them and when not to. Pulling the trigger because of frustration and a sense of being bullied is one of the deadliest mistakes made in shorthanded hold'em. My living at online shorthanded NL hold'em is the result of constantly setting people up to make this mistake. The other deadly mistake in shorthanded NL hold'em is calling too much—there is a huge advantage to being the aggressor, and passive play will generally not cut it. Do not get me wrong—there are times when the best line of play will be to call down an opponent. However, against typical players, aggressive play is what takes the money in shorthanded games.

Shorthanded cash games are my favorite form of poker because of the many layers of thinking that begin with preflop play. One aspect of shorthanded play is particularly interesting. To this point, we've been considering the EV of individual hands; however, in shorthanded NL hold'em, it's actually sometimes desirable to make moves that are slightly –EV for a particular hand in the interest of executing an overall strategy that yields huge +EV. I've made some general statements based on my experience to get you in the mind frame of thinking about shorthanded hold'em. Without further ado, let's get on with the show, and as you read, see if you take some of these tricks to your full-handed games as well.

## The Flop Usually Hits Neither You nor Your Opponent

In shorthanded games, most of the time you see the flop, you have one or two opponents, especially if you're usually entering pots with a raise. Recall that a single opponent will miss the flop approximately one third of the time. This is the starting point of short handed play on the flop.

Let's examine this starting point more thoroughly using the following scenario. You're on the button, and you open for a raise to 3BB. The SB folds, and the BB calls. Players in shorthanded games, especially in the BB, are more liberal with calling raises, so a reasonable distribution for some of your opponents may be something like [JJ,22]|||[AJ,A5]||| [KQ,K8]|||[QJ,QT]|||[JT,65]. In reality, your opponents will have widely varying distributions. Some may be on [AA,JJ]|||[AK,AQ] while others may be on [All], but let's just take this as our model. Let's see the profitability of raising with *any* two cards preflop and then continuation betting into various flops, making the assumption that we *always* miss the flop.

The first flop to consider is a flop of unpaired low cards. I'll consider low cards to be 9's and below and high cards to be 10's and above. As a specific example, suppose the flop is 258. Furthermore, suppose there are two suited cards on the board, meaning your opponent could possibly have a flush draw. Your opponent's hand distribution, with respect to combinations, is given in table 6.1.

**TABLE 6.1: Hand Distribution of Opponent on [JJ,22]||[AJ,A5]||[KQ,K8]||[QJ,QT]||[JT,65] When the Flop Is 2♣5♣8♠ and You Haven't Hit the Flop**

| HOLE CARDS | COMBINATIONS | HOLE CARDS | COMBINATIONS |
|---|---|---|---|
| JJ | 6 | KQ (flush draw) | 1 |
| TT | 6 | KJ (no flush draw) | 15 |
| 99 | 6 | KJ (flush draw) | 1 |
| 88 | 3 | KT (no flush draw) | 15 |
| 77 | 6 | KT (flush draw) | 1 |
| 66 | 6 | K9 (no flush draw) | 15 |
| 55 | 3 | K9 (flush draw) | 1 |
| 44 | 6 | K8 (no flush draw) | 11 |
| 33 | 6 | K8 (flush draw) | 1 |
| 22 | 3 | QJ (no flush draw) | 15 |
| AJ (no flush draw) | 15 | QJ (flush draw) | 1 |
| AJ (flush draw) | 1 | QT (no flush draw) | 15 |
| AT (no flush draw) | 15 | QT (flush draw) | 1 |
| AT (flush draw) | 1 | JT (no flush draw) | 15 |
| A9 (no flush draw) | 15 | JT (flush draw) | 1 |
| A9 (flush draw) | 1 | T9 (no flush draw) | 15 |
| A8 (no flush draw) | 11 | T9 (flush draw) | 1 |
| A8 (flush draw) | 1 | 98 (no flush draw) | 11 |
| A7 (no flush draw) | 15 | 98 (flush draw) | 1 |
| A7 (flush draw) | 1 | 87 (no flush draw) | 11 |
| A6 (no flush draw) | 15 | 87 (flush draw) | 1 |
| A6 (flush draw) | 1 | 76 (no flush draw) | 15 |
| A5 (no flush draw) | 12 | 76 (flush draw) | 1 |
| A5 (flush draw) | 0 | 65 (no flush draw) | 12 |
| KQ (no flush draw) | 15 | 65 (flush draw) | 0 |

*Total number of combinations = 347*

Suppose your opponent calls your continuation bet with middle pair or better, any flush draw, or any straight draw (both inside and outside draws). In that case, your opponent gives you resistance with 140 hole-card combinations, meaning that there are 347 − 140 = 207 hole-card combinations that your opponent folds. The probability of getting such an opponent to fold to a continuation bet is therefore $\frac{207}{347} \approx .60$. If you make a $\frac{2}{3}$pot continuation bet, your EV is therefore.

$$\left(\tfrac{207}{347}\right)P + \left(\tfrac{140}{347}\right)\left(-\tfrac{2}{3}P\right) \approx +.33P \qquad (6.1)$$

If you are playing in a NL game with \$1–\$2 blinds, the size of the pot on the flop will be \$13. Equation 6.1 indicates that the EV associated with your continuation bet on a flop with all low cards is (.33)(\$13) = \$4.29.

Now consider the case where one high card flops. To consider the worst-case scenario, assume it's an ace (this is the worst-case scenario because the most prevalent high card in your opponent's distribution is an ace). Table 6.2 shows your opponent's hand combinations if the flop is A♠5♣2♣.

**TABLE 6.2: Hand Distribution of Opponent on [JJ,22] || [AJ,A5] || [KQ,K8] || [QJ,QT] || [JT,65] When the Flop Is 2♣5♣A♠ and You Haven't Hit the Flop**

| HOLE CARDS | COMBINATIONS | HOLE CARDS | COMBINATIONS |
|---|---|---|---|
| JJ | 6 | KQ (flush draw) | 1 |
| TT | 6 | KJ (no flush draw) | 15 |
| 99 | 6 | KJ (flush draw) | 1 |
| 88 | 6 | KT (no flush draw) | 15 |
| 77 | 6 | KT (flush draw) | 1 |
| 66 | 6 | K9 (no flush draw) | 15 |
| 55 | 3 | K9 (flush draw) | 1 |
| 44 | 6 | K8 (no flush draw) | 15 |
| 33 | 6 | K8 (flush draw) | 1 |
| 22 | 3 | QJ (no flush draw) | 15 |

| HOLE CARDS | COMBINATIONS | HOLE CARDS | COMBINATIONS |
|---|---|---|---|
| AJ (no flush draw) | 11 | QJ (flush draw) | 1 |
| AJ (flush draw) | 1 | QT (no flush draw) | 15 |
| AT (no flush draw) | 11 | QT (flush draw) | 1 |
| AT (flush draw) | 1 | JT (no flush draw) | 15 |
| A9 (no flush draw) | 11 | JT (flush draw) | 1 |
| A9 (flush draw) | 1 | T9 (no flush draw) | 15 |
| A8 (no flush draw) | 11 | T9 (flush draw) | 1 |
| A8 (flush draw) | 1 | 98 (no flush draw) | 15 |
| A7 (no flush draw) | 11 | 98 (flush draw) | 1 |
| A7 (flush draw) | 1 | 87 (no flush draw) | 15 |
| A6 (no flush draw) | 11 | 87 (flush draw) | 1 |
| A6 (flush draw) | 1 | 76 (no flush draw) | 15 |
| A5 (no flush draw) | 9 | 76 (flush draw) | 1 |
| A5 (flush draw) | 0 | 65 (no flush draw) | 12 |
| KQ (no flush draw) | 15 | 65 (flush draw) | 0 |

*Total number of combinations = 339*

Your opponent resists with 147 combinations and folds 339 – 147 = 192 combinations. Your EV for a $\frac{2}{3}$pot-sized continuation bet is given in equation 6.2.

$$\left(\tfrac{192}{339}\right)P + \left(\tfrac{147}{339}\right)\left(-\tfrac{2}{3}P\right) \approx +.28P \qquad (6.2)$$

Now, let's see what happens when the board contains two high cards. Again, we'll consider the scenario in which your opponent gives you the most resistance, meaning we'll assume that both an ace and a king flop. Your opponent's distribution is in table 6.3.

Your opponent resists with 200 combinations and folds 129 combinations. Your EV for a $\frac{2}{3}$pot-sized continuation bet is given by equation (6.3).

$$\left(\tfrac{129}{329}\right)P + \left(\tfrac{200}{329}\right)\left(-\tfrac{2}{3}P\right) \approx -.01P \qquad (6.3)$$

**TABLE 6.3: Hand Distribution of Opponent on [JJ,22] || [AJ,A5] || [KQ,K8] || [QJ,QT] || [JT,65] When the Flop Is 2♣K♣A♠ and You Haven't Hit the Flop**

| HOLE CARDS | COMBINATIONS | HOLE CARDS | COMBINATIONS |
|---|---|---|---|
| JJ | 6 | A5 (flush draw) | 1 |
| TT | 6 | KQ | 12 |
| 99 | 6 | KJ | 12 |
| 88 | 6 | KT | 12 |
| 77 | 6 | K9 | 12 |
| 66 | 6 | K8 | 12 |
| 55 | 6 | QJ (no flush draw) | 15 |
| 44 | 6 | QJ (flush draw) | 1 |
| 33 | 6 | QT (no flush draw) | 15 |
| 22 | 3 | QT (flush draw) | 1 |
| AJ (no flush draw) | 11 | JT (no flush draw) | 15 |
| AJ (flush draw) | 1 | JT (flush draw) | 1 |
| AT (no flush draw) | 11 | T9 (no flush draw) | 15 |
| AT (flush draw) | 1 | T9 (flush draw) | 1 |
| A9 (no flush draw) | 11 | 98 (no flush draw) | 15 |
| A9 (flush draw) | 1 | 98 (flush draw) | 1 |
| A8 (no flush draw) | 11 | 87 (no flush draw) | 15 |
| A8 (flush draw) | 1 | 87 (flush draw) | 1 |
| A7 (no flush draw) | 11 | 76 (no flush draw) | 15 |
| A7 (flush draw) | 1 | 76 (flush draw) | 1 |
| A6 (no flush draw) | 11 | 65 (no flush draw) | 15 |
| A6 (flush draw) | 1 | 65 (flush draw) | 1 |
| A5 (no flush draw) | 11 | | |

*Total number of combinations = 329*

Now, suppose you miss the flop and it contains three high cards and a flush draw; A♣K♣Q♥ is the worst-case scenario. Your opponent's hand distribution, in terms of combinations, is given in table 6.4 (opposite).

**TABLE 6.4: Hand Distribution of Opponent on [JJ,22] || [AJ,A5] || [KQ,K8] || [QJ,QT] || [JT,65] When the Flop Is A♣K♣Q♥ and You Haven't Hit the Flop**

| HOLE CARDS | COMBINATIONS | HOLE CARDS | COMBINATIONS |
|---|---|---|---|
| JJ | 6 | KQ | 9 |
| TT | 6 | KJ | 12 |
| 99 | 6 | KT | 12 |
| 88 | 6 | K9 | 12 |
| 77 | 6 | K8 | 12 |
| 66 | 6 | QJ | 12 |
| 55 | 6 | QT | 12 |
| 44 | 6 | JT | 16 |
| 33 | 6 | T9 | 16 |
| 22 | 6 | 98 (no flush draw) | 15 |
| AJ | 12 | 98 (flush draw) | 1 |
| AT | 12 | 87 (no flush draw) | 15 |
| A9 | 12 | 87 (flush draw) | 1 |
| A8 | 12 | 76 (no flush draw) | 15 |
| A7 | 12 | 76 (flush draw) | 1 |
| A6 | 12 | 65 (no flush draw) | 15 |
| A5 | 12 | 65 (flush draw) | 1 |

*Total number of combinations = 321*

We will assume like before that your opponent gives you resistance with top pair or better, a flush draw, or a straight draw. This means that your opponent resists with 213 combinations and folds 321 − 213 = 108 combinations. Your EV for a $\frac{2}{3}$pot continuation bet is given by equation 6.4.

$$\left(\tfrac{108}{321}\right)P + \left(\tfrac{213}{321}\right)\left(-\tfrac{2}{3}P\right) \approx -.11P \qquad (6.4)$$

The EVs for continuation betting into the different board types are summarized in table 6.5 (on p. 232).

**TABLE 6.5: EV for Continuation Betting Flops with 0–3 High Cards**

| NUMBER OF HIGH CARDS | EV |
|---|---|
| 0 | +.33P |
| 1 | +.28P |
| 2 | −.01P |
| 3 | −.11P |

Table 6.5 shows that continuation betting into boards with no high cards or 1 high card is highly profitable. Continuation betting into a board containing 2 high cards is just barely –EV, and continuation betting into a board containing 3 high cards is the only play that carries large –EV. The point to be made is that continuation betting is a potentially powerful play, especially in the shorthanded setting where you are forced to play more hands, but where you and your opponents will miss the flop a majority of the time.

## EV Across Multiple Hands

To this point, we have thought about EV in terms of individual hands. For the most part, if you're playing your cash game poker by thinking about optimizing your EV on a hand-by-hand basis, you're going to do well. There's one interesting point to consider, though. In short-handed games, you'll end up in repeated one-on-one encounters against the same opponents. If your opponents get a line on your play, it's going to be very difficult for you to profit. You *may* not lose a lot, but you certainly aren't going to win a lot if this happens. Thus, you need to throw some deception into your play.

When I first sit in most online 6-max games, I immediately put my foot on the gas. For about the first two or three orbits, anytime I'm in an unraised pot, I raise preflop with any two cards, and as long as I'm heads-up, I make a continuation bet into any flop (even a flop with three high cards like AKQ). Our previous discussion showed that these continuation bets into scary boards are most likely –EV plays. However, this initial per hand –EV is compensated by the huge boost in EV that I gain for future hands in the session.

My initial aggression accomplishes many tasks. I identify the players who will fight back and the players who will allow me to bludgeon them. By forcing my opponents to adapt in ways that make them uncomfortable and quickly figuring out the ways that my opponents adapt, I put myself at a huge advantage.

The players who "fight back" typically do so in two ways: The first possibility (the more likely from my experience) is that your opponents will fight back by calling you a lot more. Some opponents may go so far as to call with any two cards on the flop. Against these opponents, you've lost any EV associated with continuation betting (the +EV from continuation betting is your fold equity). You are forced to switch from continuation betting mode to value betting mode. On one hand, this stinks, because you are only hitting flops about one third of the time. However, when players are calling you down to the river with ace high, the value that you get from your made hands is quite high. In addition, if I raise with AX against these types and miss the flop, I can continuation bet on the flop as a value bet—in other words, my continuation bet is made with the actual intention of betting the best hand despite missing the flop.

The second possibility is that your opponents will begin fighting back by fighting fire with fire. They will start reraising you and throwing lots of bluffs at you across all rounds of play. If these opponents do this by keeping their bets proportional to the pot size, you have a tough battle ahead. Your best bet is to hunker down and make sure that you are in with hands that you can comfortably play across all rounds of betting. These guys will make mistakes, and when they do, you need to be confident in pushing your statistical edge when you have it. Most players who fight fire with fire will not do so by betting proportionately with respect to the pot. They will fight back by grossly overbetting the pot preflop or on the flop. They are afraid of playing with you and want to end pots as quickly as possible without having to face any tricky decisions. Against these types, you can comfortably sit back and play hit-to-win poker, for their overbetting gives you more than sufficient odds to do so.

You should occasionally throw in token raises with hands that you'll dump to a reraise to train them to continue with their overbetting. These raises are –EV, but are an essential part of a battle plan that's overwhelmingly +EV. Most likely, you'll end up going to war against these types of players with hands like top pair/top kicker (TPK). You'll find that you often get action from middle pair (and sometimes even bottom pair).

While some players will choose to fight, some players won't change much. They may loosen their preflop requirements a tad, but for the most part, they'll still play hit-to-win. While against these opponents, simply run them over with an endless barrage of raises and continuation bets. When these players fight back, they have the goods, so don't get carried away with TPTK. Don't assume that *all* your opponents are fighting back at you with less.

To summarize, your profit against loose opponents is most likely to come from value betting your made hands, and your profit against tight opponents is most likely to come from continuation betting. One very interesting dynamic occurs when you're at a table consisting of both loose and tight players (which is most likely going to be the case). You can toss tons of profitable continuation bets at the tight players for image while sitting back and betting made hands for value against your loose opponents. The one problem is that it's sometimes hard to open for a raise in shorthanded games with loose players, so this opportunity may not present itself. If it's there, then by all means, take full advantage. This particular overall approach to shorthanded poker is an example of the idea that EV, even in cash games, is something that can materialize over the play of many hands. Sometimes, –EV plays at specific pots need to be made to accomplish the task of optimizing your EV across an entire session.

### "Third Time's the Adjustment"

I've discussed so much poker with JV that it's hard to distinguish between what he says and what he writes. When I read his material, I see many JVisms that he uses in conversation. One such saying I'm sure I've seen in print is that the "third time's the adjustment." What JV means by this is, if your opponent does something three times in a row, you need to make an adjustment starting with the third time. There's compelling mathematical evidence corroborating this idea.

Here's a common situation. You've been sitting at a table, and the first three times you post your BB, the action folds to the button who raises. What's the probability that this player is actually raising with legitimate hands? Assume that "legitimate hands" are hands in the following distribution: [AA,66]|||[AK,A8]|||[KQ,K9]|||[QJ,QT]|||[JT]. These hands comprise 262 out of 1,326 possible combinations of hole cards. The probability that your opponent has one of these hands

$n$ consecutive times is $\left(\frac{262}{1326}\right)^n$. The values of this expression as a function of $n$ are in table 6.6.

**TABLE 6.6: Probability That Your Opponent Has [AA,66] || [AK,A8] || [KQ,K9] || [QJ,QT] || [JT]**

| CONSECUTIVE TIMES | PROBABILITY |
|---|---|
| 1 | .2 |
| 2 | .04 |
| 3 | .008 |
| 4 | .002 |

Table 6.6 indicates that there's actually justification for adjusting after the second consecutive raise from the button, and if the button opens for a raise three consecutive times, it's very likely that he's no longer raising with just these hands, meaning that you should make an adjustment. In a ten-handed ring game, you can afford to get your blinds stolen every orbit, but when you're playing shorthanded, the blinds become more significant. In a five- to six-handed game, you don't need to expand your starting requirements a lot—remember the disadvantages of playing heads-up pots out of position. Once you get down to three-four players, you need to begin mixing it up. How you mix up calls and reraises is a function of your opponent, but you somehow need to find an adjustment to win.

Another important scenario is to see whether an opponent is playing hit-to-win poker against your continuation bets. Your opponent only hits the flop one third of the time, meaning that your opponent should be folding to about two thirds of your continuation bets. Accounting for possible draws, saying that an opponent looking to hit flops will fold with a probability of .6 is a good starting point. If his true folding rate is .6, the probability of your opponent calling three consecutive continuation bets is $(.4)^3 \approx .06$, which is quite low.

Shorthanded poker is about deciphering your opponents' betting patterns. Each opponent is a puzzle, and it's your job to solve each one. In solving each puzzle, the saying that "third time's the adjustment" can be useful. In the next section, we'll look at the consequences of short buying into a short handed game (especially heads-up or possibly three handed) when your opponents have deep stacks.

### Never Buy In for Less Than 25BB in a Game with a 100 + BB Max Buy-In When Your Opponent Has 100 + BB

An interesting playing dynamic evolves when a short stack encounters a deep stack heads-up. The deep stack is essentially guaranteed to take all the short stack's money through blind aggression. The short stack, by not exercising the right to reload, indicates that he's afraid of losing money. As a result, the deep stack can take some chips initially by raising every unraised hand with the intention of continuation betting every flop. Eventually, the short stack gets sick of being bullied, and he begins to fight back with worse cards than he's accustomed to playing. When he finally hits a flop, he typically plays back by overbetting since he's sick of being bullied.

Once he starts overbetting, the short stack has put himself in a noose. At this point, the deep stack continues making his cursory flop bets, and eventually, he'll hit a flop with top pair or better. When he hits his hand, he can go all-in against the overbetting short stack, and he'll usually end up being about a 70–75% favorite to win the hand (the short stack will usually have only 5 or 6 outs—either a draw to two pair draw or an overpair). It's very important that the deep stack waits for this opportunity. He shouldn't give away more than the cursory flop bet with second pair and top kicker. There's no point in gambling with worse than top pair when a short-stacked heads-up opponent is overbetting.

Now, here's where the numbers do the talking. The 25% of the time the deep stack loses, he'll still have about a 2:1 chip advantage in a situation where the short stack thinks he's an absolute maniac. The playing dynamic is preserved, meaning that the deep stack will easily get the short stack all-in, most likely in another situation where he has a .75 chance of winning the hand. The probability of losing two 75% shots in a row is $(.25)^2 \approx .0625$. If the deep stack does lose two in a row, he buys back in to the full buy-in amount and has one more chance to stack his opponent. At that point, both players have 100BB, so it's a lot tougher to get into an all-in confrontation. Still, this preliminary analysis indicates that the short stack is donating his money to the deep stack about 95% of the time. I don't know about you, but I'll certainly take donations any day of the week!

Note that you will most likely bleed some chips in the beginning of these matchups by taking this route as a deep stack. Also, your short-stacked opponents will not always start overbetting, and they might not be overly frisky with their reraises (meaning that they have at least two pair when they reraise). By maintaining a high degree of aggressiveness, though, your opponent will eventually take a wrong step. Therefore, the short stack is still essentially donating his chips. The moral of the story is not to buy into a heads-up game short-stacked and to take merciless advantage of players who do!

## Chapter Summary and Preview of What's to Come

In this chapter, we explored the dynamic that's created when your game is short-stacked and you can no longer play hit-to-win poker. The flop usually doesn't hit anyone, and to succeed, you need to take advantage of the situation. Because the emphasis in shorthanded poker is aggressive betting, it's imperative that you get a handle on your opponents' betting patterns. Thoughts such as "third time's the adjustment" are helpful in this regard. We also considered the interesting idea that even in cash games, the EV of some plays is something that manifests itself over many hands. Plays that are individually –EV may yield more +EV results in later hands because they may force your opponents to make big mistakes.

Much of the thought process of cash game NL hold'em has been unveiled thus far. Many interesting situations and lines of play haven't been covered, but the examples discussed serve as a solid foundation. In the next chapter, we discuss NL Texas hold'em tournaments. The percentages involving hitting hands remain the same, but some extremely complicated playing dynamics develop because of how tournaments work. The biggest idea is associated with this chapter's discussion of EV developing over many hands. The goal in tournaments is to maximize your expected payout, and to do that, you aren't always going to make moves that maximize your *chip EV.* The *type* of thinking is similar, but the way the thinking is *implemented* is quite different. Before we get to that stuff, here are some problems to review the concepts covered in this chapter.

## Problems

1. You are playing in a four-handed $200NL game with $1–$2 blinds. A hyperaggressive maniac at the table raises almost every hand to $15 preflop. It is a short-handed game, so the blinds are going to eat you up fairly fast. However, with the bad odds you are getting, it is tough to justify calling the raises. What mixture of hands should you consider playing, and why (assume that for the duration of the session, both you and your hyperaggressive friend have at least $200 in front of you)?

2. Your opponent calls raises with a distribution of [AA,22]|||[AK,A2]|||[KQ,K9]|||[QJ,Q9]|||[JT,J9]|||[T9,T8]||| [98,65]. The flop comes 4♣4♥2♥, and your opponent is willing to call bets on paired boards with as little as KQ.

   a. What's your line of play if you raised preflop with AK?

   b. What if you raised with KT instead?

3. You are playing some $100NL with $0.50–$1 blinds online. Dutifully, you are running Poker Tracker and PokerAce HUD. You are in a five-handed game. It folds to the button who has seen 9% of flops and has raised 1% of hands over 200 hands. He raises to $5 and has $25 left. The SB folds and you have KK in the big blind. What do you do?

## Answers to Problems

1. You are going to be sitting and waiting for premium starting hands like [AA,TT] and [AK,AQ]. The exact distribution may vary slightly, but the general idea is to tighten up and to go in with starting hands that leave no ambiguity for what's likely to be very heavy postflop action.

   *Explanation:* Your opponent is overbetting quite a bit. If you call his preflop raises, you are getting just barely better than 1:1 odds. The game is 4-handed, meaning that every 4 hands, you are losing $3 if you fold all 4 hands. After 5 orbits, you lose $15 to the blinds, the same amount that the hyperaggressive player is raising to. You can afford to fold 20 consecutive hands, and in all honesty, you can afford to fold many more. Most players who overbet like this preflop tend to continue like this postflop. If you constrict yourself to just playing [AA,QQ], you will get dealt a hand from this distribution $\frac{18}{1{,}326}$ times. The probability of not getting such a hand in the span of 50 hands is $\left(\frac{1{,}308}{1{,}326}\right)^{50} \approx .50$.

   Now, if you are folding so often, you may not get proper implied odds if your hyperaggressive opponent is observant. Your strategy may be, in fact, to reraise with [AA,TT] and to call with [AK,AQ]. The calls with AK and AQ are tough, because you are relying on implied odds when you hit your top pair. One could assert that playing against this opponent with ace high is +EV, and I would not disagree. You are leaving yourself with very tough decisions on the turn and the river, though. When you are against opponents who are aggressive and bet in proportion to the pot, you are forced to open your game up quite a bit. However, when you are up against aggressive opponents who typically overbet, they are actually giving you an invitation to sit and wait for powerhouse cards.

Note that if you have many buy-ins in your bankroll (at least 50), you can fight fire with fire and reraise with a slightly wider distribution of hands [AA,88]|| [AK,AT]. You can possibly include [KQ] as well. If your opponent reraises most of your reraises all-in, then be prepared to call a good chunk of them (I'd let go of KQ). If your opponent backs down, then you have neutralized his aggression. Tightening up a lot, as suggested in my answer, guarantees that you will eventually take this aggressive player's stack with minimal risk to your bankroll. However, in all honesty, your EV is probably much higher if you play a slightly wider distribution than suggested and play every hand in your distribution very aggressively. The key not to blow a bunch of buy-ins is to test the waters by seeing how your opponent reacts to your first few reraises. His reaction to your first few reraises will dictate whether you compete against his reraises or fold.

2a. Make a $\frac{2}{3}$ pot continuation bet.

*Explanation:* If you raised with AK (assume you don't have a heart), your opponent's distribution is in table 6.7. Out of these combinations, your opponent gives you resistance with 237 hands. If we assume the worst-case scenario where your opponent wins every time he gives you resistance, your EV of a $\frac{2}{3}$ pot continuation bet is $\left(\frac{237}{420}\right)\left(-\frac{2}{3}P\right) + \left(\frac{183}{420}\right)(+P) \approx +.06P$. This is +EV even in the worst-case scenario. The actual scenario is much better because most of

**TABLE 6.7: Distribution of Opponent's Hands for Problem 2a.**

| HAND | COMBINATIONS | HAND | COMBINATIONS |
|---|---|---|---|
| AA | 3 | A♥3♥ | 1 |
| KK | 3 | A2 | 9 |
| QQ | 6 | KQ (no flush draw) | 11 |
| JJ | 6 | K♥Q♥ | 1 |
| TT | 6 | KJ (no flush draw) | 11 |
| 99 | 6 | K♥J♥ | 1 |
| 88 | 6 | KT (no flush draw) | 11 |
| 77 | 6 | K♥T♥ | 1 |
| 66 | 6 | K9 (no flush draw) | 11 |
| 55 | 6 | K♥9♥ | 1 |
| 44 | 1 | QJ (no flush draw) | 15 |
| 33 | 6 | Q♥J♥ | 1 |
| 22 | 3 | QT (no flush draw) | 15 |
| AK (no flush draw) | 8 | Q♥T♥ | 1 |
| A♥K♥ | 1 | Q9 (no flush draw) | 15 |
| AQ (no flush draw) | 11 | Q♥9♥ | 1 |
| A♥Q♥ | 1 | JT (no flush draw) | 15 |
| AJ (no flush draw) | 11 | J♥T♥ | 1 |
| A♥J♥ | 1 | J9 (no flush draw) | 15 |
| AT (no flush draw) | 11 | J♥9♥ | 1 |
| A♥T♥ | 1 | T9 (no flush draw) | 15 |
| A9 (no flush draw) | 11 | T♥9♥ | 1 |
| A♥9♥ | 1 | T8 (no flush draw) | 15 |
| A8 (no flush draw) | 11 | T♥8♥ | 1 |
| A♥8♥ | 1 | 98 (no flush draw) | 15 |
| A7 (no flush draw) | 11 | 9♥8♥ | 1 |
| A♥7♥ | 1 | 87 (no flush draw) | 15 |
| A6 (no flush draw) | 11 | 8♥7♥ | 1 |
| A♥6♥ | 1 | 76 (no flush draw) | 15 |
| A5 (no flush draw) | 11 | 7♥6♥ | 1 |
| A♥5♥ | 1 | 65 (no flush draw) | 15 |
| A4 | 6 | 6♥5♥ | 1 |
| A3 (no flush draw) | 11 | | |

*Total number of combinations = 420*

the time that your opponent calls, he has an ace that you dominate. Of course, play on the turn and the river has to be considered as well. If you are up against someone who calls on the flop with the intention of bluffing, you are justified in playing this pot, as long as you are comfortable with calling with ace high. Of course, if your opponent bluffs disproportionately with respect to the pot, then you might be forced to fold on the turn or the river, meaning that the best action on the flop might be to check. However, against most opponents like the one presented in this problem, the analysis seems to indicate that betting on the flop with your AK is the play of choice.

2b. Do not continuation bet.

*Explanation:* If you raised with KT (you are not holding a heart), your opponent's distribution is in table 6.8.

**TABLE 6.8: Distribution of Opponent's Hands for Problem 2b.**

| HAND | COMBINATIONS | HAND | COMBINATIONS |
|---|---|---|---|
| AA | 6 | A♥3♥ | 1 |
| KK | 3 | A2 | 12 |
| QQ | 6 | KQ (no flush draw) | 11 |
| JJ | 6 | K♥Q♥ | 1 |
| TT | 3 | KJ (no flush draw) | 11 |
| 99 | 6 | K♥J♥ | 1 |
| 88 | 6 | KT (no flush draw) | 8 |
| 77 | 6 | K♥T♥ | 1 |
| 66 | 6 | K9 (no flush draw) | 11 |
| 55 | 6 | K♥9♥ | 1 |
| 44 | 1 | QJ (no flush draw) | 15 |

| HAND | COMBINATIONS | HAND | COMBINATIONS |
|---|---|---|---|
| 33 | 6 | Q♥J♥ | 1 |
| 22 | 3 | QT (no flush draw) | 11 |
| AK (no flush draw) | 11 | Q♥T♥ | 1 |
| A♥K♥ | 1 | Q9 (no flush draw) | 15 |
| AQ (no flush draw) | 15 | Q♥9♥ | 1 |
| A♥Q♥ | 1 | JT (no flush draw) | 11 |
| AJ (no flush draw) | 15 | J♥T♥ | 1 |
| A♥J♥ | 1 | J9 (no flush draw) | 15 |
| AT (no flush draw) | 11 | J♥9♥ | 1 |
| A♥T♥ | 1 | T9 (no flush draw) | 11 |
| A9 (no flush draw) | 15 | T♥9♥ | 1 |
| A♥9♥ | 1 | T8 (no flush draw) | 11 |
| A8 (no flush draw) | 15 | T♥8♥ | 1 |
| A♥8♥ | 1 | 98 (no flush draw) | 15 |
| A7 (no flush draw) | 15 | 9♥8♥ | 1 |
| A♥7♥ | 1 | 87 (no flush draw) | 15 |
| A6 (no flush draw) | 15 | 8♥7♥ | 1 |
| A♥6♥ | 1 | 76 (no flush draw) | 15 |
| A5 (no flush draw) | 15 | 7♥6♥ | 1 |
| A♥5♥ | 1 | 65 (no flush draw) | 15 |
| A4 | 8 | 6♥5♥ | 1 |
| A3 (no flush draw) | 15 | | |

*Total number of combinations = 441*

Now, your opponent gives you resistance with 277 hands. Assuming your opponent always wins when he gives you resistance, your EV for a $\frac{2}{3}$pot continuation bet is $\left(\frac{277}{441}\right)\left(-\frac{2}{3}P\right) + \left(\frac{164}{441}\right)(+P) \approx -.05P$. Of the times that you are called, you are beaten virtually all of them—you are usually drawing to a 6 outer with two cards to come, and sometimes you are drawing to a 3 outer. It seems that the best action here is to check—do not continuation bet here.

Now, if we reverse roles, it seems that giving resistance with ace high on paired boards is the way to go against aggressive opponents. If the betting is proportional to the pot, I sometimes call on the flop and then either bet or raise the turn. Other times, I raise immediately on the flop. One problem with raising on the flop is that some players typically assume that you don't have a 4—they'd normally slowplay a 4, and they expect that you would as well (this is why I usually don't slowplay when I actually have trips). This can lead to some tricky dynamics on the turn and the river. The key, as usual, is to know your particular opponents and to deduce the best line of play against each.

3. Fold.

   *Explanation:* There seems to be a small population of online players who "10 table" and have stats like these. If 1% is the true percentage of hands this guy raises with, that means he has 13.26 combinations of cards that he raises with. AA makes 6 combinations, and KK accounts for another 6 combinations. QQ may also be in his raising distribution (with such a small raising percentage, 200 hands is unfortunately not enough to have accurate statistics). Most likely, though, this player is on [AA,KK]. Since you have KK, there are 6 AA combinations and only 3 KK combinations, meaning that two thirds of the time, you are beaten by AA. Situations like these are usually great opportunities for attempting to draw to a set heads-up—your opponent has a huge pocket pair, meaning you should get a lot of money in if you flop your set. Unfortunately, your opponent in this particular hand doesn't have enough money in his stack to give you proper implied odds. Thus, the play here is to fold.

# 7

# TOURNAMENT PLAY

♧♤♢♡

## Introduction

To this point, our discussion has focused on cash game situations. A fair amount of the thought processes that motivated that discussion can be applied to the play of tournament hands. Some of the results derived can also be used. After all, your chances of hitting a flush when you flop a four flush are the same in both cash games and tournament play. Some interesting playing dynamics happen in tournaments as a result of the short-stack poker that is played late in tournaments. In addition, the big question in tournament play is whether optimal play is to optimize your chip EV on every hand. Despite the way that most people think about tournaments, the answer to this question is surprisingly no.

As we advance through this chapter, we'll be looking at the differences between chip EV and *monetary EV* and we'll do some introductory analysis about determining your monetary EV. Play of individual hands is more complicated in cash game poker because the play typically occurs across four rounds of play. In contrast, an individual hand of tournament poker is quite simple, and often inelegant—most of the time, toward the end of a tournament, the small stacks make tournament poker a battle of preflop or flop all-ins. Even though an individual hand of tournament poker is simple, the strategy that determines which simple plays to use is surprisingly complicated; because of all the variables involved, to get a precise analytic grasp of the available plays is extremely difficult. This chapter serves as a beginning to getting such an analytic grasp.

## Chip EV vs. Monetary EV

Tournament poker is about understanding the difference between chip EV and monetary EV. At the beginning of a tournament, you have so many chips with respect to the blinds and you have so many people who will be eliminated, that the best strategy resembles a cash game strategy where you simply look to accumulate chips; however, you will typically only look to risk large quantities of chips in highly favorable situations. Only as the endgame of a tournament approaches will other factors creep in. The nature of hold'em tournaments is that everyone starts with a set number of chips, and as time passes, the blinds increase. As the blinds increase, people become increasingly short stacked relative to the blinds, and eventually, the blinds are high enough so that the average stack at the table is usually less than 20BB. At that point you have reached the condition of "endgame play." Let's take an example tournament hand and examine a few lines of play. Take a look at the hand described in table 7.1 (pp. 250–51).

Your options are to fold, call, or raise. If you call, you'll be left with 810 chips. If the small blind folds and the big blind checks, the pot will be 1,000 chips. If the small blind calls, the pot will be 1,200 chips. Either of those situations is favorable for a bet on the flop—your bet will be between $\frac{2}{3}$ pot and $\frac{4}{5}$ pot. However, what if one of your opponents raises preflop? In that case, you're forced to surrender. By limping with a 3BB stack, you're trying to sell a powerhouse hand, and a raise by one of the blinds indicates one of two things: (1) he has a powerhouse or (2) He knows what you're trying to represent, but he's fairly sure that you don't have it. Either way, you don't want to place yourself in a situation where you have to call 2BB all-in with J6o. Furthermore, your opponents can bet into you on the flop, and you already know from previous chapters that the probability of hitting the flop is something on the order of $\frac{1}{3}$.

Limping with a small stack isn't such a good idea unless you're trapping with AA or possibly KK, and even then, it's not a good move—since this is a pretty well-known trap, why not just go all-in? When you have AA or KK, going all-in here is a great way of disguising your hand. You'll get called by plenty of stuff, meaning that most likely you'll double up. I've played in many tournaments where my opponent has limped with AA, and I have had something like AT in the big blind. If the short stack had pushed all-in, he would have gotten a call. However, since he limped, I knew he had a huge hand, and I simply check-folded when I missed the flop (or even when I hit it).

Well, you do not hold AA or KK—you hold J6o—so let's get back to business. Ignoring the possibility of successfully executing an advanced bluff, you seem to have two possible plays: pushing all-in or folding. In general, this is always your decision at the end of tournaments, unless everyone is still deeply stacked. People push all-in with various hand distributions and call all-ins with various hand distributions. Your job is to figure out these distributions and then to act accordingly. You want to make all-in moves that are +EV, and you want to make calls of all-ins that are also +EV.

**Table 7.1: Sample Hand from a Single-Table Tournament**

**Game:** $100 + $9 Online Single-Table Tournament

**Structure:** Blinds are at 200–400. The payout is 1st: $500; 2nd: $300; 3rd: $200

**Comments:** Online single-table tournament down to 4 players out of an original 10. UTG folds, and it's your turn to act.

| | 1(SB) | 2(BB) | 3 | *4(B)* |
|---|---|---|---|---|
| | XX | XX | XX | J♦6♥ |
| **STACKS** | 3272 | 2092 | 3426 | 1210 |
| **PREFLOP** | b200 | b400 | >-<br>- | |
| **STACKS** | | | | |
| **FLOP** | | | | |
| **STACKS** | | | | |
| **TURN** | | | | |
| **STACKS** | | | | |
| **RIVER** | | | | |
| **HOLE** | | | | |

**Comments:** None.

**Legend:** SB = Small Blind; BB = Big Blind; B = Button; X = Unknown Hole Card; b = Blind or Straddle; > = Beginning of Betting Round Action; < = End of Betting Round Action; - = Fold; d = Action in the Dark; c = Call; r = Raise; E = Exposed Card; M = Main Pot; S = Side Pot; AI = All-In; R = Rake

**POT**

Now, here's where it gets tricky. Except for some talk in chapter 6, I have mostly discussed EV in the context of specific hands. In a specific pot of a tournament, you have an EV corresponding to how many chips you can expect to have at the end of a hand. While looking at this EV will be a part of our analysis, it's imperative to note that individual hand EV is not the bottom line late in tournaments. The EV that ultimately determines your decisions is your monetary EV. The decisions that you make in a tournament are based on achieving a distribution of finishes with the highest EV. EV problems of all types are similar in theory, but the tournament decision process is different from the decision process that occurs in cash games. This is why there are successful tournament players who donate money in cash games and vice versa.* Only a very small percentage of the poker playing population excels at both cash games and tournaments.

To illustrate this difference between chip EV and monetary EV, let's consider a very simple example. Suppose you're in a tournament with five players left. The payout structure is given in table 7.2.

**TABLE 7.2: Hypothetical Tournament Payout**

| FINISH | PRIZE |
|---|---|
| 1st | $65,000 |
| 2nd | $35,000 |
| 3rd | $25,000 |
| 4th | $20,000 |
| 5th | $15,000 |

* Excellent tournament players who bleed money in cash games tend to do so because of grand overbetting that they do preflop and on the flop. These players tend to have less skill in playing the turn and the river.

It is your turn to act. You have 5BB, and you face a decision where you can either fold or push all-in. The all-in move is –EV with respect to chips. Table 7.3 gives your chances of finishing in each place if you fold and if you push all-in.

**TABLE 7.3: Hypothetical Distributions of Finishes for When You Push or Fold**

| FINISH | ALL-IN | FOLD |
|---|---|---|
| 1st | .15 | .05 |
| 2nd | .1 | .05 |
| 3rd | .05 | .3 |
| 4th | .05 | .35 |
| 5th | .65 | .25 |

If you go all-in, your expected payout is given by equation 7.1.

$$(.15)(\$65{,}000) + (.1)(\$35{,}000) + (.05)(\$25{,}000) + (.05)(\$20{,}000) + (.65)(\$15{,}000) = \$25{,}250. \tag{7.1}$$

If you fold, your expected payout is given by equation 7.2.

$$(.05)(\$65{,}000) + (.05)(\$35{,}000) + (.3)(\$25{,}000) + (.35)(\$20{,}000) + (.25)(\$15{,}000) = \$23{,}250 \tag{7.2}$$

This calculation shows that even though pushing all-in is –EV with respect to chips, it's actually +EV with respect to money (+$2000 to be exact). Because of the top-heavy payout schedules in most tournaments, this situation is com-

---

Excellent cash game players who don't fare well in tournaments tend to struggle in tournaments because they fail to put their foot on the gas late in tournaments.

mon, and the willingness to be aggressive in these types of situations is what separates top tournament players from everyone else. Chip EV and monetary EV are two separate issues, and since our goal in poker is to maximize our winnings (money), what is ultimately important in tournament poker is maximizing monetary EV. There's sometimes correlation between the two types of EV, but there are also times where there isn't.

Now that we're clear on your goal of maximizing monetary EV in tournament situations, let's further examine the decision of pushing or folding your J6o (recall the hand in table 7.1). Let's first explore what happens if you push. You have just over 3BB. In this situation, players in the BB with very large stacks may call an all-in with any two cards. However, in this particular circumstance, the BB has slightly over 4BB left if he folds. If you push all-in, and he calls and loses, he is down to 2BB, which isn't a powerful position to be in. Most likely, he is waiting for cards, even though he's not going to be overly tight unless he's really trying just to make the money. The SB is richer, but he's in a similar mode. In this circumstance, if your all-in gets one caller, he'll have something like [AA,22]|||[AK,A2]|||[KQ]. If both players call, the second caller most likely has [QQ,AA]. Players are aware that pushing all-in here is a standard bluff, so some players may call with a wider distribution. At the same time, most of the advantages that a player has preflop range from 60:40 to 65:35. If a player has a medium stack (6BB–15BB), he may not want to risk a chunk of it on what may be a 60:40 proposition. Thus, the calling distribution may be narrower. Other players may eliminate the lower pocket pairs but introduce hands like [KJ] and [QJ] to the mix.

What's important is that we're at least going through the process of thinking about what our opponents will do before they even do it. I've said it before, and I'll say it many more times: your optimal action is a function of how *your* opponents play—not the ones I make up based on my perceived averages of my experiences. I can't give some magical strategy that'll work against all foes. What I can give you are the tools that'll enable you to dissect your foes and find out how to beat them for yourself.

We now know the possibilities of what happens after you push all-in. First, both blinds can fold, and you can steal the blinds. Second, you get one caller, and you know what distribution of hands he has when he calls. Third, both opponents call, and again, you know what distributions they have. Having put your opponents on calling distributions, you can calculate the probability that they fold, and using Poker Stove, you can also calculate the probability that you win the hand, given that you get one or two callers.

The probability that your opponents fold is equal to the probability that your first opponent folds times that probability that your second opponent folds. We know both opponents are calling with [AA,22]|||[AK,A2]|||[KQ]. The probability that your first opponent folds is $\frac{1{,}040}{1{,}326}$. The probability that your second opponent folds isn't the same (recall the idea of independence). In earlier chapters, I made a blanket claim stating that using an independence approximation doesn't introduce a lot of error. However, blanket claims aren't really sufficient. So, one important issue is determining whether the error introduced by using an independence approximation is significant.

Another issue similar to the independence issue is that if we know the folding distributions of players acting before us, we can adjust to the expected number of combinations for each starting hand for the remaining players. As an extreme example, suppose you are the small blind and everyone at your table who acts before you only plays [AA]|||[AK,A2]. When your opponents fold, you know that they do not have an ace. If you get eight players like this folding in front of you, that means that out of the 16 cards in the muck, none of them is an ace. Now, if you do not have an ace either, that means that there are a total of 18 known non-aces. Ignoring this knowledge, and assuming that there are 50 cards left in the deck, the probability of the BB not having an ace is $\left(\frac{46}{50}\right)\left(\frac{45}{49}\right) \approx .84$. Accounting for the 18 non-aces, the probability of your opponent not having an ace drops down to $\left(\frac{30}{34}\right)\left(\frac{29}{33}\right) \approx .78$. This knowledge has a noticeable impact on the probability of running into an ace, and this effect is called *clumping.*

Tournament endgame analysis and a lot of other poker analysis, such as the profitability of stealing blinds in cash games, would be much easier if clumping could be ignored—especially since most of the time, the clumping analysis is much more complicated than the example I give here. Imagine if you had to account for clumping by considering folding distributions like [AA,88]|||[AK,A9]|||[KQ,KJ]|||[QJ] for nine players in front of you—not fun! If your opponents will be on distributions wider than [AA]|||[AK,A2], there's a chance that we can make a reasonable approximation to actual playing conditions by ignoring clumping.

One final consideration to make analysis simpler is to see how much overcalling matters. Having to do separate calculations for when you get 1, 2, 3, or 4 callers can get quite tedious. If the number of times that you receive 3 or more callers is rare enough, we can simply ignore them. Before we can go any further with our analysis of the J6o push, we must address independence, clumping, and overcalling.*

* Credit goes to Ryan Patterson who performed all the simulations whose results I refer to in this chapter. Without the computing power available to him, I don't know how I would have gotten these results!

## Independence

To test whether assuming independence introduces big errors, simulations consisting of 1 billion hands each were run. For each simulation, I assumed that I was the first player to act, and I assigned a calling distribution for the players remaining behind me. I found out the probability of not running into a hand from each distribution as a function of the number of players remaining to act. The distributions used for each of the simulations are in table 7.4.

**TABLE 7.4: Opponent's Calling Distributions for Each Independence Simulation**

| | CALLING DISTRIBUTION |
|---|---|
| Distribution #1 | [AA,JJ] |
| Distribution #2 | [AA,22] |
| Distribution #3 | [AK]\|\|[QJ]\|\|[T9]\|\|[87]\|\|[65]\|\|[43]\|\|[22] |
| Distribution #4 | [AA,88]\|\|[AK,AT] |
| Distribution #5 | [AA,22]\|\|[AK,A2]\|\|[KQ,KT]\|\|[QJ,QT]\|\|[JT]\|\|[98s,65s] |

Some of these distributions, especially Distribution 3, aren't realistic calling distributions. The point here is to test the mathematical validity of the independence approximation, though. By showing that it's valid to use the independence approximation for a wide range of calling distribution, you're more likely to find that such an approximation is actually valid for most, if not all, calling distributions.

In each of the five independence simulations, the error in the probabilities was on the order of ten-thousandths. Everything we've been doing in this book has been to hundredths, so essentially the numbers I obtained in these simulations are exact.

The data analysis I did was as follows: I took the probabilities from the simulations and I compared them to the numbers you get by taking the probability of one player folding and raising it to the power of the number of players remaining behind. For example, if you hold 22 and you have one opponent, the probability that he will fold if he calls with Distribution #1 is .980. If you have two opponents, the probability that they both fold from the simulation is .961. If you take .980 and square it (the independence approximation), you get .960. The difference between the independence approximation and the result for the simulation is .001 in this case.

I looked at the highest changes as a function of the number of players for each simulation (note that as the number of players remaining increased, so did the difference between the simulation results and the independence approximation). For Distribution #1, the highest error was .005; for Distribution #2, the highest error was .005; for Distribution #3, the highest error was .005; for Distribution #4, the highest error was .022; and for Distribution #5, the highest error was .021. For Distributions #4 and #5, errors on the order of .01 were encountered beginning with about four players to act behind.

These results are encouraging for the validity of using independence approximations. The error incurred by assuming independence was found to be small for a wide range of calling distributions. The errors that were noticeable were just barely so, and for the distributions tested, errors were meaningless until there were three to four players remaining behind. Based on the results of these simulations, I'm going to assume independence when doing any further analysis. Using independence is much better than wading through tons of tables of data (I've done that work for you so that you don't have to!).

## Clumping

The first approximation, independence, has been validated. Let's now examine the impact of clumping. Players are more apt to play good cards. Thus, if there are ten players at a table and the first eight players have folded, that means that none of those players had good hands. Since none of those players had good hands, it's more probable that the remaining player has good cards. To test how much more probable it is that the remaining player has good cards, I again ran simulations consisting of 1 billion hands each.

I assigned folding distributions to the players in front of you, and as a function of the number of players who folded in front of you, I found the probabilities of hands existing behind you as a function of players remaining to act. I ran simulations for all numbers of players in front and players behind (for all table sizes). However, the case for which clumping has the largest effect is the time that you're at a 10-handed table, you're the SB, and all 8 players have folded in front of you. If the probability of the BB having a playable hand isn't much different than when you don't consider this information, we can ignore clumping.

The distributions of hands that players before you enter the pot with are summarized in table 7.5 (p. 260). The distribution, [None], means that the players in front of you fold no matter what. In terms of information, this is equivalent to when you are the first to act and no one else has done anything yet. The folding distributions are the complements of the playing distributions. The calling distributions for play-

**TABLE 7.5: Playing Distributions for Players Who Act Before You in the Clumping Simulations**

| | CALLING DISTRIBUTION |
|---|---|
| Distribution #1 | [AA,77] \|\| [AK,A9] \|\| [KQ] |
| Distribution #2 | [AA,22] \|\| [AK,A2] \|\| [KQ,KT] \|\| [QJ,QT] |
| Distribution #3 | [AA,22] \|\| [AK,A2] \|\| [KQ,KT] \|\| [QJ,65] \|\| [QT] |
| Distribution #4 | [None] |

ers behind you, given that you push all-in, are given in table 7.6.

**TABLE 7.6: Calling Distributions for Players Behind You After You Push All-In in the Clumping Simulations**

| | CALLING DISTRIBUTION |
|---|---|
| First Caller | [AA,22] \|\| [AK,A2] \|\| [KQ] |
| Second Caller | [AA,QQ] |
| Third Caller | [AA] |
| Fourth Caller | [AA] |

The analysis here is to look for substantial differences between Distributions 1-3 and Distribution #4 (table 7.5). If clumping isn't a significant effect, we shouldn't see much difference.

In the simulations, the folding percentages were found with the error being in the thousandths place, meaning that my numbers are good to the hundredths place. For Distribution #1, clumping decreased the probability of folding by .01 in the best case and .02 in the worst case. For Distribution #2, clumping decreased the probability of folding by .04 in the best case and .07 in the worst case. For Distribution #3, clumping decreased the probability of folding by .04 in the best case and .07 in the worst case. These results are trouble for ignoring clumping—Distributions #2 and #3 are representative of the types of distributions that players in front of you will be playing. Unfortunately, I can't give you a separate table of results for every combination of playing distributions the players in front of you have. The next best thing, then, is to analyze the error as a function of folders in front of you so that you can ignore clumping at first and then make an appropriate correction after. Approximate clumping corrections based on my simulation data are in table 7.7.

Keep in mind that the adjustments in table 7.7 are simply estimates that I've come up with based on the minimum and maximum deviations from my simulations. I'm not proclaiming these to be exact; I'm just proclaiming them as being potentially helpful in simplifying tournament endgame analysis since you won't have access to networks of computers to do simulations for you on the spot. One thing I will note is that for narrower playing distributions, the data from my simulations indicate that you want to use corrections on the lower end of my suggested ranges. Meanwhile, wide playing distributions will necessitate using corrections on the upper end of my suggested ranges. What's most important is that we can initially ignore clumping as long as we provide an appropriate correction to your fold equity based on the number of opponents who folded in front of you.

## Overcallers

So far, we've addressed independence and clumping. The final issue we need to address is accounting for instances where

**TABLE 7.7: Clumping Errors as a Function of the Number of Folders in Front of You**

| FOLDERS | DIST. #1 MIN. | DIST. #1 MAX. | DIST. #2 MIN. |
|---|---|---|---|
| 1 | 0 | 0 | 0 |
| 2 | 0 | .01 | .01 |
| 3 | 0 | .01 | .01 |
| 4 | .01 | .01 | .01 |
| 5 | .01 | .01 | .02 |
| 6 | .01 | .02 | .02 |
| 7 | .01 | .02 | .03 |
| 8 | .01 | .02 | .04 |

you get more than one caller. In general, your chip EV is equal to the following qualitative expression:

Chip EV = (P(All Fold))(Chips Won) +
(P(One Caller))(P(Win If One Caller))(Chips Won) –
(P(One Caller))(P(Lose If One Caller))(Chips Lost) +
(P(Two Callers))(P(Win If Two Callers))(Chips Won) –
(P(Two Callers))(P(Lost If Two Callers))(Chips Lost) +
(P(Three Callers))(P(Win If Three Callers))(Chips Won) –
(P(Three Callers))(P(Lose If Three Callers))(Chips Lost) . . .

Eliminating terms from this expression would be convenient. To do that, we need to find out at what point the number of *overcallers* is negligible. To test the worst-case scenario with respect to debunking the validity of approximating, I ran a simulation that had somewhat wide overcalling distributions. The calling and overcalling distributions are in table 7.8.

| DIST. #2 MAX. | DIST. #3 MIN. | DIST. #3 MAX. | APPROX. ADJUSTMENT |
|---|---|---|---|
| .01 | 0 | .01 | ≈.00–.01 |
| .01 | .01 | .01 | ≈.01 |
| .02 | .01 | .02 | ≈.01–.02 |
| .03 | .01 | .03 | ≈.01–.03 |
| .04 | .02 | .04 | ≈.01–.03 |
| .05 | .02 | .05 | ≈.02–.04 |
| .06 | .03 | .06 | ≈.02–.05 |
| .07 | .04 | .07 | ≈.02–.06 |

**TABLE 7.8: Calling Distributions for Players Behind You in the Overcalling Simulations**

| | |
|---|---|
| First Caller | [AA,22] \|\| [AK,A2] \|\| [KQ] |
| Second Caller | [AA,JJ] \|\| [AK,AQ] |
| Third Caller | [AA,QQ] |
| Fourth Caller | [AA,KK] |
| Fifth Caller | [AA] |
| Sixth Caller | [AA] |

The important simulation with respect to overcallers is the case where you have the most players remaining to act behind you. Thus, to test the validity of when to ignore *overcallers*, I used the simulation for which you are UTG at a ten-handed table—you are pushing all-in with 9 players remaining to act. The probabilities of getting 0, 1, 2, 3, 4, 5, or 6 callers were found as a function of your starting hand. The minimum and maximum probabilities are in table 7.9 (p. 264).

**TABLE 7.9: Probabilities of Getting 0–6 Callers When Players Are on the Distributions Defined in Table 7.8 and There Are 9 Players to Act Behind You**

| NUMBER OF CALLERS | MIN. PROBABILITY | MAX. PROBABILITY |
|---|---|---|
| 0 | 0.07 | 0.19 |
| 1 | 0.71 | 0.77 |
| 2 | 0.1 | 0.19 |
| 3 | 0 | 0.01 |
| 4 | 0 | 0 |
| 5 | 0 | 0 |
| 6 | 0 | 0 |

From table 7.9, we see that we can ignore instances where 3 or more players call your all-in; the probabilities are so small that those cases have a very small impact on the chip EV of an all-in.

## Approximations Taken Care of . . . Let's Take Care of Business

We've addressed independence, clumping, and overcallers. With all of that squared away, we can now resume figuring out your expected tournament payouts for the hand described in table 7.1. Four players remain in the tournament, and there's some probability distribution governing your expected finish. For every decision you make, there's a $P(1^{st})$, $P(2^{nd})$, $P(3^{rd})$, and $P(4^{th})$. Your EV is given by equation 7.3.

$$P(1st)(\$500) + P(2nd)(\$300) + P(3rd)(\$200) + P(4th)(\$0) \qquad (7.3)$$

To figure out your expected payout, all we need to do is calculate P(1st), P(2nd), P(3rd), and P(4th)! The general theoretical framework looks very elegant when expressed like this, and when it comes down to it, filling in equations such as equation 7.3 is all there is to optimal decision making in tournament poker. Unfortunately, figuring out the probability distribution of finishes is *damn* tough (years of frustration are expressed in that italicized damn). Extreme difficulties arise with just four players left—imagine trying to get a precise handle on things in a multi-table tournament where there are twenty players left! As someone who likes to be theoretically rigorous, I find this is the most downright frustrating aspect of tournament poker.

We can't do much else at this point, so let's examine the outcomes when you push all-in. Assume your opponents are on the calling distributions in table 7.10.

**TABLE 7.10: Calling Distributions for Players Behind You After You Push All-in**

| CALLER | DISTRIBUTION | COMBINATIONS, GIVEN YOU HOLD J6O |
|---|---|---|
| First Caller | [AA,22]\|\|[AK,A2]\|\|[KQ] | 272 |
| Second Caller | [AA,QQ] | 18 |
| Third Caller | [AA] | 6 |
| Fourth Caller | [AA] | 6 |

There are 50 cards left in the deck after accounting for your J6o, meaning that there are 1,225 total available hole-card combinations for your opponents. The probability of everyone folding is $\left(\frac{953}{1,225}\right)^2 \approx .61$. The probability of getting one caller is $\left(\frac{953}{1,225}\right)\left(\frac{272}{1,225}\right) + \left(\frac{272}{1,225}\right)\left(\frac{1,207}{1,225}\right) \approx .39$. The probability of getting two callers is negligible (less than .01). Table 7.11 gives your outcome space with respect to your stack (winning, tying, and losing probabilities in each scenario were found with Poker Stove):

**TABLE 7.11: Outcome Space for When You Push All-In**

| STACK SIZE | PROBABILITY |
|---|---|
| 1,810 (everyone folds) | .61 |
| 2,620 (You win against P2) | (.172)(.33) ≈ .06 |
| 2,820 (You win against P1) | (.219)(.33) ≈ .07 |
| 1,310 (You tie against P2) | (.172)(.01) ≈ .00 |
| 1,410 (You tie against P1) | (.219)(.01) ≈ .00 |
| 0 (You lose when you get called) | (.172)(.66) + (.219)(.66) = .26 |

Your chip EV is (.61)(1,810) + (.06)(2,620) + (.07)(2,820) = 1,459. Not only is this move +EV with respect to chips, but perhaps more importantly, you have chips .61 + .06 + .07 = .74 times—you will still be in the tournament about three fourths of the time.

What happens if you fold this hand and push all-in on the next hand no matter what two cards you get? We don't know what P1 and P2 will do if you fold, but let's just assume that the stacks are about the same. Instead of pushing all-in with 2 players remaining, you are now pushing all-in with 3 players remaining. Again, assume that all players behind you are on the calling distributions outlines in table 7.10. The probability that all 3 players fold is $\left(\frac{953}{1,225}\right)^3 \approx .471$. The probability that you get one caller is $\left(\frac{272}{1,225}\right)\left(\frac{1,207}{1,225}\right)\left(\frac{1,207}{1,225}\right) + \left(\frac{953}{1,225}\right)\left(\frac{272}{1,225}\right)\left(\frac{1,207}{1,225}\right) + \left(\frac{953}{1,225}\right)\left(\frac{953}{1,225}\right)\left(\frac{272}{1,225}\right) \approx .52$. The probability that you get 2 callers is the leftover .01. The outcome space for when you push all-in is given in table 7.12 (cases with 2 or more callers are ignored to simplify the calculation, and winning, tying, and losing probabilities in each scenario were found with Poker Stove):

**TABLE 7.12: Outcome Space for When You Push All-In into 3 Opponents with a Random Hand**

| STACK SIZE | PROBABILITY |
|---|---|
| 1,810 (everyone folds) | .47 |
| 2,620 (You win against P3) | (.13)(.36) ≈ .05 |
| 2,820 (You win against P2) | (.17)(.36) ≈ .06 |
| 3,020 (You win against P1) | (.22)(.36) ≈ .08 |
| 1,310 (You tie against P3) | (.13)(.02) ≈ .00 |
| 1,410 (You tie against P2) | (.17)(.02) ≈ .00 |
| 1,510 (You tie against P1) | (.22)(.02) ≈ .00 |
| 0 (You lose when you get called) | (.52)(.62) ≈ .32 |

Your EV is (.47)(1,810)+(.05)(2,620)+(.06)(2,820)+(.08)(3,020) ≈ 1,393. Like the push from the button with J6o, this move is +EV with respect to chips; however, it isn't quite as high. Furthermore, you only have chips .47 + .05 + .06 + .08 = .66 times—the probability that you are still in the tournament after making this move is .08 less than the probability that you are in the tournament when you push from the button with J6o.

Against opponents on the [AA,22]|||[AK,A2]|||[KQ] calling distribution, your best move is to push from the button with the J6o. In general, when your opponents are sufficiently tight, most of your EV comes from your fold equity, meaning that your best move is opening by pushing all-in when in as late position as possible. If your opponents are not sufficiently tight, more of your EV comes from actually winning hands, meaning that you need to be waiting for pocket pairs, AX, and KX. In the next section, we'll see that being handicapped by cards is undesirable because of the winning and tying probabilities associated with all-in preflop matchups.

## Preflop All-In Matchup Probabilities and the Importance of Being the Aggressor

The tournament poker endgame is mostly about hands where players get all-in preflop. Preflop all-ins happen in cash games as well, but not nearly as often, which is why I have waited until now for this analysis. We will find some potentially surprising results that will motivate us to say that aggression is the path to walk in the tournament endgame.

There are 169 possible starting hands, meaning that there are 169•169 = 28,561 possible heads-up all-in matchups. Memorizing P(win), P(lose), and P(tie) for all these combinations is infeasible. We need a classification scheme so that we can consider representative hands whose results we can refer to for estimates of all matchups. The first order of classification is to separate matchups involving pocket pairs from matchups not involving pocket pairs. For the matchups not involving pocket pairs, there are cases where there is no *domination* and cases where there is domination (domination occurs when one rank is common in both hands—for example, AK dominates over AQ because an ace is no good for AQ). In the cases of no domination, there are a few different scenarios.

Let's start with the pocket pair scenarios. One scenario is to have a pocket pair against a pocket pair. Table 7.13 (opposite, top) shows results from a few representative matchups.

Table 7.13 suggests that an overpair wins the hand approximately 80% of the time—the odds against the underpair winning are approximately 4:1. Another scenario is to

**TABLE 7.13: Pocket Pair vs. Pocket Pair**

| HAND 1 | HAND 2 | P(1 WIN) | P(1 LOSE) | P(TIE) |
|---|---|---|---|---|
| AA | KK | .8171 | .1782 | .0046 |
| AA | QQ | .8133 | .1824 | .0044 |
| AA | 77 | .8031 | .1935 | .0034 |
| AA | 22 | .8195 | .1751 | .0054 |
| 33 | 22 | .7794 | .1708 | .0498 |

have a pocket pair against unpaired cards, both of which are lower in rank than the rank of the pocket pair. Table 7.14 shows results from a few representative matchups:

**TABLE 7.14: Pocket Pair vs. Two Unpaired Undercards**

| HAND 1 | HAND 2 | P(1 WIN) | P(1 LOSE) | P(TIE) |
|---|---|---|---|---|
| AA | KQo | .8692 | .1268 | .0040 |
| AA | KQs | .8273 | .1686 | .0042 |
| AA | 76o | .8116 | .1850 | .0034 |
| AA | 76s | .7734 | .2229 | .0036 |
| AA | 86o | .8248 | .1719 | .0034 |
| AA | 86s | .7858 | .2106 | .0036 |
| AA | K3o | .8863 | .1092 | .0044 |
| AA | K3s | .8435 | .1521 | .0044 |
| AA | 94o | .8755 | .1205 | .0040 |
| AA | 94s | .8334 | .1625 | .0040 |

Table 7.14 shows that P(1 win) varies depending on the type of undercards held. Suited undercards reduce P(1 win) by approximately .04. This .04 difference corresponds to the probability of hitting a flush with five cards to come. There isn't a substantial difference between connected cards and

1-gaps, but cards with no connectivity fare badly in comparison to connectors and 1-gaps. A good way of summarizing table 7.14 is that P(1 win) ranges from about .77 (when the pair is against suited, connected cards) to about .88 (when the pair is against unconnected, unsuited cards).

Next we have a pocket pair facing unpaired cards so that there is only one overcard. Table 7.15 shows the results of some representative calculations:

**TABLE 7.15: Pocket Pair vs. One Overcard**

| HAND 1 | HAND 2 | P(1 WIN) | P(1 LOSE) | P(TIE) |
|---|---|---|---|---|
| KK | AT | .6991 | .2969 | .0040 |
| TT | AT | .6706 | .3077 | .0216 |
| 77 | J3 | .6933 | .2995 | .0072 |
| 33 | A2 | .6764 | .3170 | .0066 |

Table 7.15 shows that domination doesn't have much of an effect. Whenever a pocket pair faces one overcard, the pocket pair will win just under 70 percent of the time.

The final case to consider is the proverbial "coin flip," a pocket pair against two overcards. Table 7.16 (opposite, top) displays some representative numbers.

Table 7.16 shows that the coin-flip situation is generally one where the pocket pair wins with a probability of about .55. When against suited cards, the probability of the pocket pair winning decreases to about .52 or .53. The one interesting case is a time where the overcards are connected. Table 7.16 shows that JT is actually a very slight favorite over an underpair such as 55, where all the straights are still available for JT. If we consider JTs specifically, the probability that JTs wins or ties against 55 is actually about .52. The rule for

**TABLE 7.16: Pocket Pair vs. Two Overcards**

| HAND 1 | HAND 2 | P(1 WIN) | P(1 LOSE) | P(TIE) |
|---|---|---|---|---|
| QQ | AK | .5584 | .4373 | .0042 |
| 88 | AK | .5430 | .4532 | .0038 |
| 55 | JT | .4901 | .5022 | .0072 |
| 55 | JTs | .4728 | .5193 | .0072 |
| 55 | A8 | .5436 | .4519 | .0044 |

the pocket pair versus two overcards scenario seems to be to assume that the pocket pair wins about .55 times, unless the overpair is a suited connector, in which case, the scales tip and the suited connector becomes a slight favorite.

We've covered all the pocket pair scenarios. Table 7.17 summarizes the results obtained so far:

**TABLE 7.17: Summary of Pocket Pair Preflop Matchups**

| HAND 1 | HAND 2 | P(HAND 1 WINS) |
|---|---|---|
| Higher Pocket Pair | Lower Pocket Pair | .8 |
| Pocket Pair | Unpaired (Two Undercards) | .77–.88 |
| Pocket Pair | Unpaired (One Overcard) | .7 |
| Pocket Pair | Unpaired (Two Unsuited, Unconnected Overcards) | .55 |
| Pocket Pair | Unpaired (Two Suited, Connected Overcards) | .48 |
| Pocket Pair | Unpaired (Two Unsuited, Connected Overcards) | .50 |

Table 7.17 suggests that calling an all-in with KK if you know your opponent is pushing in with AX is potentially

not as strong a move as pushing all-in from the button with any two cards. If you call an all-in with KK and your opponent has AX, the probability of surviving the all-in is around .68–.70. Meanwhile, pushing all-in from the button against sufficiently tight opponents leaves you with chips with a probability of around .73–.75. Granted, your probability of doubling up with KK is greater; however, you can't afford to sit around several orbits while you wait for hands like [AA,JJ]. The blinds continually hit you in tournaments, and they do nothing but increase, meaning that to succeed in tournaments, you must be willing to make moves without good cards when the opportunity presents itself.

Having summarized the preflop matchups involving pocket pairs, let's proceed to talk about preflop matchups not involving pocket pairs. The first scenario to consider is a hand where the lowest card from one set of hole cards outranks the highest card from the other set of hole cards. Table 7.18 shows the results from some representative hands:

**TABLE 7.18: Two Higher Cards vs. Two Lower Cards**

| HAND 1 | HAND 2 | P(1 WIN) | P(1 LOSE) | P(TIE) |
|---|---|---|---|---|
| AK | QJ | .6411 | .3541 | .0048 |
| AK | 76 | .6142 | .3817 | .0040 |
| AT | 98 | .6240 | .3719 | .0040 |
| AJ | 84 | .6558 | .3396 | .0046 |
| KT | 54 | .6240 | .3689 | .0070 |
| JT | 54 | .6288 | .3593 | .0118 |

Table 7.18 suggests that the higher unpaired cards win with a probability of about .63. The next case to consider is the matchup between hands that have alternating relative

ranks—matchups such as AQ vs. KJ. Table 7.19 shows results for various alternating matchups:

**TABLE 7.19: Alternating Relative Ranks**

| HAND 1 | HAND 2 | P(1 WIN) | P(1 LOSE) | P(TIE) |
|---|---|---|---|---|
| AQ | KJ | .6222 | .3731 | .0048 |
| AQ | K5 | .6375 | .3577 | .0048 |
| KT | Q8 | .6446 | .3488 | .0066 |
| A7 | Q5 | .6282 | .3673 | .0046 |

Table 7.19 suggests that the case of alternating relative ranks is similar to the case of two higher cards vs. two lower cards, with the average probability of the better hand winning being about .63. The last type of matchup between sets of unpaired hole cards occurs when one set of hole cards lies between the ranks of the cards from the better hand. An example of such a matchup is A5 vs. JT. The results from these "tweener" matchups are in Table 7.20:

**TABLE 7.20: Tweener Matchups**

| HAND 1 | HAND 2 | P(1 WIN) | P(1 LOSE) | P(TIE) |
|---|---|---|---|---|
| AT | KQ | .5931 | .4023 | .0046 |
| A5 | JT | .5434 | .4521 | .0046 |
| A2 | 87 | .5419 | .4534 | .0048 |
| T7 | 98 | .5640 | .4167 | .0192 |
| A2 | Q6 | .5835 | .4115 | .0050 |

Table 7.20 shows that the underdog hand in a tweener matchup isn't in quite as bad shape. P(win) for the favored

hand ranges from .54 to .59, with the suited, connected tweeners being in the best shape. For matchups between unpaired hole cards where there's no domination, the hand with the highest hole card generally wins in .63 unless it's a tweener matchup, in which case, the probability of the favored hand winning fluctuates between about .55 and .60, depending on the suitedness and connectivity of the tweener hand.

The final class of matchups to consider is matchups between unpaired hole cards involving domination (hands like AK vs. AQ). The results from some domination matchups are in Table 7.21:

**TABLE 7.21: Domination Matchups Between Sets of Unpaired Hole Cards**

| HAND 1 | HAND 2 | P(1 WIN) | P(1 LOSE) | P(TIE) |
|---|---|---|---|---|
| AK | AT | .7070 | .2476 | .0454 |
| AK | KT | .7271 | .2616 | .0114 |
| A7 | A6 | .4920 | .2354 | .2726 |
| A7 | 76 | .6826 | .2919 | .0254 |
| A7 | 97 | .6917 | .2863 | .0220 |
| AQ | KQ | .7319 | .2568 | .0114 |
| A2 | 82 | .7321 | .2514 | .0164 |

Table 7.21 suggests that in most cases, the dominating hand will win with a probability of about .7. This breaks down in cases such as the A7 vs. A6 matchup, where P(tie) is really high because of the probability of the low hole cards from each hand not playing.

By breaking the various matchup types into groups, we were able to accomplish some very meaningful analysis relating to preflop all-in matchups. The winning percentages associated with these matchups are vital to your decision-making process when considering calling an all-in. Table 7.22 summarizes the results from all the preflop all-in analysis:

**TABLE 7.22: Summary of Preflop All-In Analysis**

| HAND 1 | HAND 2 | P(HAND 1 WINS) |
|---|---|---|
| Higher Pocket Pair | Lower Pocket Pair | .8 |
| Pocket Pair | Unpaired (Two Undercards) | .77–.88 |
| Pocket Pair | Unpaired (One Overcard) | .7 |
| Pocket Pair | Unpaired (Two Unsuited, Unconnected Overcards) | .55 |
| Pocket Pair | Unpaired (Two Suited, Connected Overcards) | .48 |
| Pocket Pair | Unpaired (Two Unsuited, Connected Overcards) | .50 |
| Unpaired | Unpaired (nontweener, nondominated) | .63 |
| Unpaired | Unpaired (tweener, nondominated) | .55–.60 |
| Unpaired | Unpaired (dominated) | Usually .7 |

Besides simply knowing these probabilities for making calling decisions, knowing these probabilities and weighing them versus the survival probabilities associated with pushing all-in is vital to any successful tournament strategy. As discussed, the aggressor has a distinct advantage against tight opponents because P(win) for even most of the premium hands is usually no more than about .7.

## Chapter Summary and Preview of What's to Come

We began this chapter by talking about the difference between chip EV and monetary EV. The difference between these two EVs is an extension of the more general notion that it's possible for EV in poker games to transcend the play of multiple hands. Understanding that optimizing tournament play equates to optimizing monetary EV, we studied the general theory that should govern our tournament decisions—our tournament decisions should yield the distribution of finishes {P(1st), P(2nd), P(3rd) . . . } that yield the highest monetary EV. Determining that having a precise handle on the distribution of finishes is exceedingly difficult, we discovered some ways of doing some individual hand analysis.

The precise way to do hand analysis is to use hand simulators. However, large-scale hand simulations take up substantial computational resources. Given that, we discussed some corrections and approximations to assist in our analysis of all-in pushes. In particular, we talked about the validity of assuming independence with a small number of players remaining to act behind and clumping corrections. With these ideas in place, we calculated the chip EV of pushing all-in against opponents on specific calling distributions. We also discussed the idea of comparing survival probabilities versus comparing chips EVs as a way of evaluating the best line of play.

To conclude this chapter, we looked at the winning, tying, and losing probabilities associated with preflop all-in matchups by breaking the matchups into a few classes. This analysis showed that AA is the only really powerful all-in hand because it will never be against overcards. All the other premium paired and unpaired hole cards have some vulnerability, and in general, when you are called and you are a favorite to win a hand, your P(win) will be somewhere in the .55–.70 range. Because of the high fold equity associated with tight opponents, we determined that the best line of play against tight opponents is to push all-in aggressively from the SB, B, or CO provided that no one else has yet to enter the pot.

In the next chapter, we wrap things up by discussing a few random topics that didn't really fit in smoothly with the material presented thus far. Before concluding this journey into highly analytic NL hold'em, here are some problems to tackle. These are the last problems in the book, so make sure you do a thorough job!

## Problems

1. You are at the final table of a large multi-table tournament. The buy-in was $500 + $45, and the prize distribution is in Table 7.23:

**TABLE 7.23: Prize Distribution for Problem 1**

| FINISH | PRIZE |
|---|---|
| 1 | $150,000 |
| 2 | $100,000 |
| 3 | $75,000 |
| 4 | $50,000 |
| 5 | $35,000 |
| 6 | $30,000 |
| 7 | $25,000 |
| 8 | $20,000 |
| 9 | $15,000 |
| 10 | $10,000 |

You are currently the button, and the stacks are in Table 7.24:

**TABLE 7.24: Stack Sizes for Problem 1**

| PLAYER | STACK |
|---|---|
| SB | $15,000 |
| BB | $50,000 |
| 3 | $35,000 |
| 4 | $125,000 |
| 5 | $500,000 |
| 6 | $200,000 |
| 7 | $100,000 |
| 8 | $300,000 |
| CO | $75,000 |
| Button (You) | $125,000 |

The blinds are $3,000–$6,000, and the table is discussing a deal. What kind of deal might you be interested in, and what factors might influence your decision? Justify.

2. You are 1 of 3 remaining players in a tournament, and you are the button. Assume that everybody starts the hand with 8,000 chips and blinds are at 1,000–2,000. You are dealt 23o.

   a. Calculate the chip EV of an all-in push and evaluate P(survival) if your opponents call with [AA,55]||[AK,A5]. If the SB calls, assume that the BB only calls with [AA,KK]

   b. Calculate the chip EV of an all-in push and evaluate P(survival) if the SB calls with [AA,55]||[AK,A5] and the BB calls with [AA,22]|||[AK,A2]|||[KQ,K2]||| [QJ,QT]|||[JT]. If the SB calls, assume that the BB only calls with [AA,JJ]|||[AK].

## Answers to Problems

1. No concrete answer; read the explanation for things to think about when making deals.

   *Explanation:* Theoretically, the deal that you should take is one where the amount of money that you get is equal to or greater than your monetary EV. You are at a ten-handed table with some relatively deep stacks, meaning that figuring out your distribution of finishes in any precise way is pretty much impossible. Many factors will affect your distribution of finishes; let's discuss a few of them.

   Since there are still deep stacks in the tournament, one important factor is your playing skill relative to your opponents. This is where it's vitally important for you to stick to the Killer Poker credo of being honest with yourself. Suppose all deep stacks at the table are better than you are. There are 4 big stacks, meaning that your most likely finishes are probably going to be in the 4–8 range. The SB only has $15,000 left, meaning that he'll be out very soon. There are a few other short stacks, and there's a good chance that at least one of them will be knocked out before you are in danger of being eliminated. Looking at the prize distribution, you should probably be willing to take any deal where you get at least $30,000.

   Take the opposite scenario, where you are a better player than the other deep stacks. The other deep stacks have a chip advantage over you; however, you still have a pretty good chance of snagging 2nd or even 1st. At this point, you may want to assign an even distribution to finishing anywhere from 8th to 1st. Your monetary EV for an even finishing distribution from 1st to 8th is given by equation 7.4.

$$(.125)(\$20{,}000) + (.125)(\$25{,}000) + (.125)(\$30{,}000) + (.125)(\$35{,}000) + (.125)(\$50{,}000) + (.125)(\$75{,}000) + (.125)(\$100{,}000) + (.125)(\$150{,}000) = \$60{,}625 \quad (7.4)$$

Thus, if you're the most skilled among the deep stacks, you shouldn't settle for a deal unless you get at least $60,625. This relative skill level is probably the most difficult concept to adjust for analytically, but it's important to be aware of it and to consider somehow if you're at a final table establishing a deal.

This doesn't seem like much of a factor in this decision, but another factor to consider when making a deal is players who are about to be eliminated. By simply refusing to make a deal until a player is eliminated, you automatically make more money if last place is among the most prevalent in your distribution. P(10th) is pretty low here, though, so there's not really a reason to hold off on making a deal, especially if you're worried about getting outplayed by the other deep stacks. However, if you have about $60,000 chips, you may wish to wait for SB's eventual all-in before consenting to a deal, unless the table somehow offers you a really good deal that you may not get once it's down to nine handed.

The next factor in making your deal is factoring in whether your opponents are risk averse. If your opponents, especially the deep-stacked ones, are risk averse, you'll be able to convince them to take less money than they're entitled to. Risk-averse players are willing to take what's guaranteed, even if it's less than their theoretical EV. At a table with a risk-averse big stack, negotiating a tough deal as a small stack is great. In this particular situation, you aren't small stacked; however, if the $500K and $300K stacks seem like they don't want to risk an 8th or 7th place finish, you may be able to get a deal going where the $500K stack takes $110K, the $300K stack takes $90K, and the remaining $260K is distributed among the other eight players. Given that you're tied for 4th in chips, you might be able to get a deal where you squeeze out $60K, which was your hypothesized EV if you had a theoretical uniform distribution of finishes from 1st to 8th. The key concept against risk-averse big stacks is that if you're a small or medium stack and you happen to know your monetary EV precisely, you'll always get a deal where you make more money than your monetary EV for playing out the tournament.

I've outlined a few factors that should be accounted for when in a deal-making scenario. The theoretical idea of deducing a distribution of finishes and using it to compute your monetary EV is very straightforward. The intricate part, and the part which may not be feasible at all except for short-handed, short-stacked scenarios, is actually deducing the distribution of finishes. The ideas presented in this solution are some ideas that are helpful in both establishing your monetary EV and getting deals where you make more money than your monetary EV.

2a. Chip EV = 8,990 and P(survival) ≈ .77.

*Explanation:* Your opponents have 10 pocket pairs

in their distributions, each with 6 available combinations, and they have 9 unpaired hole cards in their distributions, each with 16 available combinations. In total, your opponents have (10)(6) + (9) (16) = 204 combinations in their distributions. Since you know your hole cards, there are 50 cards left in the deck. The probability of both players folding is $\left(\frac{1,021}{1,225}\right)\left(\frac{1,021}{1,225}\right) \approx .69$. The probability of getting one caller is $\left(\frac{204}{1,225}\right)\left(\frac{1,213}{1,225}\right) + \left(\frac{1,021}{1,225}\right)\left(\frac{204}{1,225}\right) \approx .30$. The probability of getting two callers is therefore about .01, which is pretty much negligible. The possible outcomes, along with their probabilities and EV contributions, are in table 7.25. Note that I didn't include tying possibilities because their probabilities and EV contributions are very small.

**TABLE 7.25: Outcomes for Pushing All-In for Problem 2a.**

| OUTCOME | PROBABILITY | EV CONTRIBUTION |
|---|---|---|
| 11,000 (You Steal Blinds) | .69 | 7,590 |
| 18,000 (You Win Against SB) | (.16)(.27) ≈ .04 | 720 |
| 17,000 (You Win Against BB) | (.14)(.27) ≈ .04 | 680 |
| 0 (You Lose) | (.30)(.72) ≈ .22 | 0 |

By pushing all-in here, P(survival) = .77, and your chip EV is 8,990.

Note that waiting an orbit for a better hand isn't necessarily a great idea. A bulk of your EV comes from your fold equity here, and if you get blinded down to 5,000 chips, you may have a lot less fold equity, especially if the other stacks confront each other and you are stuck heads-up against a 19,000 chip stack.

2b. Chip EV = 7,860 and P(survival) = .64.

*Explanation:* The SB has the same distribution as in problem 2a, meaning that he calls with 204 combinations and folds 1,021 combinations. The BB is calling with a much wider range of holdings now. He has 11 pocket pairs consisting of 6 combinations each and 2 pocket pairs consisting of 3 combinations each. He has 10 unpaired aces consisting of 16 combinations each and 2 unpaired aces consisting of 12 combinations each. He has 9 unpaired kings consisting of 16 combinations each and 2 combinations of unpaired kings consisting of 12 combinations each. He has 16 combinations each of [QJ,QT]|||[JT]. In total, the BB calls with 472 combinations when the SB folds. The probability that both players fold is $\left(\frac{1,021}{1,225}\right)\left(\frac{753}{1,225}\right) \approx .51$. The probability that the SB calls is $\left(\frac{204}{1,225}\right)\left(\frac{1,213}{1,225}\right) \approx .16$, and the probability that the BB calls is $\left(\frac{1,021}{1,225}\right)\left(\frac{472}{1,225}\right) \approx .32$. From the answer to problem 2a we know that the probability of winning against the SB's distribution is .27. The probability of winning against the BB's distribution is .29. Table 7.26 (p. 284) summarizes all the possibilities, and again, ties are ignored along with the possibility of both blinds calling because both cases have negligible contributions.

P(survival) = .64, and your chip EV is 7,860. This play is negligibly –EV with respect to chips. P(survival) is a tad low, but its slightly better than the .63 chance of winning that you are most likely going to

**TABLE 7.26: Outcomes for Pushing All-In for Problem 2b.**

| OUTCOME | PROBABILITY | EV CONTRIBUTION |
|---|---|---|
| 11,000 (You Steal Blinds) | .51 | 5,610 |
| 18,000 (You Win Against SB) | (.16)(.27) ≈ .04 | 720 |
| 17,000 (You Win Against BB) | (.32)(.29) ≈ .09 | 1,530 |
| 0 (You Lose) | (.16)(.73) + (.32)(.71) ≈ .34 | 0 |

have by waiting for an ace. Whether pushing all-in here is a good play is a large function of how aggressive your opponents are. If your opponents are passive and there is a chance that both players will fold when you are BB, then passing and waiting for a better hand to push with may be the best play. If your opponents are very aggressive, you can fold and reduce your calling requirements for the hands ahead, but if you are going to do that and end up in a situation where you are likely to be about .6–.65 to win the hand, you might as well just push all-in here with your P(survival) of .64. These are the types of tricky decisions that separate tournament play from cash game play.

# 8

# CLOSING THOUGHTS

♧♤♢♡

## Introduction

We've thoroughly dissected the game of Texas hold'em from a mathematical, logical perspective. Unfortunately, I wasn't able to cover every scenario possible, but the tools you've learned will serve you well into the future as you tackle the poker situations that you encounter. It's been a fun journey, but we aren't quite done yet. There are a few topics that I didn't fit into the flow of my main content, but I thought that this book would be incomplete if these topics weren't at least mentioned: pot-commitment and the impact that jackpots can have on play.

## Pot Commitment

You are pot-committed when you are forced to make a call, knowing you are behind in the hand, because of the favorable pot odds being offered. In cash games, being pot committed is usually the result of one or more players having a short stack relative to the blinds at the start of the hand. In tournaments, being pot committed is usually the result of having to call an all-in reraise or being the BB in a situation where the pot is raised a small amount.

Being pot-committed in some cash game situations is unavoidable if short stacks exist. The key concept in cash games is avoiding lines of play that are normally +EV but where ending up pot-committed when your opponent reraises results in an overall line of play being –EV. One good way to avoid this situation is to adjust your betting size so that you are not pot-committed when your opponent goes over the top. Unfortunately, most players assign meanings to bet sizes, so your opponent may not be raising all-in with the hands you think he is when you decrease your bet size (poker is such a complicated game, isn't it!). The point is that if you *can* adjust your bet sizes without encountering problems, do so.

Being pot-committed in tournaments is a different concept. When watching hold'em tournaments on TV, most announcers use pot odds having to do with chip EV to determine whether a player should call an all-in bet. What I'm about to say may meet with much controversy, but I assert that most situations where players are presumed to be pot committed in tournaments are situations where players are, in fact, not pot committed. This is an endless debate that I constantly engage in, and I'd like to bring you into the fray.

Take the following situation: You are five handed. Blinds are 1,000–2,000, and you post the big blind. You have 7,000 remaining in your stack. Everyone has stacks ranging from 3BB to 8BB, and the players have very tight calling distributions (even though they are fairly liberal with their all-ins). Action folds to the button who pushes all-in to 3,500. The SB folds and you have 83o—what do you do? Looking at pot odds, you are getting 6,500:1,500 ≈ 4.33:1 to call. You are positive chip EV to call any distribution that the button is on at this point. However, by calling, you are most likely entering a situation where you will only win the pot with a probability between .12 and .36. By calling, you are most likely leaving yourself in a situation where you are only going to have 5,500 chips. If you push all-in with a 5,500 stack, a BB who is thinking strictly about chip EV is getting 8,500:3,500 ≈ 2.43:1 to call, meaning that against such a player, your fold equity is gone. By folding, you leave yourself with a 7,000 stack that gives you more fold equity, and as we've learned, fold equity is your major weapon in the tournament endgame. It's situations like that that lead me to believe that players in tournaments default to thinking that they are pot-committed way more than they actually are.

An interesting note about being pot-committed in tournaments is that it may be possible for situations to arise where you're forced to make a call because of the huge expected boost in monetary EV. Just like in the cash game discussion, just be careful that you don't let such calls arise because you take lines of play that carry an overall negative monetary EV.

## Impact of Jackpot

Many casinos have bad beat jackpots, and some of them even have high-hand jackpots. The idea is that some money (usually from $0.25 to $1) is taken from each pot. The money goes toward a progressive jackpot. When the jackpot is hit, the players at the table receive money, and the house also takes a cut (I should stop playing poker and writing about it so that I can open up my own casino!). In a typical bad beat jackpot in L.A.'s cardrooms, the jackpot is hit when a hand at least as good as aces full of tens (AATTT) is beaten by a hand at least as good as quads. To qualify for the jackpot, both hands must go to showdown, and both hole cards from both players' hands must play. Usually, the loser of the hand gets 50% of the table share, the winner of the hand gets 25% of the table share, and the rest of the table share is evenly divided among the other players dealt in the hand. High-hand jackpots (seen mostly in Las Vegas cardrooms and online) occur when a player shows down some qualifying hand. Sometimes, only the player with the qualifying hand gets the money. Other times, there will be some money divided among the other players at the table.

There are two jackpot considerations: The first is the value of the jackpot that makes the jackpot bet +EV. Unfortunately, if it is –EV, some players out there may still be stuck having to play with it, but it is at least good to know these things. To figure out whether the jackpot is +EV, we must first calculate the amount of jackpot money you pay per hand. This is relatively simple, in theory. Suppose you are in a game with a $1 jackpot rake. Furthermore, suppose that you know that you win 12 percent of the hands played at the table on average. In that case, you are playing $0.12 per hand. Suppose the odds against the jackpot in the game you are at are 1,000,000:1. In that case, you need an expected jackpot payout of $120,000 for the jackpot to be +EV. As with some other concepts we've encountered, this is all good in theory.

Unfortunately, two problems prevent us from going further: First, it's tough to know the precise percentage of hands that you'll win at a specific table. Sure, you may be playing online where you have Poker Tracker statistics, one of which is your overall percentage of hands won. However, the percentage of hands that you win in a particular session is partly a function of the particular players sitting at your table. Second, the probability of hitting the jackpot is a large function of how your opponents play. Simulations that deal hands from start to finish can only provide minimal insight because in most games, even the loosest of jackpot games, players aren't calling any hand down to the river every hand just to hit the jackpot.

The second consideration having to do with the jackpot is much more real. When facing an all-in call in a NL game, the jackpot must be counted as part of the pot in EV calculations. Suppose you have QQ preflop, and you put your opponent on [KK,AA]. If the jackpot is high enough, you may have odds to call a reraise all-in where you are not getting the approximately 4:1 odds from the pot itself because of the additional money that the jackpot contributes.

Whether you love the jackpot or hate it, the bottom line is that it has an impact on the play. If you are a Killer Poker player, you will account for this impact.

## Closing Words

Finishing this book has been like approaching an asymptote—no matter how close I got, it seemed like I'd never get here. No matter how close I was, the perfectionist in me was never satisfied. I wish I could've written some sections in more detail, and I wish I could've squeezed in some omitted material. However, I'm happy with the way the book works, emphasizing process over results in a world single-mindedly obsessed with results (though this wasn't an encyclopedia of results, I think I still managed to give more than enough results).

Having made it all the way through, you are now well versed in a rigorous, analytic approach to poker. Now that you have this weapon, no one can take it from you—well, no one except for yourself. As humans, we are sometimes slaves to emotional impulses, and there is no more dangerous place for emotional impulses than the poker table. The math and the results I derived are significant, but the unifying idea is that poker is about successful data acquisition and interpretation, complementary processes that must coexist in a Killer Poker player's mind.

# Glossary

Most of these are terms and acronyms used in the text. I've included a few terms here not used in the text that are, nonetheless, commonly used in talking about poker. There are a few entertaining terms in here as well.

**Aggressive:** A player who bets and raises more often than he checks and calls. This term is the opposite of passive (note that aggressive players can be either loose or tight).

**Autopilot:** Mental mode where your decisions are automatic and not completely thought out. You think that you've been in a situation so many times that you simply act before thoroughly thinking. For me, I have to fight autopilot because I'm used to playing many online games simultaneously with the aid of Poker Tracker and Poker Ace HUD. Autopilot for you may have other causes. The bottom line is that autopilot is to be avoided at all costs.

**Backdoor:** A draw that needs two cards to complete the hand: one on the turn, and the other on the river.

**Big Blind (BB):** The big blind is a forced bet made before a hand is dealt. It is usually placed by the player two positions to the left of the button, and it is typically twice the small blind. If no one raises, the player who posts the big blind has an option of raising. BB is also used to designate the player who posts the BB in a hand.

**Blinds:** Forced bets that are made before the hand starts. In a Texas hold'em hand, there are usually two blinds: a small blind and a big blind. The player immediately to the left of the button posts the small blind, and the player immediately to the left of the small blind posts the big blind. The word "blinds" can be used to refer to both the bets and the players who post them.

**Broadway:** The ace-high straight, TJQKA.

**Broadway Cards:** Cards that are 10 or higher.

**Bubble:** The last few spots in a tournament before the money. In a multi-table tournament, the bubble is usually when there's one table of players to eliminate before payouts begin. In single table tournaments where the top 3 get paid, bubble time is when the tournament is down to 4 players. If you finish on the bubble, you are said to have "bubbled out."

**Burn:** In a brick-and-mortar game, this is the action of mucking the top card of the deck before dealing the flop, the turn and the river. Cards are burnt to protect against cheaters who mark cards.

**Bust:** Usually refers to when you get eliminated from a tournament. However, this can also refer to when you lose money in a cash game and have no more money with which to buy in.

**Button (B):** The player who acts last on all betting rounds except the first round. The button is denoted by a white disk that usually has the word "dealer" written on it. Online, "dealer" is replaced by D since the disk on screen is too small.

**Check-Raise:** Play where you initially check only to raise later in the same round of betting. For example, you have four opponents. You flopped a set and are first to act. You check. The person to your left bets, everyone folds, and you raise when the action gets back to you.

**Clean Outs:** Outs where your hand is improved and you are not beaten by another hand. Say the board is J52, and you have

AQ. If your opponent has JT, aces and queens are clean outs. However, if your opponent has AJ, aces are no longer clean outs since your top pair will be beaten by your opponent's two pair.

**Chip EV:** Expectation value in terms of the number of chips you have in front of you. In cash games, your decisions are usually based on optimizing your chip EV. In tournaments, there is chip EV associated with each hand, but your goal isn't necessarily to optimize chip EV.

**Clumping:** Effect in which players in late position are more likely to have good cards given that all the early position players folded.

**Combination:** A particular set of objects for which ordering does not matter.

**Complete Information:** A game is said to be a game of "complete information" when all players have the same state of knowledge. The board game, Monopoly, for example, is a game of complete information since there is no hidden information—everyone has their property, money, and "Get Out of Jail Free" cards laid out for everyone to see.

**Conditional Probability:** The chance of an outcome that is dependent on previous outcomes.

**Connectors:** Hole cards containing cards of consecutive ranks (e.g., JT and 54).

**Continuation Bet:** A bet made by a preflop raiser on the flop when he misses the flop.

**Crippled Deck:** Situation that occurs when you have a monster hand and hold most of the cards that could make good hands for your opponents. For example, if the flop is AAK and you hold AK, there aren't many cards left that your opponents could have so that they could justify staying in the hand with you.

**Cutoff (CO):** The player to the right of the button. Aggressive players in the CO will often open for a raise, cutting the button off from entering the hand.

**Domination:** Situation in which players have hole cards with one card in common. The set of hole cards with the higher kicker is said to dominate. For example, preflop, AQ dominates AJ.

**Double Gutshot Straight Draw:** A straight draw where you simultaneously have two inside straight draws. If you hold 75, and the flop is 369, you have such a draw. Notice that you have 8 outs with a double gutshot, which is the same number of outs you have with an outside straight draw.

**Double-Paired Board:** Board with two pair on it. An example of a double-paired board is KK552.

**Early Position (EP):** At a full-handed table, this term usually apply to UTG, UTG+1, and UTG+2. More generally, it refers to approximately the first third of players to act in a hand, so at a six-handed table, UTG and UTG+1 can be considered to be EP.

**Event Odds:** The odds corresponding to an event happening. These are usually simply referred to as "odds," but sometimes a distinction needs to be made between event odds and pot odds. As an example, the event odds against drawing an ace from a full deck of cards are 12:1.

**Expectation Value (EV):** The amount of money you expect to win or lose in the long run per random event. If I flip a coin and I make a bet where I profit $5 for a head and lose $10 for a tail, my EV would be –$2.50. Negative EV events like this one are to be avoided.

**Exposed Card:** A card that shouldn't be known but is somehow shown to one or more players at the table. Cards are usually shown via dealer mistakes or by players who expose their cards either willingly or unwillingly.

**Fixed Strategy:** Game plan in which a player always performs the same action in a specific situation. An example of a fixed preflop strategy is always raising with [AA,JJ]|||[AK,AQ], limping with [AJ,A9]|||[KQ,K9]|||[QJ,Q9]|||[JT,J9]|||[TT,55], and folding all other hands.

**Flat Call:** To call a bet, often with the intent of changing from passive play to aggressive play later in the hand. A flat call may be a trap, or it might be a call with nothing, with the intent of bluffing later in the hand.

**Fold Equity:** The part of EV that arises from considering the probability that an opponent will fold and multiplying it by the amount of money to be won when he folds.

**Full Ring Game:** Cash Game consisting of 7–11 players. Contrast this to a shorthanded game, which consists of 6 or less players.

**Gutshot Straight Draw:** A straight draw where only one rank can complete the straight, meaning that there are only 4 outs to complete the straight. An example is if you hold AK and the board is QJ5.

**Hand Distribution:** The group of hands that you assign to your opponent.

**Hand Simulator:** Software that takes as its input hole cards and a board and outputs the winning, losing, and tying probabilities associated with each hand.

**Hand-Tracking Software:** Software that keeps track of hands played online and sorts the data according to many statistics. These statistics include such things as the percentage of which players who voluntarily put money in the pot (VPIP), the percentage with which a player attempts to steal blinds (ASB), and the percentage of times an opponent will fold to a bet on the flop.

**Heads-Up Display (HUD):** Software that takes the data stored in a hand tracker's database and displays your opponents' statistics in real time while playing online.

**Hit-to-Win Poker:** Approach to game where you sit and wait to catch good hands. In loose games where 3+ opponents see the flop, a hit-to-win strategy will typically be profitable.

**Idiot End of Straight:** Straight made with a board of 4 connected cards that can be beaten by a higher straight. Suppose the board is 4567. If you make a 7-high straight with a 3 in your hand, you have the idiot end of the straight. This is sometimes also referred to as the "ass end" of the straight.

**Implied Odds:** Payout odds gained because of money that opponents are expected to put in the pot on future betting rounds.

**Incomplete Information:** State in a game where not all players have the same state of knowledge. Poker is not a game of complete information since players' cards are unknown to other players.

**Independence:** Term from probability referring to events whose outcomes do not influence each other. Independent events are convenient to work with because the probability of both events happening is equal to the product of their individual probabilities. An example of independent probabilities is the outcome of consecutive coin flips (the coin doesn't remember what the result of the previous flip was).

**Interval Notation:** Way to communicate a range of hands concisely. The beginning and end hands in the range are contained within brackets and separated by commas. To derive the other hands in the range, start with the first set of hole cards and simultaneously step through both cards until you arrive at the second set of cards. The interval [55,AA], for example, represents all the pocket pairs from pocket 5's to pocket A's.

**In the Dark:** Phrase referring to an action (betting, checking, raising) done to begin the next betting round before the board card(s) for the next betting round is/are exposed.

**ITM:** Acronym meaning In The Money. Refers to the time that players reach the point in a tournament where payouts begin.

**JV:** Nickname (and probably not coincidentally the initials) for the founder of Killer Poker, John Vorhaus.

**Ka-chingaling:** Word synonymous with "major payday." Here's an example. In the last hour of cash game play on the Party Poker Million IV (PPMIV) cruise, I was playing $2–$5 blind

NL hold'em with a $200–$500 buy-in. UTG raised to $25, UTG+1 called, and UTG+2 raised to $50. UTG+3 folds, and I look down to see AA. I reraise to $150. I get 5 cold callers. The blinds fold, along with UTG and UTG+1. UTG+2 reraises all-in to $1,250, I call my remaining $750 or so, and everyone else folds except for the button who calls off his remaining $500. UTG+2 had KK, and the button, believe it or not, called his remaining $500 with 22! I take down a $3,000 pot—ka-chingaling!

**Ka-chingo:** Term my friends and I sometimes use when referring to the casino. "Our pockets go ka-chingo after visiting the casino."

**LAG:** Acronym referring to a generally loose-aggressive player.

**LAP:** Acronym referring to a loose player who is aggressive preflop and passive postflop.

**Limp-Reraise:** Play where you limp in only to raise later within the same round of betting.

**Loose:** A player who plays a lot of hands. Loose is the opposite of tight (loose players can be either passive or aggressive).

**LPA:** Acronym referring to a loose player who is passive preflop and aggressive postflop.

**MCU Poker Chart:** Chart used to relay the play of poker hands. These charts were first introduced by Mike Caro in *Mike Caro's Book of Poker Tells*.

**Mixed Strategy:** Game plan in which someone executes different actions given the same situation. In the most ideal sense, the action chosen for a specific instance is determined by a random event having the same probability distribution as the mixed strategy to be employed. An example of a mixed strategy is calling with KK 10% of the time and raising with KK 90% of the time. To accomplish this, you can use the second hand of a watch. If the hand is from 0–53, you raise, and if the hand is from 54–59, you call. A second hand is appropriate because with respect to the play of hands, the location of a second hand is a random event.

**Monetary EV:** Your expected payday. In cash games, chip EV and monetary EV are synonymous. In tournaments, chip EV and monetary EV are different. In tournaments, your goal is ultimately to optimize your monetary EV.

**Nuts:** The absolute best hand that someone can have given the board cards. If the board is T♠J♠Q♠, you have the nuts if you have A♠K♠ for the royal flush.

**Odds:** Term referring to the ratio of (Outcomes of Interest): (Outcomes Not of Interest)

**1-Gap:** Hole cards such as 8T, where there's a single rank in between the two cards.

**Open:** The first person to put money in a pot voluntarily in a particular betting round is said to "open."

**Outcome Space:** Set of all possible outcomes for a random event. If I'm flipping a coin, the outcome space is (heads, tails).

**Outcomes of Interest:** Outcomes for which a probability, the odds in favor of or the odds against, are calculated.

**Outs:** Cards available in the deck that can improve your hand. If you have two hearts in your hand and there are two hearts on the board, you have 9 outs with which you can complete your flush.

**Outside Straight Draw:** Straight draw where you have 4 consecutive cards and you have 8 outs. For example, if the board is 674 and you hold 89, you have an outside straight draw. Note that even though you have 4 consecutive cards with JQKA, this is not considered an outside straight draw because you only have 4 outs.

**Overcaller:** If there's a raise and a call, any additional players who call the raise are referred to as "overcallers."

**Overcard:** This term has multiple applications, but it has the same fundamental meaning. First, an overcard is a hole card that is bigger than any of the cards on the board. Reciprocally, an overcard is also a board card greater than a pair you have (either a pocket pair or a pair made using a board card).

**Paired Board:** A board with a pair on it (e.g., TTJ2).

**Partial Outs:** After considering your opponents' hand distributions, partial outs are cards that win the hand for you against some, but not all, hands in your opponents' distributions. For example, suppose your opponent is on [AA,KK], you have AK, and the board is 4567. Aces are partial outs, because they only win the hand for you when your opponent has KK.

**Passive:** Term referring to a player who checks and calls more often than he bets and raises. This term is the opposite of aggressive (passive players can be either loose or tight).

**Payout Odds:** For a wager, this ratio is defined as (money available to win):(money you wager).

**Permutations:** Number of arrangements that exist for a set of objects.

**PFR:** Acronym referring to the "preflop raising percentage," meaning the percentage of times that a player raises preflop.

**Physical Deck**: The deck that the dealer actually holds. The physical deck does not include the burn cards or the muck. It's not used in probability calculations unless for some strange reason all the burn cards and mucked cards are known.

**Pot Odds:** The payout odds when only factoring the money currently in the pot.

**Probability:** The relative frequency with which an outcome occurs. If you take a probability and multiply it by 100%, you get the percentage with which an outcome occurs.

**Probe Bet:** A type of bet, particularly on the flop, where a player who was not the last aggressor on the previous round's betting makes a bet into the previous round's final aggressor.

**Push:** To bet all your chips. Sometimes, you'll hear this as "I pushed all-in." Other times, it'll be abbreviated as "I pushed."

**Put (On a Hand or Hand Distribution):** The act of assigning possible holdings to your opponents.

**Rake:** The amount of money that the cardroom takes from a pot. Casinos usually take a rake in low-and medium-stakes games (a timed collection is usually employed at high-stakes games). As poker players, it's desirable to play in games with the lowest possible rake; however, we should also acknowledge that cardrooms couldn't possibly exist without the rake. Every business needs to make money, and quite frankly, I wouldn't be able to make my money if the cardrooms couldn't make theirs. Remember to account for the rake when calculating your pot odds.

**Random Event:** An occurrence where the precise outcome is unknown, and each possible outcome has a known or unknown probability associated with it.

**Reverse Domination:** Situation where a hand that is originally dominant falls behind because the other player hits his kicker. For example, before the flop, AQ dominates over AJ. However, when the flop comes J52, the AQ becomes dominated because an ace gives AJ two pair.

**Reverse Implied Odds:** Payout odds lost because of money that you may lose on future betting rounds.

**Ring Game:** Synonymous with "cash game." Chips in play at a ring game can be exchanged for actual money at any time.

**ROI:** Acronym referring to "return of investment." ROI is used as a measure of tournament success (particularly single-table tournaments). To find your ROI, take your net profit or loss, divide it by the total amount of entries and fees, and then multiply by 100%. Usually, players calculate ROIs for different stakes separately. As an example of an ROI calculation, assume that I play ten \$20 + \$2 single-table tournaments, and I've won \$240. I've paid \$220 in entries and fees, so my net profit is therefore \$20. My ROI would be $\left(\frac{\$20}{\$220}\right)(100\%) \approx +9.09\%$.

**Runner-Runner:** Refers to a draw made by hitting both the turn and the river cards. For example, if you hold two hearts and there's one heart on the flop, you need to "hit runner-runner" to complete your flush.

**Semi-Bluff:** Play where you bet or raise with a hand that is currently behind but has the potential to improve to the best hand on a later round. An example of a semi-bluff is raising with a four-flush.

**Small-Blind (SB):** Forced bet made by the player to the left of the button. It's usually equal to half the big blind, but it can range from one third of the big blind to two thirds of the big blind.

**Sniffer:** Term referring to a hand tracker.

**Squeeze Play:** Sophisticated play, usually preflop, where after a raise and one or more callers, you reraise representing a monster hand. Against most opponents, you usually end up squeezing the original raiser and all the subsequent callers out of the hand unless they have monster hands.

**Stop-and-Go:** Line of play from early position where you check/call the flop or turn and then bet out immediately on the next round.

**Straddle:** A voluntarily posted blind equal to double the big blind. Since it's a blind, the person posting the straddle has an option to raise if no one else raises. There are different types of straddles. The usual straddle bet is made by the player immediately to the big blind's left. Another type of straddle, referred to as a "Mississippi Straddle," is a straddle where the option to straddle works from the button to UTG. If a person posts a Mississippi straddle, he acts last preflop—preflop action skips him and returns to him after the big blind acts.

**TAG:** Acronym referring to a player who is generally tight-aggressive.

**TAP:** Acronym referring to a tight player who is aggressive preflop and passive postflop.

**Theoretical Deck:** The pool of all the unknown cards (includes burn cards and the muck). Because of burn cards and mucked cards, the theoretical deck and the physical deck are different things. The theoretical deck is the deck that must be used in probability calculations.

**Tight:** Term referring to a player who does not play a lot of hands. This term is the opposite of loose (tight players can be either aggressive or passive).

**TPA:** A tight player who is passive preflop and aggressive postflop.

**Tree Diagram:** Visual aid in which different outcomes and actions are represented by branches.

**Tripped Board:** Board with three of a kind (e.g., KKK54).

**Under the Gun (UTG):** Player immediately to the left of the big blind. He is the first one to act preflop.

**Variance:** Numerical measure of the spread of payouts pertaining to a random event. Take the following two sets of outcomes: A = {$5, $0, –$5} B = {$500, $0, –$500} (assume that each outcome has an equal probability). Set B has a much higher variance associated with it even though both A and B have the same EV.

**VPIP:** Acronym referring to the percentage of hands for which a player "Voluntarily Puts money In the Pot." You'll sometimes see VP$IP used instead of VPIP.

**Wheelhouse Card:** A card that completes a huge hand. For example, if you hold A♠K♠, and the board is Q♠J♠5♣, T♠ would be considered a "wheelhouse card."

# Index